The Baltic States
in Peace and War
1917–1945

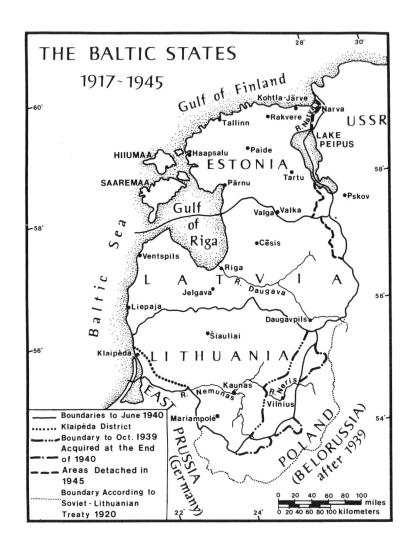

THE BALTIC STATES

1917 - 1945

Gulf of Finland

Kohtla-Järve
Tallinn
Rakvere
Narva
R. Narva
USSR
LAKE PEIPUS

HIIUMAA
Haapsalu
Paide
ESTONIA
SAAREMAA
Pärnu
Tartu
Pskov

Gulf
of
Riga
Valga Valka

Cēsis

Ventspils
Riga
Baltic Sea
LATVIA
Jelgava
R. Daugava
Liepaja
Daugavpils

Šiauliai

Klaipėda
LITHUANIA
Kaunas
R. Nemunas
R. Neris
Vilnius

Mariampolė
PRUSSIA
(Germany)
POLAND
(BELORUSSIA)
after 1939

EAST

Boundaries to June 1940
Klaipėda District
Boundary to Oct. 1939
Acquired at the End of 1940
Areas Detached in 1945
Boundary According to Soviet - Lithuanian Treaty 1920

0 20 40 60 80 100
miles
0 20 40 60 80 100 kilometers

The Baltic States in Peace and War

1917–1945

Edited by

V. STANLEY VARDYS

ROMUALD J. MISIUNAS

The Pennsylvania State University Press
University Park and London

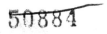

Published with the cooperation of
the Association for the Advancement of Baltic Studies

Library of Congress Cataloging in Publication Data

Main entry under title:

The Baltic States in peace and war, 1917–1945.
  Includes index.
    1. Baltic States—History—Addresses, essays,
lectures. I. Vardys, V. Stanley, 1924–
II. Misiunas, Romuald J.
DK511.B3B2827   320.9'47'4   77-88472
ISBN 0-271-00534-3

Composition by Asco Trade Typesetting Limited, Hong Kong
Printed in the United States of America

Contents

Preface

This book consists of essays originally presented at Baltic studies conferences in the United States and in Europe and revised especially for this collection. The idea of organizing a volume on Baltic domestic and international development grew from our work on the program of the Fourth Conference on Baltic Studies, co-sponsored by the Association for the Advancement of Baltic Studies, Inc., and the University of Illinois-Chicago Circle on May 16–19, 1974. The other conferences at which some of the book's essays were presented were held at the Hoover Institution on War, Revolution and Peace, Stanford University, on April 13–15, 1973, and at the Hässelby Castle in Stockholm on June 13–16, 1975. The Hoover conference was co-sponsored by the Association for the Advancement of Baltic Studies while the Stockholm meeting was organized by the Baltic Scientific Institute in Scandinavia. It was the third such conference held in Sweden.

The focus on Baltic States in war and peace was chosen not just because it concentrates on Baltic nation building in modern times—a unique experience in itself—but also because more than any other European countries, the Baltic nations were existentially affected by the conditions of war and peace in the twentieth century. Estonia, Latvia, and Lithuania were both beneficiaries and victims of the two world wars. Peace, too, did not always bring a period of independent creative development for the Balts. Indeed, in this century, the Baltic States enjoyed peace for some seventy years, albeit with interruptions. Of these, however, only twenty-two allowed an independent shaping of the Balts' own societies.

In the technical preparation of this book, our main problem was related to the use of toponomy. Since the Baltic region historically has been dominated by German, Russian, Polish, or even Swedish influence, the names of Baltic towns, rivers, and villages were formulated, articulated, and recorded in these languages. Between the two world wars, the independent Baltic States returned to the use of local language toponomy, but on the international level, this new practice spread slowly and gained momentum only after World War II. Soviet geographers and historians employ native toponomy. We, too, have generally used Estonian, Latvian, and Lithuanian toponomy. However, to aid the reader in identifying the historical scene, we have provided, in parentheses as well as in a special table, the old and diverse forms sometimes still employed by European or American scholars. For the transliteration of Russian names and references we generally followed the Library of Congress system of transliteration.

We are happy to acknowledge the aid of the Association for the Advancement of Baltic Studies in the preparation and publication of this volume. We are also thankful to Professor Alfred Erich Senn, University of Wisconsin, Professor Edgar Anderson, California State University at San Jose, and Dr. Jonas Jakštas of Cleveland for their advice on specific problems. Finally, we are indebted to the Lithuanian Foundation for subsidizing the preparation of the map of the Baltic States.

V. STANLEY VARDYS
ROMUALD J. MISIUNAS

Introduction: The Baltic Peoples in Historical Perspective

This book examines the rise, the struggle for life, and the fall of the three Baltic States—Estonia, Latvia, and Lithuania. The immensely rich and tense drama of Baltic nation building—from birth to death—was played within a single generation between the two world wars of 1914–1918 and 1939–1945. The Baltic peoples themselves, however, are of ancient lineage, their roots going back into the early history of the Christian era.

The Differences and Similarities of Historical Development

A historical survey of Estonia, Latvia, and Lithuania is faced with the question of diversity and similarity. Until recent times, observers tended to assert the diversity of the area almost as an expression of the obvious. The British authors of the prewar survey *The Baltic States*[1] deemed "the grouping together of the three Baltic states [as] to some extent arbitrary" in that their differences were at least as striking as their similarities. Most German scholars used to classify Estonia and Latvia alone as "Baltic provinces" or "Baltic" countries, and it was only in 1970 that Georg von Rauch, the dean of German Baltic historians, crossed the Rubicon with the publication of *Geschichte der baltischen Staaten*.[2] In the book he felt it necessary to explain why he chose the "unusual" approach of tying together Lithuania's history with that of the other two countries. The old separation has become inoperative. The Baltic identity has been forged by fate. The interwar political and social experiences, the wartime occupation by great-power belligerents, and the postwar imposition of the Russian embodiment of Marxism have illuminated the existence of past bonds. The new sense of community, of a distinct culture bloc, has been reinforced by a self-perception of differences from the rest of the Soviet Union. The one unalterable difference lies in ethnic and linguistic diversity. The Finno-Ugric Estonians speak a language radically different from those of their two neighbors to the south. Latvian and Lithuanian are the only living varieties of the Indo-European Baltic family.

While it would be a great distortion to negate the historical differences among the three peoples—or, more accurately, between the Estonians and Latvians on the one hand and the Lithuanians on the other—it still remains possible to posit some general basic trends engendered by geographical proximity. The entire eastern littoral of the Baltic Sea remained a pagan backwater to both of the great civilizations of medieval Europe —the Latin West and the Orthodox East—and straddled the commercially important waterway from the Varangians to the Greeks. Serious outside incursions began only toward the end of the twelfth century. The military monastic order of the Teutonic Knights, having suffered crusading reverses in the eastern Mediterranean, moved to the southeast Baltic and conquered the lands of the Baltic Prussians. This proved to be the first stage in a process that in the course of several centuries led to the extinction of the Prussians, with only their name left (at least until 1945) to designate the land that they had once inhabited. At about the same time the Danes entrenched themselves in northern Estonia while German merchants began to move into the area of the mouth of the river Daugava (Dvina). In 1201 the Riga bishopric was established. The land on both sides of the river was subjugated by the Order of the Brothers of the Sword—a counterpart of the Teutonic Knights. Native Estonian resistance suffered a serious setback in 1217 with the death in battle of its leader Lembit.

Within a decade the conquest of what was to become Estonia and Latvia was complete. As a result, both peoples were absorbed into the world of Western Christendom before they could develop a native political system. The foreign conquerors colonized, Christianized, and enserfed the indigenous populations, thus establishing the northeastern frontier of the Latin Christian world. After the Danes sold their portion of Estonia to the Order in 1346 the entire area became a loose confederation of ecclesiastical estates ruled by princes of the Holy Roman Empire, the lands of the Order, and a few independent and prosperous Hansa towns. The identity of the natives was reduced to an ethnic character, which remained politically dormant until the age of modern nationalism. This situation introduced the first and most important difference between them and their neighbors to the south, the Lithuanians.

The foreigners proved unable to overwhelm the less accessible Lithuanians during their initial drive of the thirteenth century. A native chief, Mindaugas (Mindovg), succeeded in forging the tribes in Lithuania, Samogitia (Žemaitija), and parts of present-day Belorussia into a lasting political entity. He inflicted a crushing defeat on the Brothers of the Sword, which led in 1237 to their amalgamation into the Teutonic Order. In an effort to secure peace with the Germanic invaders, he converted to Latin Christianity and was crowned king on the authority of Pope Innocent IV. While his attempt to secure peace with the West through an entry into its body politic proved abortive, his political creation, the Lithuanian state, survived his violent demise in 1263 at the hands of his compatriots and a return of its society to paganism.

Led by a series of particularly able rulers, Gediminas (Gedymin), Algirdas (Olgerd), and Kęstutis (Kenstut), the fourteenth-century Lithuanian state managed not only to contain the assaults of the Teutonic Order but also to take advantage of the recession of Tatar power in the southeast and to absorb large areas of the former Kiev state, thus turning Lithuania into a major power in the area. The extensive state, whose rulers and ethnic core maintained their pagan religion, became a cultural battleground between Latin influences and the Orthodox traditions of the incorporated East Slav population. The West won when, in 1386, Great Prince Jogaila (Jagiełło) as a condition of his marriage to Jadwyga, the heiress of Poland, and of his accession to the Polish throne agreed to bring his pagan Lithuanian subjects into the fold of the Latin faith. The personal union of the two realms, politically ill-defined for almost two centuries, lasted until 1569. The rule of Jogaila's cousin Vytautas (Vitovt) saw the apogee of Lithuanian power. The realm stretched from the Baltic to the Black seas, from the outskirts of Moscow to Poland. Its ruler was the arbiter of East European politics. In 1410 a combined army of Poles, Lithuanians, and Vytautas' East Slavs and Tatars inflicted a crushing blow on the Teutonic Order at Grünwald (Tannenberg).

The period of personal union between Lithuania and Poland had two lasting cultural effects: the Christianization of the Lithuanians according to the Latin Rite and the Polonization of the Lithuanian nobility. The older, more developed, and culturally richer Polish social structure proved irresistible to the Lithuanian nobility, which eventually became indistinguishable from its Polish counterpart. While the elite succeeded for a long time in preserving a sense of political separation, the Lithuanian peasants suffered the same fate as in Estonia and Latvia—enserfment to a nobility that could not speak their language. The Latin Christianization of the Lithuanian peasantry—a process that extended into the sixteenth century —failed to introduce an element of similarity with Estonia and Latvia, since it occurred just before the Lutheranization of the latter.

The Reformation rendered the Order and the ecclesiastical estates politically anachronistic. Unable to defend themselves adequately, they looked for outside protection. In 1521 the Swedes established themselves in northern Estonia. The major political realignments in the area, however, were triggered by the Livonian War, launched by Ivan IV in his search for a Russian outlet to the Baltic. Faced with the onslaught from the east, the Livonian nobility in 1560 sought Lithuanian protection. The eastern and northern parts of Livonia were incorporated into Lithuania while the western part became the Duchy of Courland, a fief of the Polish and Lithuanian sovereign. Soon thereafter Lithuania itself formalized its personal union with Poland. While the duality of sovereignty was retained in a federal Commonwealth structure, a common sovereign and legislature was established (Lublin, 1569).

The Commonwealth proved sufficiently strong to push Muscovy out of the Baltic. However, it could not expel Sweden. In 1626 Livonia was divided. Its northern half including the city of Riga became a Swedish possession. Its eastern portion, Latgale, remained under Lithuanian rule, and the status of Courland did not change. Except for Latgale, whose 200-year-long association with Lithuania had made it distinct from the rest of Latvia, the cultural boundary between Lithuania and the north acquired a lasting character. It was the boundary between the Lutheran and Catholic worlds, between German and Polish social and administrative practices. It reinforced and perpetuated the differentiation of the Lithuanians from their neighbors to the north.

Estonians and Latvians tend to regard the Swedish period rather fondly. Sweden itself had never had an enserfed peasantry. As a result, the sympathies of the Stockholm government were not automatically on the side of the Baltic barons, and a somewhat more liberal regime prevailed. Sweden depended on the barons for military service, however, and could not afford to alienate them either.

The Baltic nobility recouped their positions after the Russian Empire acquired Livonia and Estonia from Sweden during the Great Northern War. The Treaty of Nystad (1721) confirmed Russian possession, and Russia in turn confirmed the local noble privileges that the Swedes had curtailed. In addition, new opportunities for advancement in the service of St. Petersburg opened up to them. The barons proved loyal subjects, and the status of their peasants decreased correspondingly. Perhaps no other place in early modern Europe saw quite the plethora of legal writing designed to extend the rights of the nobility over the peasantry. In effect, a closed corporation of 172 families succeeded in establishing a monopoly on landholding.

In addition to absorbing Livonia and Estonia, Russia established a *de facto* protectorate over the Duchy of Courland, which during the preceding century had been a virtually independent state. The formal annexation of Courland was delayed until 1795 when its suzerain, the Polish-Lithuanian Commonwealth, perished at the hands of Russia, Prussia, and Austria. As a result of the Third Partition (1795), the bulk of the ethnically Lithuanian population became subjects of the Russian Empire. A period of relative similarity—experiences stemming from the rule of a common overlord, the awakening to a sense of national identity during the second half of the nineteenth century, and the social problems attendant to this rise of national consciousness—ensued. However, the cultural heritage of the past provided an element of differentiation to these processes.

The Baltic provinces of Estonia, Livonia, and Courland were the first regions of the Russian Empire in which serfdom was abolished. Alexander I first tried to limit it in 1804, but the barons were able to nullify the practical effects of the measure. However, by 1819 personal emancipation, though without land, had been effected. With a series of measures from the 1840s to the 1860s that enabled peasants to acquire leased land as personal landholding the social structure began to be differentiated from that in the rest of the Russian Empire. The concurrent abolition of compulsory guild membership for urban craftsmen allowed the development of an Estonian and Latvian urban class. The coming of the railways, which increased the significance of Libau (Liepāja), Riga, and Reval (Tallinn) as ports and industrial cities, also changed the character of the population in the Baltic provinces. A Latvian and Estonian middle class began to crowd out the Germans, and a Latvian and Estonian proletariat appeared. Reval, already more than 50% Estonian in 1871, became nearly 70% Estonian by 1897. Riga's Latvian population during the same period nearly doubled—from about 23% to 42%. Education in the native languages expanded with urbanization. By the end of the century this was one of the few regions of the Russian Empire that had virtually eliminated illiteracy.

The Estonian and Latvian national consciousness received an indirect boost from the Russification policy pursued under Alexander III. The provincial administration, courts, and educational systems, all bastions of German privilege, were the principal targets. Increased political activity by the Estonians and Latvians resulted in electoral successes on the municipal level. In 1904 Estonians for the first time gained political control of a major city by constituting a majority in the municipal council of Tallinn. Between 1897 and 1906 Latvian majorities were elected in four large Latvian towns.

A radical wing of the nationalist movement influenced by Socialist ideas appeared quite early in both Estonia and Latvia. Police persecution of radical nationalism forced a number of Socialists to flee abroad, where they developed ties with the European Social Democratic movement. August Bebel, for instance, took a keen interest in the development of Latvian Socialist Democracy. In 1904 various Latvian Socialist groups fused to form the Social Democratic party of Latvia. Two years later it joined the Russian SDP and provided several prominent leaders for both the Mensheviks and the Bolsheviks. An Estonian SDP was formed in 1906.

The Lithuanian national renaissance emerged in radically different circumstances. Although in one portion of the country—the Suvalki province, which had belonged to Napoleon's Grand Duchy of Warsaw— the peasants were freed during the first decade of the nineteenth century, emancipation with the right to limited landholding came to the rest of the country only in 1861. A social struggle with the Polonized nobility ensued. Russification, aimed primarily at the Polonized nobility, had been constant since the 1831 revolt. However, this was not always beneficial to the Lithuanian national renaissance. During the revolt of 1863 the Lithuanian peasantry showed itself to be more revolutionary than its Polish counterpart. Thereafter, Russianization also hit the national renaissance. In 1865 the publication of Lithuanian books in the Latin alphabet was prohibited, a measure that was not repealed until 1904. Attempts were made to settle Russians in rural areas and to proselytize for the Russian Orthodox Church. The rights of the Catholic Church were restricted. In 1894 Roman Catholics were prohibited from holding administrative positions.

Unlike the industrializing Latvia and Estonia, Lithuania remained an overwhelmingly agrarian country. Rural overpopulation at a time of intense anti-Russian sentiment engendered emigration—mostly to the United States and Canada. It is estimated that on the eve of World War I one out of every three Lithuanians lived in North America.

Too, unlike the Estonian and Latvian national self-consciousness, the Lithuanian national awakening initially had a strong religious connection. Greater persecution by authorities led to the use of the Lithuanian population across the border in East Prussia as a *point d'appui*. It was here that the first Lithuanian journal was published. Books printed in Tilsit and elsewhere were smuggled into Lithuania. They were used in secret, religiously oriented Lithuanian schools. This flowering of Lithuanian culture in a non-Catholic area added a secular perspective to the national renaissance movement. Socialism, however, remained alien to Lithuania. Although the Lithuanian SDP (1895) antedated its Latvian and Estonian counterparts by almost a decade, it never flourished among the agrarian Lithuanian population and remained largely confined to the non-Lithuanian urban elements.

The disorders that swept the Russian Empire in 1905 affected the entire Baltic region, but the degree of turbulence varied considerably between Lithuania and its neighbors to the north. Urban unrest was particularly severe in Tallinn and Riga. Students at the University of Dorpat (Tartu) hoisted red flags. Petitions were circulated for freedom of the press and of assembly as well as for a universal franchise. A Provisional Revolutionary Government was formed in Riga. Jacqueries swept the countryside—the targets were the German nobles and the clergy. Some 184 manor houses were burned and 82 nobles killed. At Tukums Latvians fought Russian troops for two days. The revolt was brutally suppressed—900 persons were executed and thousands were either imprisoned or exiled to Siberia.

The disorders in Lithuania, largely confined to rural areas, lacked the social-protest aspects of the revolution to the north and were directed primarily against Russian schoolteachers and Orthodox clergy. Excesses were comparatively few. The political aspect of the 1905 Revolution in Lithuania was highlighted by a massive National Congress of 2000 delegates, which met in Vilnius (Wilno) in December 1905. It resolved to work for autonomy, a centralized administration for the ethnic Lithuanian area of the Russian Empire, and the use of the Lithuanian language in administration.

Like the revolt itself, the postrevolt reaction was at its mildest in Lithuania. Measures undertaken to establish a rural class of prosperous farmers throughout the empire even benefited many Lithuanian peasants. At the same time small German landholders were encouraged to immigrate into Latvia and Estonia as support for the *status quo*. All three Baltic nationalities were represented in the four Dumas. The events of 1905 had forced many of the Estonian and Latvian leaders into exile, however. The general cultural relaxation after 1906 and the elimination of restrictions against the press in the native languages allowed national consciousness to grow steadily among the three peoples.

The Baltic States, 1918–1940: Years of Independence

An analysis of the rise of modern Baltic statehood reveals further interplay of diversity and similarity in social and political development, though from 1918 on the similarities overwhelm the historically accumulated

differences. All three peoples successfully seized the rare historical opportunity—provided by the collapse of the Russian and German empires—
to create their own states. In 1918, before the end of the war, Lithuania
and Estonia declared their independence on February 16 and 24, respectively. Latvia followed suit on November 18. In each case the goal was
accomplished in a different way. As Olavi Arens describes it in his study of
the early Estonian legislative assembly, the Estonian movement for separate
statehood began as an aspect of the dissolution of the Russian Empire.
Estonia was the first—and actually the only—national region of Russia
to which the Provisional Government, during the initial euphoria of
democratic sentimentality, granted an autonomy. The Estonians ultimately
expanded this autonomy into complete independence, which was formally
announced a day before the German troops occupied Tallinn. Further
political progress was delayed by the German military occupation, but
the Kaiser's downfall at the end of the same year cleared the way for
implementing the decision to be free. Estonian efforts were both aided
and complicated by the Allied sponsorship of the White Russian general
Iudenich whose army, based in Estonia, planned to seize Bolshevik-ruled
Petrograd. Allied supervision of the defeated German troops in Latvia
aided Latvian efforts to free themselves from German tutelage. Estonia's
birth pains were sharpened by Germany's diplomatic and military action
in Latvia where German aid was needed to help stem the Red tide. Using
this need as a political lever, the Germans attempted to salvage influence
and land for colonization in Latvia and, the Estonians suspected, in their
country as well. However, on June 22, 1919, the army of General von
der Goltz, who had established a pro-German puppet regime to replace
a government created by Latvian democratic parties, was defeated by the
Estonians and Latvians in the battle of Cēsis (Wenden). This victory eased
the Latvian situation. The pro-German government fell, the terms of
armistice demanded a quick withdrawal of all German military, and it
seemed possible to concentrate all efforts on clearing the Baltic region of
Red Army troops. Von der Goltz organized another army, however, this
one containing also White Russian units under the command of Colonel
Avalov-Bermondt. This military adventurer decided to take Riga.
Charles Sullivan describes how the Latvians won the battle and thus
ended German efforts to regain a foothold in the region. Everyone could
now concentrate on fighting the Red Army. At the turn of 1919–1920
the Estonians won full control of their territory, and though Trotsky
routed Iudenich at the gates of Petrograd in November, Lenin sued for
peace.

Conditions in Latvia, as discussion of the German, Estonian, White and Red Russian, and Allied involvement shows, were more complicated. As the most industrialized part of the Tsarist empire, Latvia had a large working class, and a strong revolutionary movement had developed in the cities as well as on land. Furthermore, the Latvian Rifle regiments—authorized by the Tsar after the Germans had reached the river Daugava in the summer of 1915—exhibited strong revolutionary proclivities. Their loyalties were split between the Latvian nationalist movement and Lenin's Bolsheviks. Because of this division and the strength of the Bolshevik movement, Latvia had serious difficulty in halting the advance of the Red Army. In addition, it had to contend with German revisionism.

While the Latvians thus maneuvered between the Germans and the Bolsheviks and eventually fought them both, the Lithuanians, as Aba Strazhas demonstrates from archival materials, at first had to concern themselves only with the Germans, who had occupied the entire country in the summer of 1915. Lithuanian efforts for independence had to be promoted under the watchful eyes of very strict German military occupation. Ultimately, however, the Lithuanian Council (*Taryba*), a group of distinguished leaders that the Germans originally had sought to use to legitimize their own expansionist aims, declared complete independence in the winter of 1918. Germany, being at the peak of its power in the East at this time, refused to recognize an independent Lithuania not perennially bound to Germany. The Council therefore was isolated and unable to institutionalize its decision until Germany's subsequent collapse made it possible to organize an administrative apparatus and a defense against the invading Red Army. In addition, the Lithuanians had to fight the retreating Avalov-Bermondt troops that occupied some districts in northern Lithuania. They were defeated on November 21–22, 1919, near Radviliškis. Moreover, Lithuania had one problem not shared by the other two countries—dealing with Poland, which with diplomatic and military vigor was pressuring Lithuania into a Polish-Lithuanian union resembling that of earlier centuries. These pressures were resisted, but they delayed Lithuania's recognition by West European powers. To make matters worse, Polish claims involved such hotly disputed territories as the city and region of Vilnius (Wilno), the ancient capital, which the Lithuanians lost to General Lucjan Żeligowski. Poland had signed an armistice that left the city on the Lithuanian side but on Pilsudski's orders Żeligowski feigned independent action and took the capital.

A portion of the history of this period belongs to the Baltic Communist parties and the Red Army's attempt to establish Soviet Baltic republics (in the Lithuanian case, the Lithuanian-Belorussian republic). These Communist efforts in Estonia and Latvia are briefly discussed in this book by Arens and Sullivan.

On February 2, July 12, and August 1, 1920, respectively, Estonia, Lithuania, and Latvia concluded peace treaties with Soviet Russia. In these treaties Lenin renounced Russian claims of sovereignty over the Baltic territories. Thus the first nation actually to complete the war of independence was Estonia, while Lithuania—because of its involvement with Poland—was the last. The Lithuanians, as a consequence, were the last to proceed with nation building as well.

As V. Stanley Vardys describes it in his chapter on domestic political development, the three Baltic States chose similar systems of government to meet their social and political needs. The assembly-type liberal democracy that was chosen is the most difficult one of its kind to operate, but it reflected European trends prevailing at that time. Unfortunately, even the highly literate Estonia and Latvia, not to speak of the almost completely agricultural Lithuania, lacked the economic, social, and political culture and structure needed to support it. Nor had they had the time to gain experience and develop institutions to guard state structures against pressures of radical interests and ideologies. As a result, their constitutional development, as elsewhere in Europe at the time, led away from democratic liberalism to authoritarianism. The roads traversed in this direction were more similar in Estonia and Latvia. The Latvians, however, shared with the Lithuanians a fear of radical leftism, while the democratic trends that surfaced and grew in the authoritarian regimes before the outbreak of World War II were common to Lithuania and Estonia. Nevertheless, seen from a historical perspective, their political development and their problems were strikingly similar. Similarities included the land reform that changed the structure of Baltic agriculture and society. Similarities were present in the treatment of ethnic minorities, which is briefly discussed by Vardys; their participation in Estonian and Latvian democratic politics is separately analyzed by Michael Garleff.

In foreign affairs the Baltic countries first had to obtain diplomatic recognition. The British and the French granted it relatively easily to Estonia and Latvia, withholding it from Lithuania until later. On July 27, 1922, all three were recognized by the United States, which remains one of the very few countries that has not withdrawn that recognition. This remains true, as Boris Meissner explains, even after the Helsinki agreements of 1975. The next foreign objective was collective security, which the three sought in the League of Nations and, when the clouds darkened in

Europe, in a declaration of neutrality. Arrangements of regional collective security, too, were considered but never realized.

Of their two big neighbors, Germany in the twenties appeared to present a lesser threat than did the Soviet Union. Weimar Germany was firmly entangled, like the giant Gulliver, in the net of arrangements imposed by the Treaty of Versailles from which it was not expected to escape quickly. The peril seemed to lie in the young Soviet state, which had demonstrated its enormous aggressive capacity in the Polish campaign and continued to persist, as a Communist attempt at a *coup d'état* in Estonia in 1924 confirmed, not only in revolutionary oratory but also in violent action. Perception of this international Soviet danger created some interest in establishing a larger international community of nations to contain this expansionist and only temporarily disabled state. However, mutual hostilities and mistaken priorities prevented the forging of a long East European chain of nations from Finland to the Black Sea. As Edgar Anderson documents, only in 1934 did the Baltic States create what would be considered a rump union at best. In fact, it was merely an "entente," which came too late and provided for too little. Its intention of pooling strength was sound, but it was so hesitant, slow, and limited in scope that in the end it did not help very much. In a world in which Germany had escaped Allied controls and the Soviet Union began to search for ways of regaining possessions it had renounced in the peace treaties of 1920, a more substantial endeavor was required.

As Alexander Dallin and Boris Meissner show, both of the giant neighbors kept a watchful eye on Baltic developments. Julius Slavenas documents the case of German interest, with Germany seeking to influence the Baltic power play to its own advantage in deciding who should possess the Klaipėda (Memel) harbor. West European attention to the Baltic region was not so solicitous. Although the British supported the Balts by mutually advantageous trade agreements regarding Baltic lumber, bacon, and dairy products, neither the British nor the French displayed commitment to their independent existence. It cannot be said that the Western Allies did not welcome Baltic statehood and freedom, but their support was limited. Nevertheless, as David Crowe shows, the British and the French supported Baltic sovereignty against Soviet designs, though they did not aid Lithuania in keeping Klaipėda—incorporated in 1923—when Hitler demanded its surrender to Germany a week after the final occupation of Czechoslovakia. The Allied defense of Baltic territorial inviolability against the Kremlin helped to spoil the British and French chances of a pact with the Soviet Union in the summer of 1939, but it was not a decisive factor in the collapse of the Allied-Soviet talks. British attitude toward preserving Baltic statehood became very ambiguous during World War II, and, as David Kirby demonstrates from archival materials, if it were not for American disapproval, Churchill's Cabinet would have by treaty guaranteed the Soviet possession of the Baltic States.

The Baltic States in World War II

The broader panorama of great-power interplay in the Baltic area is examined by Dallin and Meissner. Proceeding from the more distant American and the closer European perspectives, they reach a similar conclusion: While concretely Baltic independence was doomed by the Hitler-Stalin nonaggression pact of August 22, 1939, in the long run the free existence of the Baltic republics was unacceptable to the totalitarian Soviet Union. Both authors suggest that Baltic independence was short-lived not because of the countries' internal weaknesses, but principally because of international factors. It was not a drift to authoritarianism or Soviet tactical cleverness in organizing synthetic revolutions, Dallin suggests, not even the Soviet need of a buffer to protect Leningrad that facilitated or motivated Stalin to annex the Baltic States. Their demise was caused largely by their geopolitical condition, that is, their proximity to Russia. Meissner, who examines, by way of the Estonian example, the Soviet annexation technique, considers the Russian intolerance of Baltic independence to be inspired by Soviet totalitarianism. This intolerance, he in effect concludes, could soften as a result of the "inner renewal" of the Soviet regime.

Painting with a historical brush, however, we note that in modern times the fate of the Baltic as well as Polish regions has depended on a competitive but not violent relationship between the German and Russian empires. Once they were allied, as at the end of the eighteenth century or again in 1939, Poland as well as the Baltic States were doomed. Conversely, their collapse at the end of World War I created a historical opportunity for Baltic statehood. The destruction of German power during World War II and the annihilation of Germany's centuries-old presence in East Prussia and Pomerania eliminated German influence, at least for this generation, and completely delivered the Baltic States into Soviet hands. Moreover, after the war, the British and French power in the equation was replaced by that of the United States.

Before this new balance of power tightly shut in the Baltic peoples within the Soviet borders, they had to survive World War II. In September–October 1939, just weeks after the division of Poland between Germany and the Soviet Union, Estonia, Latvia, and Lithuania were forced to accept mutual assistance pacts that authorized the Kremlin to keep Red Army bases on Baltic territory. The Estonians signed the pact on September 28, the Latvians on October 5, and the Lithuanians on October 10. The latter, in addition, had their pill sugarcoated by the Kremlin's return of the city of Vilnius, which the Red Army had captured from Poland. The old capital was returned, together with a small piece of territory that the Soviet Union had originally conceded to Lithuania in the peace treaty of 1920. For all practical purposes, the installation of Soviet garrisons reduced the Baltic republics to the status of Moscow's protectorates, both constrained as well as relatively free to act, as is contemporary Finland. This political tutelage, however, was terminated by an outright occupation in June 1940.

The subsequent Soviet policy in the Baltic republics reinforced the trends of parallel or even identical development that had become so pronounced since World War I. In the summer of 1940 the Soviets ran in the Baltic area a six-week compressed course in "people's democracy," one that after World War II at a more relaxed pace (1944–1948) was applied in all East European countries. Sovietization was speeded up in August after the three republics had become formally absorbed by the Soviet Union. Wholesale nationalization and a new land reform that pulverized land holdings initiated an economic system similar to, and for the time being stricter than, the NEP of the early Soviet state. Next, ideological uniformity was imposed. A glimpse into this policy is offered by Dennis Dunn, who examines the relations of the new rulers with the Vatican and the Catholic Church in the Baltic States.

A sustained and vigorous attack on the old social structure and the forcible methods of introducing the Stalinist system were accompanied, as many East Europeans were to learn later, by police terror and widespread arrests that culminated in massive deportations of more than 60,000 adults and children in June 1941, just a week before the German attack on the Soviet Union. These deportations were the most traumatic single historical experience of the Estonians, Latvians, and Lithuanians. It was bound to turn the population violently and even recklessly against the Soviet rule. As a consequence, the news of the outbreak of German-Soviet hostilities on June 22 was received with a sigh of relief. At the same time, the armed conflict between the two giants who just yesterday had conspired to destroy the independence of Poland and the Baltic States raised hopes of national restoration. A revolt against the Soviets broke out on June 23 in Lithuania, and armed Latvian and Estonian units battled the Soviets before the arrival of the German troops. These events, genuine and spontaneous as they were, had been encouraged by Berlin, which hoped to benefit from the Baltic anger against the Soviets and intended to use Baltic opposition as a "fifth column" in the war against the Red Army. The Germans sought to do it without incurring any political obligations to the Baltic peoples themselves. Their game, however, was understood.

Contrary to German expectations, the insurrectionists in Lithuania managed to capture major cities and on June 23 proclaimed the restoration of independence. The establishment of a Provisional Government was also announced. The Latvians followed suit on June 28. The Estonians in the meantime learned of the actual German attitude and therefore merely stressed to the occupant the necessity of establishing a legal Estonian government.[3] The Lithuanians and Latvians hoped that by confronting the Germans with a *fait accompli* they could force a recognition of Baltic sovereignty. Lithuanian events were instructive of Berlin's response. As a price for German recognition of Lithuanian independence, the Provisional Government offered to mobilize Lithuanian manpower in the war against the Soviet Union.

The Germans, however, did not accept this suggestion, but instead obstructed the government almost in the same way in which the Kaiser had obstructed the Lithuanian Council in 1918. On July 17 Berlin announced the establishment of von Rosenberg's Ministry for the Occupied Eastern Territories and put the Baltic republics under a *Zivilverwaltung*. Within ten days Nazi commissars had assumed power in the capitals of Tallinn, Riga, and Kaunas, and Heinrich Lohse was established as the chief of *Ostland* in Riga. It became clear that a mutually advantageous collaboration with the Germans was impossible, and the Provisional Government suspended itself "against its will" (the Germans reported that the government had been "dismissed"). As a parting shot, its acting prime minister, Juozas Ambrazevičius, accused the occupation authorities of obstructing its work, making it impossible for it to function and to prevent, among other matters, the perpetration of outrages, as he put it, against the Jewish population.[4] The *Zivilverwaltung* then found others who consented to work for the Germans in the capacity of "counselors." Hitler legitimized the "self-government" of such counselors in 1942. In all three countries these officials and their administrative apparatus treaded the thin line between outright subservience to the Germans and loyalty to the interests of their own native societies.

Eventually, by force, by propaganda, and by cajoling the leadership the Germans obtained native manpower for military and labor duty, most successfully in Estonia and Latvia, which were more sensitive to Soviet danger because of their proximity to the front lines. However, by September 1941 an anti-Nazi underground of Baltic nationalists had developed, stretching from Tallinn to Vilnius and being especially strong in Lithuania. This underground deeply penetrated the existing administrative apparatus, schools, and economic organizations, but offered primarily passive resistance to the Germans, organizing and saving resources for the moment when, they thought, Western Allied pressure or intervention would make their own strength count against the Soviets in a sort of repetition of the events and the final outcome of World War I. The essay by Romuald Misiunas shows that this confidence in the West has become an extremely touchy point in Soviet evaluation of the events of World War II. This historiographic essay also reports on the Soviet interpretation of wartime developments.

The story of the Baltic peoples in World War II is of course much more involved and complicated than these extremely short notes can indicate. The Nazi oppression in some aspects equaled and in others exceeded the worst destructive policies of the preceding Soviet regime. In comparison to Western Europe, however, Baltic responses to it were immensely complicated by the fact that the Balts did not have a clear choice between their own national governments and the Nazis, a choice that in Western Europe rendered the Soviets allies of occupied nations. In the Baltic region native political aspirations for independence were opposed not only by the Nazis but also by the Soviets. The room for maneuvering between the two was extremely small. In the words of Tomas Venclova, the son of a prominent Lithuanian Communist and a dissident poet of the 1970s, during the war the native leaders' choice was among "Hitler, Stalin, and death, neither of the first two alternatives necessarily excluding the third." [5]

The outcome of World War II was not favorable to the Balts. Germany's destruction was complete. The influence of the Western Allies was totally eliminated from the region. Thus there was no repetition of the events of 1918 that allowed the native Baltic forces to achieve independence. In the new circumstances the Kremlin could confidently take possession of the three republics, where it established a firm and severe rule. However, the Baltic societies refused to peacefully accept this rule. While in 1940

Baltic governments considered it futile militarily to resist occupation by the Red Army, in 1944–1945 various Baltic groups went underground to organize armed resistance to the new Soviet occupation. As a result, armed insurgency spread through the region, only sporadically in Estonia and Latvia, but reaching massive proportions in Lithuania. In that republic a guerrilla war against the Soviets was fought for eight years, 1944–1952, causing tens of thousands of casualties.[6] However, this new resistance as well as the new sovietization against which this struggle was directed lie beyond the scope of our study.

I

The Road to Independence

The Estonian *Maapäev* during 1917

OLAVI ARENS

The Estonian *Maapäev*,* or Diet, has played an important transitional role in modern Estonian history. The *Maapäev* was created as an institution of self-government with limited political functions by a law of the Russian Provisional Government at the end of March 1917. Yet in the course of 1917 the *Maapäev* was to claim for itself far more political authority than had been assigned to it originally. Indeed, by the end of a period of four and a half months from its initial session, the *Maapäev* laid claim to being the highest political authority in Estonia. In February 1918 the Committee of Public Safety of the Committee of Elders of the *Maapäev* issued a declaration of Estonian independence and named a provisional government for Estonia.

Because of its importance in modern Estonian history a number of controversial points surround the history of the *Maapäev*. Among these is the question of the original area of competence of the *Maapäev*—was its authority one of self-government only or did it reach that of an institution of an autonomous Estonia? Also under dispute is the significance of the declaration of November 15, in which the *Maapäev* proclaimed itself the highest authority in Estonia; some commentators argue that this was in fact a declaration of Estonian independence. Furthermore, there is a controversy over the elections to the *Maapäev*, hence over the mandate that the *Maapäev* actually received. Finally, the internal history of the *Maapäev* itself has so far received only passing mention.[1] This

---

* This chapter is part of the research done under a grant from the Foreign Area Fellowship Program in Helsinki, Finland, in 1970–1971. *Maapäev*—the Estonian translation of the German word *Landtag*—is used here to denote the self-governmental institution formed in July 1917. The official name of the institution when it was founded was *Maanõukogu* in Estonian and *zemskii soviet* in Russian. In Estonian newspapers of the period the institution came to be referred to as *Maapäev*. *Maakond* is the Estonian word for the Russian *uezd* and German *Kreis*. *Vald* is the Estonian word for the Russian *volost* and German *Landgemeinde*. Dates throughout this chapter refer to the old or Julian calendar.

chapter focuses on these points of controversy and also delineates the internal history of the *Maapäev* from its initial meeting to the declaration of November 15.

Politics and the Law of March 30

Estonian political leaders reacted to the success of the February Revolution in Petrograd much faster than they had in 1905. Already on March 4 Jaan Tõnisson, the head of the North Baltic Committee, convened a meeting in Tartu of representatives of Estonian social organizations to consider what steps should be taken in the new circumstances. On the same day a telegram was dispatched in the name of the North Baltic Committee to the Provisional Government, requesting the establishment of a new provisional administrative order based on autonomy in Estonia.[2]

To press this demand, Tõnisson paid a personal visit on either March 7 or 8 to Prince Lvov, the prime minister of the Provisional Government, and gained his support for the introduction of new self-governmental institutions into Estonia. As a result of this meeting and of another approach to Lvov by Jaan Raamot, an Estonian Duma deputy, Raamot was appointed commissar of the Provisional Government with the authority to gather Estonian opinions on the nature of the proposed governmental reorganization.[3] Shortly afterward a joint call went out from Raamot and the North Baltic Committee for a conference to be held in Tartu on March 11 to work out a proposal that could be forwarded to the Provisional Government for its approval.[4]

Estonian leaders agreed that, while autonomy should be a long-term goal, Estonians should first settle for a minimal self-government that would have a chance of being approved by the Provisional Government. Estonian differences over the question whether Estonia should consist of one *guberniia* or two (Estland and Northern Livland) were resolved in favor of the latter, but with the provision that they be ruled by a common governor-general and have a single *Maapäev*. On March 26 a mass demonstration of Estonians in Petrograd petitioned the Provisional Government to act quickly on the proposal. As a result, the Law on the Provisional Organization of Administration and Local Self-Government of the Estonian *Guberniia* was approved and promulgated four days later, on March 30.[5] It eliminated the subdivision that Estonian leaders had proposed, but made a concession to Tõnisson's two-*guberniia* idea by naming two vice-commissars for the two halves.

The law of March 30 signaled a major change in Russian policy toward Estonia. It showed that the new Russian government was prepared to work with a new partner in the Baltic area—Estonian liberal intellectuals and, in a larger sense, Estonian nationalists—and had completely abandoned the Baltic Germans who had been the traditional political partner of Tsarist Russia in the Baltic area. The old historic *guberniia* boundaries were eliminated in favor of new boundaries between Estonians and Latvians based on ethnic considerations. Furthermore, the institutions of the Baltic German aristocracy (the *Landtage*) were to hand over their functions to the new Estonian institutions to be created by the law. Finally, the Tsarist Russification policy was modified to include the option of conducting *Maapäev* affairs in Estonian and to authorize the new Estonian institutions to take over some of the functions of Russian officials in Estonia. However, the Russian Provisional Government did not fully understand its new political partner, Estonian nationalism, and dealt with Estonia not in a framework of nationality policy, but in an older framework of local self-government.[6] Moreover, the law did not fully spell out the administrative functions that were to revert to the new Estonian institutions and did not clearly demarcate between the functions of these institutions and those of the Russian officials and the *guberniia* commissar [7]

Implementation of the Law of March 30

After its adoption the law of March 30 was forwarded to the Main Administration for Affairs of Local Economy in the Department of Interior to work out the provisions for implementing it. Here the initial reaction to the law was negative; it was called "a mistake" and "foolishness." Apparently Department officials were especially irked by the lack of a clear distinction between administrative and self-governmental affairs and the fact that the law, if interpreted liberally, could lead to the control of all administrative affairs in Estonia by a self-governmental institution.[8]

After the February Revolution the Department of Zemstvo Affairs in the Main Administration was taken over by the Kadet expert on zemstvos, B. Veselovskii. The Department had begun to reorganize zemstvos all over Russia, and Veselovskii tried to bring the introduction of self-government into Estonia in line with the Russian zemstvo statutes. Brought up for discussion at a public hearing on May 26, however, Veselovskii's proposal for the implementation of a zemstvo statute in Estonia met with Estonian opposition, forcing Veselovskii to drop the idea, and work was begun afresh on the basis of the March 30 law.[9] In June a number of public hearings were held on the question, and the measure was finally hammered out. The major dispute at these hearings was over the administrative functions that would be assumed by the new self-governmental institutions in Estonia. Estonian representatives especially wanted to eliminate the offices of the commissars for peasant affairs and school directors and inspectors appointed by the Ministry of Education. In the end, the rules of implementation approved by the Provisional Government on June 22 retained both the commissars for peasant affairs and the educational officials for the time being, but a proviso allowed for their removal once agreement from the appropriate ministries had been secured.[10]

As soon as Jaan Poska was confirmed the commissar for the new Estonian *guberniia* in April, he ordered preparations in Estonian rural areas for the elections to the institutions of self-government. Despite Bolshevik objections to early timing, the initial election was held in each *vald* or rural commune on May 23. Each *vald* was to send electors to a *maakond* or district electoral college meeting on the basis of one elector for 1000 inhabitants.

Voter participation in the rural elections was small; the available fragmentary statistics suggest that because of apathy and the low level of politization in the countryside only approximately 30% of the eligible voters voted.[11]

Generally speaking, political parties did not run electoral slates at the *vald* level. Estonian political parties, still in the process of formation at this time, were simply not equipped to conduct a campaign. The voters either could choose between two slates representing the landed peasants and the landless peasants or were presented with a single compromise slate representing both groups.

The electoral assemblies that met toward the end of June elected deputies to both the *guberniia Maapäev* and to the *maakond* councils. Electors who represented landless peasants voted for a Socialist (Social Democrat, Social Revolutionary, or Laborite), while those who represented landed peasants voted for a non-Socialist. In a number of the *maakond* councils Socialists were able to obtain a majority of seats.[12] The lack of support for the Bolsheviks in the Estonian countryside at this time is demonstrated by the Bolshevik inability to elect more than one deputy to the *guberniia Maapäev*.

The First Month and a Half of the *Maapäev*

When the *Maapäev* convened on July 1, only deputies from Estonian rural areas were present. Urban deputies could not be selected until the new city and town assemblies had been elected. It was not until October that the last urban deputies from Tartu took their seats.

On its first vote, the *Maapäev* agreed unanimously to adopt Estonian as its language of proceedings. The next two votes, however, showed the *Maapäev* to be split into two blocs of roughly equal size. The democratic bloc consisted of Tõnisson's Democratic party, Radical Democrats from northern Estonia, and representatives of landed peasantry who were in the process of forming an agrarian party. The Socialist bloc consisted of Estonian SDs, Estonian SRs, Laborites, and initially one Estonian Bolshevik. The Socialists prevailed in electing their own man, A. Vallner, as presiding officer, but failed to have the Assembly send a telegram of greetings to the All-Russian Soviet. A telegram was dispatched to the Provisional Government only. Both decisions won by a margin of only one vote.

The first month and a half of *Maapäev* activity was spent largely on organizational matters. A five-member administrative board was elected to organize the administrative functions of the *Maapäev* in agriculture, education, labor, public health, and general administrative affairs. Here, again, the basic cleavage in the *Maapäev* came into evidence, with the two blocs bargaining over specific positions and reaching a compromise that the democratic bloc would hold three (education, agriculture, and public health) of the five administrative posts.[13]

Maapäev's relations with the Provisional Government deteriorated with the passage of time. This was largely because the Provisional Government refused to turn over to the *Maapäev* a number of functions that the *Maapäev* considered to have been promised to it and because the remaining Russian bureaucrats actively worked against attempts by the *Maapäev* to remove them. An example of this is the administration of education in Estonia. One matter that excited most Estonians in the weeks after the February revolution was the prospect of Estonian-language schools and an end to Russification in education. Yet despite promises and the removal of a number of Russian educational officials, nothing of note happened during the spring and summer of 1917. The *Maapäev* worked out a project for local control of education in July and early August, and a number of *maakond* councils began moving toward administering education in September by taking the power of appointment of teachers into their hands. Nevertheless, school funds remained in the hands of the

Russian school directors and inspectors. Together with the educational curator for the Baltic region, they did their best to hinder the introduction of Estonian as the language of education in elementary schools in Estonia. As a result, education in Estonia in the fall of 1917 presented a chaotic picture with regard to both administration and language of instruction. Too, the Provisional Government failed to eliminate the office of the commissars of peasant affairs, even though its main function—the overseeing of the activity of *vald* institutions—was in fact being performed by the new *maakond* councils.[14]

The only area of government that came under immediate Estonian control in the spring of 1917 was the police. One of the effects of the February revolution had been the removal of the entire Tsarist police force. It was then left to local authority to organize a new police force. In Estonian towns and cities the town assemblies and town soviets administered the new police or *miilits*. In the rural areas the *vald* councils and at the *maakond* level the new *maakond* councils took over the administration of the *maakond* police. The Provisional Government forwarded funds to the *maakond* councils, which matched the previous expenditure on the police by the Tsarist government. By October the entire management of the police in Estonia was in local hands.[15]

The Special Session of the *Maapäev*

On August 25, following the German capture of Riga, the *Maapäev* was called together for a special session to discuss what action it should undertake in the event of a continued German advance and occupation of Estonia. The meeting was opened by a statement from Tõnisson:

> Internally Russia is mortally sick. If we look at developments at the front, it becomes evident that Russia lacks the internal strength and order to repel the enemy. . . . If the Baltic area falls under the power of the German armed forces the question of our country will change into an international question. . . .
>
> With a German victory in the Baltic Sea, the English would be excluded from the Baltic Sea. . . . England would never consent that the Baltic area remain under Germany. For that reason it should be possible to create a buffer state from the Baltic lands by reconciling the conflict of interest of the great powers. . . . If the Lithuanian, Latvian, Estonian, Finnish, and Scandinavian people unite, they would have, as a union of thirty million

people, a certain amount of influence during the negotiations at the peace conference. In the same way as with England, the general interests of the United States would also coincide more or less with the interests of the Baltic-Scandinavian people.[16]

Besides the possibility of a Baltic-Scandinavian union, a number of other possibilities for Estonia were also discussed or at least mentioned at this meeting: union with Germany, an independent Estonian state, federative union with the western nationalities of Russia, and a state in a Russian federation. Generally speaking, the Estonian Socialists, both SRs and SDs, showed greater faith in Russian "democracy" and a greater reluctance to endorse any proposal that might separate Estonia from Russia than did non-Socialists. A note somewhat different from that of the other Socialists was struck by the Estonian SD, Karl Ast, who argued on the basis of *Realpolitik* rather than ideology:

> We should look with suspicion on the idea of a Baltic-Scandinavian federation. We should not forget that Russia will still remain next to us. It is not thinkable that Russia could do without the Baltic Sea. It cannot penetrate anywhere else except here in order to reach the sea. Russia has been beaten before, but she has never remained so weak that she need not be taken into consideration. She will recover again.[17]

Three resolutions were adopted. One assented to the principle of appointing representatives of the *Maapäev* to defend Estonian interests outside Estonia. In the second resolution the Estonian members of the *Maapäev* declared themselves to be the representatives of the Estonian nation and as such the defenders of its interests. Finally, the *Maapäev* resolved to urge Estonians not to flee into Russia in case of a German occupation of Estonia.[18]

It was in these resolutions that the *Maapäev* clearly overstepped the authority granted to it by the Provisional Government in the law of March 30. It had declared itself an Estonian national institution and proceeded to make a number of decisions—to send representatives abroad and to continue to function during a German occupation—that could for the first time be correctly labeled "separatist" by the Russian state.

The *Maapäev* also had to deal with Kornilov's attempt to seize power in Petrograd. After prolonged discussions that indicated a further division between the Socialist and Democratic blocs, the Assembly adopted a Socialist resolution that opposed Kornilov and called for cooperation with the workers' and soldiers' soviets.

The Last Regular Session

When the *Maapäev* returned for what proved to be its last regular session on September 25, it was augmented by nine deputies from Tallinn. On October 6 two more deputies from Tartu took their seats, and the selection process for the *Maapäev* at last reached its completion, with sixty-two members elected in all.[19] Three of the nine deputies from Tallinn were Bolsheviks, and during the next week and a half they took the initiative by bringing forward a number of political issues. Though almost every resolution that the Bolsheviks introduced was defeated, they did thus force the other political parties to take a stand on these questions.

Bolshevik tactics are exemplified by their handling of the issue of Estonian-language use in elementary schools. When the curator for educational affairs in the Baltic provinces attempted to slow down the introduction of Estonian in elementary schools by proposing that it be handled case by case—that is, on the basis of each *vald* petitioning for the change—the Estonian Bolsheviks proposed that, unless there were protests from a particular *vald*, the schools immediately go over to Estonian.[20] The basis of such tactics was disregard for legality and directives of the Provisional Government and the promotion of Estonian through "democratic" (revolutionary) means. While this worked in the city assemblies, it did not work in the *Maapäev*, because here the Bolsheviks were in a much weaker position, and the non-Bolsheviks had greater hope of obtaining concessions from the Provisional Government on the issue of Estonian-language schools than on the use of Estonian in city assemblies. In fact, on October 10 it was announced in the *Maapäev* that the minister of education, possibly influenced by a major exodus of Russian officials, had finally given his consent to Estonian-language instruction in elementary schools.

While the Bolsheviks had their own ideas on other matters, such as the distribution of food, the crucial challenge of their presence in the *Maapäev* was to attack the very existence of the Assembly. On September 25, immediately after the seating of deputies from Tallinn, the Bolsheviks introduced the following resolution:

> Since the Estonian *guberniia* Provisional *Maapäev* has not been elected on a democratic basis and for that reason it cannot decide any questions concerning the inhabitants of Estonia, the *Maapäev* Bolshevik fraction proposes that the Estonian *guberniia* Provisional *Maapäev* be reelected on the basis of general, direct, secret, equal, and proportional voting.[21]

This definition of democratic elections was, of course, the standard Social Democratic one. Measured against this definition, the *Maapäev* elections fell short. Direct elections could probably not have been held in the Estonian countryside in the spring of 1917 because Estonian political parties were not sufficiently organized to be recognized at the *vald* level and the necessary election machinery to conduct such elections was lacking. Still, criticism against indirect elections had already been voiced by Estonian Socialists at the Tartu conference of March 11–13, and it was generally accepted that future elections would be direct ones. Indeed, there was a provision in the law of March 30 for direct elections to the assembly, which was to emerge from the statute on self-government that was going to be worked out for Estonia. The real reason for the Bolshevik demand for direct elections was a political one, however. Demand for reelections was the tactic of the moment for Bolsheviks all over Russia. Moreover, the Estonian Bolsheviks had done extremely well in a number of city and town assembly elections in August 1917 and had also increased their representation in the Tallinn soviet in reelections of factory delegates in August. In any reelection of the *Maapäev* the Bolsheviks would have gained the most.

In parrying the Bolshevik thrust to its existence, the *Maapäev* turned to the provision in its law that authorized it to discuss the adoption of an administrative statute for Estonia. Over Bolshevik opposition, a resolution drawn up by the Estonian SD, Karl Ast, was approved. It declared the *Maapäev* to be the legal representative of the people of Estonia until the election of a more competent institution. Furthermore, it authorized a commission of the *Maapäev* to start work on a permanent statute for Estonia that was to be presented to an Estonian Constituent Assembly chosen in direct and proportional elections. Finally, going beyond the provisions of the law of March 30 which talked only about the creation of institutions of self-government for Estonia, the *Maapäev* resolution called for the creation of an autonomous Estonia within a federal Russia.[22]

In addition to the Bolshevik challenge, the *Maapäev* had difficulties in reelecting the administrative board. Since the Bolsheviks refused to support the Socialist bloc, the Democratic groups gained majority. Konstantin Päts was elected board chairman.

Another problem that the *Maapäev* had to face was the question of finances. As a result of the delay in transferring the functions of Russian government officials in Estonia to the *Maapäev* (particularly in education) and partly no doubt because of the financial straits of the Provisional Government, the *Maapäev* was unable to obtain sufficient funds from the central government to cover its operations. The only major area for which money from the government was received was for the operation of the *maakond* police or *miilits*.

The *Maapäev* began to receive a certain amount of tax money from the *maakond* councils in northern Estonia in September after it had taken over the functions of the Estland *Landtag*. A report of October 7, however, showed that instead of the expected 180,000 rubles only 130,000 had been collected.[23] It was mainly the latter sum, plus a number of loans, that enabled the *Maapäev* to survive financially. On October 12 the *Maapäev* passed a taxation measure that imposed a property tax of 2,000,000 rubles to be collected by December 15.[24]

The *Maapäev* Meeting of November 15

The Bolshevik seizure of power in Petrograd at the end of October and the simultaneous proclamation of power by the Bolsheviks in Estonia presented the *Maapäev* with an entirely new political environment. Despite the initial skepticism about the Bolshevik ability to hold and consolidate their might in Russia, the first political steps taken by the leadership of the *Maapäev* in meetings of the Committee of Elders at the beginning of November were conciliatory. The chairman of the administrative board of the *Maapäev*, Konstantin Päts, and the leader of the democratic bloc, Jaan Tõnisson, tried to reach an understanding with Jaan Anvelt, the chairman of the Executive Committee of Estonian Soviets. But these failed.

As a result, the Committee of Elders decided to convene a meeting of the entire *Maapäev* on November 15 to pass a number of resolutions on the existing situation. Before the *Maapäev* could convene, the Executive Committee of Estonian Soviets issued a decree on November 12 declaring the *Maapäev* to be dissolved. This decree called upon the administrative personnel of the *Maapäev* administrative board to continue performing its tasks; furthermore, it fixed the date of elections (January 21–22) for an Estonian Constituent Assembly which was to convene on February 15 with the task of working out a statute of self-government for Estonia.[25]

The Committee of Elders met again on November 14, when it decided to ignore the decree of the Executive Committee of Estonian Soviets and proceed with the convening of the *Maapäev* on the following day. Furthermore, the meeting was to take place in Tallinn, rather than in Haapsalu

where the First Estonian Regiment could have given the *Maapäev* protection.[26]

The November 15 meeting lasted approximately twenty minutes and
was to be the last meeting of the full assembly for over a year. By the time
Bolshevik-led demonstrators burst into the meeting hall, the *Maapaev* had
passed all its key resolutions. The most important of these declared:

> Since state authority has been entirely destroyed in Estonia because of
> general disorder and because of conflict among individual parties and since
> central authority under which the separate parts of the state would place
> themselves is missing, the provisional Estonian *Maapäev*, as a legally and
> democratically elected representative of a land and people, declares as its
> duty the following in order to protect against the growing disorder in
> Russia and against the consequences of a threatening civil war and in
> order to insure the future of Estonian national politics.
>
> 1. The Estonian *Maapäev* declares itself to be the sole bearer of supreme
> power in Estonia, in accordance with whose laws and decrees everyone
> in Estonia has to comply until the convening of the Estonian Constituent
> Assembly elected on the basis of a democratic electoral law of the
> *Maapäev*. . . .
>
> 3. During the time the Estonian *Maapäev* is not in session, the *Maapäev*
> leadership and the Committee of Elders together with the administrative
> board is given the authority as the representative of supreme authority in
> Estonia to proclaim and enforce emergency orders and decrees on the
> ordering of life in Estonia.[27]

An analysis of the political meaning of the *Maapäev* declaration of
November 15 should deal with its effects on both the Estonian political
scene and on Estonia's relations with Russia. The *Maapäev* delaration did
deny the legitimacy of the Russian government formed by the October
Revolution. It did not, however, constitute a declaration of independence
from Russia. Were a new Russian government to emerge from the Russian
Constituent Assembly, were it able to stop the German advance into
Estonia, and were it to accept the autonomous status of Estonia, the
Maapäev, in the thinking of its members in November, would probably
have recognized its legitimacy in Estonia. In the meantime, the *Maapäev*
had declared that *de facto* it would function as an institution of an autonomous Estonian state that would issue decrees and presumably also enforce
them.[28]

Within Estonia, the declaration meant a denial of the legitimacy of the
claim of the Executive Committee of Estonian Soviets to political author-

ity. As a result, after November 15 there were two political institutions
with conflicting claims to legitimacy in Estonia. Of the two, the *Maapäev*
proved to be politically the weaker in the three months following the
October Revolution as it was unable to exert its authority in a positive
sense. It did, however, exercise a strong blocking influence on the authority
of the Executive Committee of Estonian Soviets. One immediate effect
of the November 15 declaration was that the administrative personnel of
the administrative board of the *Maapäev* went out on strike and refused
to serve Soviet authority despite continued attempts by Soviet authorities
to employ them.[29] The *Maapäev* declaration also had the effect of preventing the Soviets from gaining effective control of Estonian military
units which were in various stages of formation. While all this had the
earmarks of the preliminary stages of a civil war, one hope of reconciliation
still remained in 1917—the elections scheduled for January 1918 to an
Estonian Constituent Assembly. Both the *Maapäev* and the Executive
Committee of Estonian Soviets proclaimed their support for these elections.

The elections to an Estonian Constituent Assembly were in fact held in
most localities on January 20–21, 1918, and were to be concluded in the
remaining places the following weekend. But before they could be concluded, the Bolsheviks became aware that they could not hope to secure a
majority of the votes and therefore declared the whole electoral process at
an end.[30] The fact that the Bolsheviks had interrupted the voting and thus
prevented the convocation of an Estonian Constituent Assembly meant
that the *Maapäev* and its institutions continued their existence. It was thus
the Committee of Public Safety, formed by the administrative board and
the Committee of Elders, that issued the proclamation of Estonian independence and formed a provisional Estonian government that was to
assume power in Estonia after the end of the German occupation in
November 1918. The *Maapäev* emerged again at that time to meet until
the new elections to an Estonian Constituent Assembly in April 1919.

The 1919 German Campaign in the Baltic: The Final Phase

CHARLES L. SULLIVAN

On July 3, 1919, the leadership of a defeated German Army was forced to sign a humiliating treaty at the village of Strazdumuiža, just outside Riga. This event seemed a somber ending to what had commenced in the spring of that year as an idealistic campaign to rid Latvia of her Soviet conquerors.

The setting for this campaign had been established in November 1918 when the victorious Allied powers had placed in the Armistice Agreement Article XII, which called for the withdrawal of German forces from the territory that had been part of the Russian Empire only, "as soon as the Allies shall consider this desirable." It was hoped that the German Eighth Army on the old eastern front could shield the Baltic area from the threat of Soviet forces. Each of the Baltic nationalities, the Estonians, Lithuanians, and Latvians, had taken advantage of the disrupted conditions in the east to declare their national independence, but Soviet troops invaded Estonia on November 22 and had captured Riga by early January.

In mid-January the front in Latvia had stabilized along the river Venta east of Liepāja. The campaign to push the Soviets from the *Baltikum* was organized under German auspices. A special command was established in East Prussia, *Armee Oberkommando Grenzschütz Nord (OKN)*. The *OKN's* fighting arm in Latvia was the *VI-Reserve Korps (VI-RK)* under Major General Rüdiger von der Goltz, the officer who had led the German Army that successfully intervened on the side of the White forces in the Finnish Civil War in 1918.

The fighting forces of the *VI-RK* were made up of Reich German volunteers, lured to the *Baltikum* by false hopes of land and settlement, local Baltic Germans, fighting to recover a privileged position in Latvia lost during the war, and Latvian national troops owing allegiance to the Provisional Government of Kārlis Ulmanis. The Spring Campaign, which liberated Latvia from the weak Soviet forces, was an easy operation, but in the process extremist leaders of the Baltic Germans in the *Landeswehr* had overthrown the Ulmanis regime and, with the cooperation of General von der Goltz, had set up a puppet government subservient to these Balt leaders. The upshot of this complicated combination of circumstances was the confrontation between the Reich and Baltic German forces and the Latvian-Estonian nationals at the Battle of Cēsis northeast of Riga from June 21 to July 3. The local nationals, with the support of the Allies, soundly trounced the Germans, seemingly bringing an end to this strange adventure with the signing of the Treaty of Strazdumuiža.[1]

The agreement, hammered out by the Allied missions in the *Baltikum*, called for the German withdrawal from Riga by July 5 and an eventual general evacuation of the area.[2] That German troops remained in Latvia for almost five more months is an indication of the power of the forces working to keep an independent German army in the east as long as possible. The intensity of this desire was evident in the closing days of the Battle of Cēsis when the *OKN* rushed massive reinforcements to von der Goltz in a vain attempt to save his deteriorating position. These troops arrived too late, but they did not soon leave. In fact, they continued to pour into the Jelgava (Mitau) area southwest of Riga for almost two weeks.[3]

Three interested parties looked with favor on the strategic position of the forces of the *VI-RK*. German nationalists and militarists centered in East Prussia were infuriated by the signing of the Versailles Treaty on June 28. Baltic Germans, still hoping to regain their special historic position in the *Baltikum*, saw possibilities in future colonization of German veterans in the east. And ultraconservative White Russian politicians centered in Berlin hoped to mount a military campaign into Russia employing former Russian POWs and German volunteers.

The reaction to the Versailles Treaty in the eastern provinces of the Reich and by German nationalists everywhere had been open hostility. The political parties of the Right boiled with indignation at the humiliating settlement. From June 29 on into July various schemes were afoot in East Prussia to thwart the execution of the Treaty, even to take the eastern provinces out of the Reich and to continue the fight. For these men, particularly Wolfgang Kapp, *Generallandschaftsdirektor* for East Prussia, the forces of the *VI-RK* were considered the best and most "reliable" unit of its size left to the army.[4] Actually, it had been taken for granted by many leaders in East Prussia that no German government would sign the Versailles *Diktat* and that hostilities would soon commence anew. In fact, the Battle of Cēsis was fought by von der Goltz, supported by the *OKN*, with the thought that in striking the Latvian-Estonian forces the German troops were actually fighting the "vassals" of the Entente, with whom they would soon be at war again anyway.[5]

For the German Balts themselves the presence of a German military force in Latvia seemed their last hope to maintain their old prewar position in that land, whether as part of the Reich itself or as part of a conservative "Russia of the future" that would welcome German settlers into the *Baltikum*. The Balt leaders had been in the forefront pushing for the recruitment of German troops for the Spring Campaign, and even after Cēsis many continued to do everything in their power to maintain a German military presence in Latvia. Heinrich von Manteuffel led the "barons" in the Jelgava area, stressing the idea of settlement among the German volunteers there. In Germany Silvio Broederich and von der Goltz's brother, Günther, continued to raise volunteers for the *Baltikum* and the *VI-RK*.[6] In early July the Balt landholders began giving courses in land management and agricultural cooperatives to the German troops there. General von der Goltz assisted by setting up a soldiers' newspaper, *Die Trommel*, which beat away at the idea of the possibilities for the German veterans' colonization in Courland after the establishment of a "friendly" government in the area.[7]

The "cover" for the second phase of the German Baltic Campaign was to be supplied by another group which now viewed von der Goltz's troops with hopeful eyes. Conservative White Russian politicians and military figures had been gravitating to Berlin for months and by April had established themselves, at least unofficially, with the German government as the West Russian Council. The idea to employ former Russian POWs as a basis for a German supported anti-Bolshevik army had a strong appeal for Gustav Noske, the German war minister. Noske encouraged the hopes of the Russians, and when von der Goltz was home for conferences in May he also met with them and indicated an interest in their plans.[8] It was early hoped that some well known Tsarist general might be found to head the West Russian Army, as it was to be known, now being formed around Jelgava, but the German military leaders on the scene finally settled on an obscure adventurer, Pavel Avalov-Bermondt, who had never held a command and had had practically no military experience. He was, however, a man whom the Germans felt they could use to advantage, and he did strike an extremely favorable pose as a leader of men. He had a flare for the theatrical and was able to elicit a powerful sense of personal devotion from the Russians in his command. Von der Goltz determined to give Bermondt a capable German staff and allow the colorful Russian to act as the figurehead for the affair.[9]

Within a week after the German withdrawal from Riga all pretense of an orderly evacuation of the *Baltikum* was dropped. August Winnig, an early supporter and organizer of the Spring Campaign, on July 4 addressed the German National Assembly and contended that the evacuation of the *VI-RK* would mean "the extermination of the remainder of German culture in the *Baltikum*."[10] Five days later von der Goltz made it clear to the Allied representatives in Latvia that the German army would not retire until the large German interests there were secure.[11] During June the *OKN* had indicated to von der Goltz that evacuation orders should not be taken seriously and that the general should prepare his troops for a transfer into "Russian" service. Through the month of July a practiced policy of duplicity was carried out by the German military leadership. Even General von Seeckt and the new High Command were willing to give the scheme a try.[12]

The deception did not stop with the military. On July 24 the Berlin government reported to the Allied Armistice Commission that there was to be no delay in the plan to evacuate the *Baltikum*. Four days earlier Mathias Erzberger, vice-chancellor and a member of the German delegation to the Commission, wrote that the withdrawal of troops was now being intentionally hindered by the High Command and the Foreign Service.[13] The Berlin government was still trying to salvage something from the sorry debacle it had underwritten in the spring,[14] and the *OKN* supplied almost everything needed for the preparation of the army.[15]

Nor did the scheme of the government and the German military go unnoticed. Leftist circles broadcast the evidence of the recruiting and the buildup, while the Independent Socialists in the National Assembly blasted away at the machinations of War Minister Gustav Noske and the Majority Socialist government.[16] Even more concerned were the Latvians in Riga. Less than a week after Strazdumuiža the Latvian press was complaining of the German-Russian "collaboration" in Jelgava, so pompously marked by the continual singing of German and Russian national anthems by troops units of both nationalities. Jelgava had become a "Wallenstein's Camp."[17]

The stage was now set to build an "independent" German-Russian fighting force on the old eastern front, one that could control a piece of territory to such an extent that a West Russian government might be set up to govern it and to supervise future conquests to the east. German nationalists, militarists, monarchists, and some industrialists saw this eventuality linked somehow with an overthrow of the current Berlin regime and a renunciation of the Versailles Treaty. To resist the Entente, Germany must be able to overcome the threat of a blockade. Arm in arm with a conservative, bourgeois "Russia of the future" this scenario might be profitably played out. It was not a new idea; in fact, General von der Goltz, while in command of German forces aiding the Whites in the Finnish Civil War, had been part of an aborted plan along these lines. In the summer of 1918, with the approval of the German High Command, von der Goltz and his immediate superior, Lieutenant General Ludwig von Estorff, had made contacts with reactionary monarchist Russian groups and were putting together preliminary plans for a German–White Russian venture against St. Petersburg.[18] The German defeat in the west brought a quick end to these plans for the moment, but it is not without significance that General von Estorff was given command of the *OKN* on July 5.[19] Three days later a secret dispatch of that command clearly indicated the intentions of von Estorff, von Fritsch, and the military leaders in East Prussia.

> The only possibility of still assisting German eastern policies lies in the *VI-RK* and in strong support of the anti-Bolshevik Russian units in the process of formation. Portions of the German troops in Latvia are ready to enter the Russian service. Support for the operation is requested from the *Oberkommando* of the *KSK* (*Kommandostelle Kolberg*).[20]

On July 6 General von der Goltz and Major Bischoff met and determined to make sure that there remained in the *VI-RK* no halfhearted troop units such as those who performed such poor service at Cēsis. These were now sent home, an action that tended to raise the general fighting reliability of von der Goltz's troop units and also gave the impression to the Allies that the evacuation of the *Baltikum* was going apace. In the meantime depleted units were filled up with new recruits raised in Germany and by troops "furloughed" by the *OKN* and transported into Latvia from East Prussia.[21]

A splendid review was held in Jelgava on July 12 for von der Goltz and Bermondt, symbolically placing a seal on the German-Russian union, but the commander of the *VI-RK* was beginning to have his doubts about the venture. He sensed correctly that without at least tacit acquiescence from the Allies and firm financial support from some quarter, the project could not succeed.[22] This feeling was intensified by his meeting on July 19 with General Sir Hubert Gough. The German maintained a coldly removed attitude bordering on hostility throughout the brief conference, but he came away much impressed by the firm position taken by the Allied representative and his staff.[23]

On July 22 a German troop leaders' meeting was held by von der Goltz at Jelgava. Here the general voiced his pessimism in very clear, practical terms. He was now sure that the evacuation was inevitable, and he said so in no uncertain terms, but his freecorps leaders would have none of it. Led by Cordt von Brandis they let it be known that they were intent on marching to Smolensk and on to Moscow. In his harangue to the hot-blooded freebooters the popular hero of Douaumont and friend of Germany's crown prince argued that the Allies would certainly support them after their first successes. "Men will pour out to us, and the Entente must support us. They do all the others. . . . Here is the place to begin cutting the barbed wire fence which has been thrown up around Germany." Much to his commander's displeasure he was given a standing ovation.[24]

Between the time of this meeting and mid-August von der Goltz acted the part of a fellow traveler in the preparation of the West Russian Army. He determined to hold on and hope. He worked feverishly to speed the arming and training of Russian units and German volunteers, but he had decided that he would probably not be able to take an active part in the coming military operations.[25] A so-called German Legion was now created in skeleton form to act as a cadre formation into which volunteer troop units would eventually be transfered to fight "under the Russian flag." On July 27 a mass meeting of troop representatives forwarded a petition to the German diplomatic mission in Riga calling for the government of Kārlis Ulmanis to carry out its promises of land settlement to the "German liberators of Latvia," promises that had never been given and, of course, would have had no legal basis now even if they had been given. The Latvian response was stepped up military preparations.[26]

The Allies, in the meantime, were developing a better picture of events in Latvia than was the Berlin government itself. The coming "union" was reported to Lord Curzon in early July, and at the Peace Conference reports from the field told of the German buildup. On July 28 General Foch demanded that von der Goltz be removed from his command. But by the first week of August the course of events in the *Baltikum* had little to do with whether that general did or did not stay on the scene. Only forceful military and political leadership from the homeland could have headed off the coming confrontation, and such leadership did not come forward.[27]

On August 12 von der Goltz's superiors in Kolberg (*KSK*) set in motion a series of events that would culminate at the end of the month in an open mutiny of German forces in Latvia. Von Seeckt ordered the evacuation speeded and demanded that further recruitment for the Bermondt adventure cease. In the meantime, however, August Winnig, with his shadow government in East Prussia, was able to gain the ear of War Minister Noske and secure tacit support from this important quarter. Noske met troop delegations sympathetically and thought they might well transfer into "Russian service." The Entente's opposition bothered him, but he wished the men success and promised no prejudicial action against those who might take part in the venture. If he were twenty again, he told one freecorps leader, "I might go along with you."[28]

On the day following the *KSK* order, representatives of the West Russian Council arrived in Jelgava from Berlin and met with General von der Goltz. In no-nonsense language the commander demanded explicit details relating to firm financial backing for the undertaking. They could give him no satisfaction, and he ordered that they make no more contacts with Major Bischoff or other troop leaders of his command.[29] Von der Goltz now raced to Kolberg and met with General Wilhelm von Groener on August 16. His superior pushed von der Goltz to speed up the evacuation of the *Baltikum*, but also present were Winnig and representatives of the *OKN* who argued that the German troops must stay in the east as long as possible.[30]

Groener was unconvinced, but the two generals now sped to Weimar finally to determine the position of the government in the matter. Both were surprised at the remarkably cordial reception from President Friedrich Ebert and his ministers. The Socialist leaders informed the commander of the *VI-RK*, probably the best fighting unit left in the German Army, that his troops might remain in the *Baltikum* as volunteers; this was a private matter for each soldier to decide. Would the government continue to supply the "Russians," or at least quietly tolerate it? The government would have no objections. The cabinet even agreed to pay the "Russian" formations for another month, War Minister Noske casting the deciding vote.[31]

General von der Goltz returned to Latvia on August 24 to find that Major Bischoff and the freecorps of the *VI-RK* had mutinied and now absolutely refused to obey any order to return to Germany. When the first troops had been drawn together to begin the long awaited evacuation on that day, Bischoff and Captain Guderian had appeared at the train station and ordered that none was to entrain or raise a finger to effect the evacuation of the *Baltikum*. That night after a gigantic torchlight parade in Jelgava, the commander of the Iron Division addressed his troops. He told them that their actions might lead to Germany's salvation. But first, "We march on Riga!"[32] All that day agents of the right-wing All German

Union were at Bischoff's side. His was the best fighting unit in the German Army. It must be held together until the right moment had arrived early in the coming year.[33]

Von der Goltz met with Bischoff and told him that he must officially object to the events of August 24. He would stay with his troops; he understood his soldiers' complaints but, of course, could not openly approve of their means.[34] The Berlin government's attempts to bring order out of this situation were downright ludicrous. Noske finally sent an officer out to the troops to speak to them personally, only to have the man threatened with physical violence by Major Bischoff himself. At the very same time the German war minister was telling the press that orders to the *Baltikumers* were of no avail and would solve nothing.[35]

Finances continued to plague the leaders of the West Russian Council in Berlin. Far more than the month-to-month accommodation of the Berlin government was necessary. Hopes to acquire guarantees from heavy industrial concerns had been tentative at best—never firm. Now the Council determined to create the collateral necessary through military victories. The "government" would issue paper money, the so-called *Bermondt Geld*, against Russian crown forests. As victory followed victory and more collateral was acquired, financial support would surely flow in from all sides. For now it was hoped that the crown lands of Courland would be enough. But it must be clear to all that they were securely in the hands of the West Russian Army.[36]

The military preparations for these victories were stepped up during September. In Germany, however, the Berlin government continued to bob and weave. The cabinet rejected Bischoff's demands and ordered the mutineers home, even going so far as to threaten eventually to cut off pay and supplies if the mutiny continued much longer. Foreign Minister Hermann Müller was instructed to deliver conciliatory notes to the Entente and to the Latvian Provisional Government, the latter for the excesses of the mutinying troops.[37] Meanwhile the battle waxed hot in the National Assembly over conditions in the *Baltikum*. Right-wing opposition members castigated the government for not supporting the troops, while the left-wing Independent Socialists, headed by Hugo Haase, hammered away at the government's irresolute and opportunistic policy in the *Baltikum*.[38]

But the real pressure now came from the Allies. After August 26 the dispatches from the British Mission in Riga were increasingly grim and pessimistic. By mid-September Lord Curzon had the idea that a truly gigantic undertaking was afoot. General Gough was called to Paris and on

September 18 he outlined the German position. On the same day Lord Curzon decided to speed the flow of material aid to the Latvian government.[39]

On September 17 the "official" transfer of the German units into the West Russian Army began, and the next day orders to the troops began appearing over Bermondt's signature. Doubtful to the last, von der Goltz still had some hopes and had determined that the entire affair must now have nothing more than the face of an anti-Bolshevik crusade. All other considerations must be set aside for the time being (e.g., settlement for the German volunteers). In the meantime the Latvians were invited to take part in the crusade. [40] Bischoff, however, was dead set that local national forces must be neutralized or won over, one way or another. No threats from the rear could be tolerated once the campaign was under way.[41]

Between September 25 and October 8 the tangled rush of events in Berlin and Latvia demonstrated the frantic and clinging hopes of the *Baltikumers*, and the almost unbelievable capacity of the German government for indecisive and opportunistic leadership. The cabinet met on September 25 and gave permission for the German troops to transfer into the West Russian Army. They also agreed to recall von der Goltz to mollify the Allies, since his name had become anathema in London and Paris. The next day Noske wired the general that German troops should decide "whether they a) will transfer into the Russian service at their own risk, or b) will return to Germany on command by railroad or on foot."[42]

The timing of the next move in this complicated chess match was truly dramatic. Forty-eight hours after Noske's permission had been secretly telegraphed to von der Goltz, the Allied leadership in Paris determined to play the game with the Germans no longer. The Armistice Commission was instructed to deliver an ultimatum to the German government. All German troops, including those masquerading as Russians, were to be withdrawn from the Baltic area. Less than immediate compliance would lead to reestablishment of the blockade.[43] The German government's change of direction was mercurial. An order was immediately sent the *VI-RK* countermanding the permission granted for the troop transfer. But this order, for unexplained reasons, did not reach the *OKN* in Bartenstein until September 30 and was not relayed to von der Goltz until October 1. By then it was too late. On reception of Noske's permission, the general had ordered a concentration of the *VI-RK* around Jelgava and the German units were transfered into the West Russian Army. On October 3 General von der Goltz dutifully replied to the government's order, stating he was ready to comply, without question, but that all the troops transferred into the Russian service, pursuant to the September 26 telegram, were now outside his command.[44]

The Berlin government made another pitiful call to the troops to come home in order to spare the fatherland more suffering. Bischoff, for his part, called for combat to break the "chains of Versailles."[45] The plan was to attack the Latvians, hit them hard, and force them to recognize the legitimacy of the West Russian Army, without actually crossing the river and taking Riga.[46] Between October 4 and 7 the German forces moved out from Jelgava in the direction of the capital city.

The German attack had been the last straw for the Allies, and on October 10 they reestablished the blockade over all German shipping in the Baltic.[47] The Allied naval command also decided to bring its guns into play on the Latvian side. The morale of the Latvian defenders rose considerably. Troops were brought from the eastern front to help shore up Riga's defenses, the Soviets remaining helpfully inactive. By October 21 the Latvian position was stabilized, although the German Army kept up a continual bombardment of the capital city. The German staff now saw that they had got themselves into a hopeless situation. They had no place to go and were depending on a move from their opponent which they could not force him to make. Supplies were growing short and no more could be counted on, even from the sympathetic *OKN*. To add to the Germans' distress, the Lithuanians had lost their patience with Bermondt's troops on their soil. From October 15 the relations between these two deteriorated, and several armed encounters took place between Lithuanian and German troops, a situation that posed an additional threat to the *VI-RK* and the West Russian Army.[48]

On November 11 the Latvians struck all along the Daugava, and by November 15 the German Legion was almost surrounded at Jelgava.[49] Four more days of bitter fighting and a Lithuanian attack in the south convinced Bischoff that he must throw in the towel. On November 17 the West Russian Army formally asked that the Iron Division and the German Legion be taken back into the *VI-RK*. General von Eberhardt, who had taken over von der Goltz's old command on October 12, acted with dispatch and announced to the Latvians the next day that the West Russian Army was now under the protection of the *VI-RK*. He requested an armistice, but the Latvians would have none of it; their troops were at this moment destroying the German forces. Meanwhile to the south the Lithuanians had placed severe pressure on the German troops just as von Eberhardt had ordered an unsuccessful counterattack against the Latvians facing him. On November 21 the Germans pulled out of Jelgava. They left the historic Couronian city in flames and headed for the Lithuanian frontier.[50]

Von Eberhardt was able to save the remainder of his broken army by working out an agreement with the truculent Lithuanians, and on November 23 the last forces of the *VI-RK* limped across the border out of Latvia, while Lithuanian troops came between the two combatants. Behind them the Germans left a scorched earth. The landscape was charred and blackened by the *Baltikumer* firebrands. Everything portable was carried off; the rest was put to the torch. Latvian civilians were subjected to unspeakable atrocities and in return no captured *Baltikumer* could count on anything milder than immediate dispatch.[51]

The German freebooters crossed the German frontier on December 13, first having been whipped together by their officers to make them look like something other than undisciplined mercenaries and adventurers. The Iron Division was marched to Memel while the German Legion moved south to Tilsit. On orders from the War Ministry the former mutineers were paid and provisioned; all talk of court-martials was now ended. Noske was as good as his word. Bischoff and von Eberhardt now worked to keep their troops together in order to maintain the physical integrity of their commands for future purposes.[52] Von der Goltz, now retired from the service, worked continually on the behalf of his "cheated" troops. He appealed to the government to take care of his *Baltikumer*s and to allow them to guard Germany's borders against the Red menace to the east.[53] But the Berlin government had finally come to see how dangerous these troops might be if kept together, particularly dangerous to the government itself. Talk of a rightist-nationalist counterrevolution was common.[54] So, by mid-March most of the *Baltikumer* units had been demobilized, and when the putschist Kapp "regime" temporarily took power in Berlin on March 13 an order to Major Bischoff to put together his old command came to naught. Many *Baltikumer*s did take part in the Kapp putsch, however, and were further embittered by its ultimate failure.[55] Later in 1923 the *Baltikumer*s, particularly Rossbach and his freecorps, were clearly in evidence when Hitler and Ludendorff attempted to overthrow the Bavarian government. In fact, one small but basic element of Hitler's following throughout the 1920s were the veterans of the Baltic freecorps. Von der Goltz was one of the first major military figures to endorse Hitler's presidential candidacy in 1932. When Hitler did take power the Baltic Campaign became a favorite patriotic tale for the Nazi regime. It well illustrated the duplicity of the Weimar government and it showed how a steadfast group of patriots might endure long suffering in pursuit of a noble goal, the salvation of the fatherland. Naturally it was carefully noted that the overwhelming majority of these patriots had supported the Nazis' struggle to power and now stood solidly behind the Nazi revolution.[56]

The ultimate responsibility for the Baltic fiasco must be assigned to the Berlin government, primarily to War Minister Gustav Noske. To have been able to please the German military and at the same time to have placated the Allies would have been an almost impossible task. But Noske was willing to succumb almost completely to the avarice and folly of his most adventurous generals in the east. Noske and his supporters in and out of the War Ministry were still intent on picking up whatever might be salvaged from Germany's crippled *Ostpolitik*, and only in the face of the most severe Allied pressures did Noske reverse his pliant, opportunistic policies. This reversal constituted the special "stab-in-the-back" for the *Baltikumer*s, which was to serve as a stock, but rather accurate, indictment in their never-ending invective directed against the Weimar Republic.

But the ultimate significance of the Baltic Campaign is, of course, not solely to be understood in the militant opposition toward republican Germany of these disgruntled veterans. The campaign in the spring of 1919 had helped clear the nascent Latvian republic of the Soviet invaders and had helped to mold a national fighting force. When called upon, this fighting force, with Allied assistance and solid support from their Estonian and Lithuanian brethren, was able to drive the Germans from Latvian soil, an act that must be considered an important element in helping to form a strong Latvian national consciousness in the years to come. Citizens of the young Latvian republic could hardly be blamed for having a strong sense of national pride whenever they reflected on the overwhelming victories that were theirs as a result of this sorry German military escapade.

The *Land Oberost* and Its Place in Germany's *Ostpolitik*, 1915–1918

ABA STRAZHAS

Germany's *Ostpolitik* during World War I is a subject on which historical literature still presents conflicting views. The purpose of this chapter is to examine Germany's policies in Eastern Europe and by means of a vertical cut to extract and analyze one segment out of the complex of these policies. The history of the so-called *Land Oberost* represents such a segment. It reveals the general lines of the eastern policy pursued by Germany's military and political authorities in World War I.

After its victories in the east in the autumn of 1915, Germany's High Command created an administrative area named Land of the Commander in Chief of the Eastern Front (*Das Land des Oberbefehlshabers Ost*), or *Land Oberost* in shortened form. It was made up of ethnographic Lithuania, Courland, the province of Grodno (with the towns Bialystok and Belsk), and two Polish districts (Suvalki and Augustovo) of the former Suvalki province, the greater part of which had been Lithuanian. Thus this territory stretched from the left bank of the mouth of the Western Dvina in the north to the Belovezh forests in the south, including them into an area of 111,911 square kilometers.

Germany's policy toward this territory was distinguished by three specific features. First, while influential personalities and groups of the German public disagreed sharply concerning the other territories of Eastern Europe that in the course of the war had come under the rule of the German Army, hardly anybody after 1915 questioned the need for Germany to annex Lithuania and Courland.[1] In the autumn of 1917 only the form of the annexation was discussed. The so-called Petition of Six Economic Associations demanded the annexation of "at least a part of the Baltic provinces and districts lying to their south." Coming in its wake, the Petition of Professors also pointed to the acquisition of the "Russian Baltic provinces" as one of the aims of the war.[2]

The great mass of German wartime literature on the aims of the war clearly shows that both the supporters of the "world policy" (*Weltpolitik*) concept and the various advocates of the "Central European idea" (*Mitteleuropa*) agreed to a direct annexation of at least Lithuania and Courland, although they differed in regard to the other eastern territories.

Also, the *Land Oberost* represented a territory with a population of 2 to 3 million on whose annexation the political and the military leadership of Germany was agreed.[3]

Furthermore, this territory attracted attention because of the extraordinary occupation regime that the Germans introduced. This administration differed not only from the one that Austria-Hungary had established in the governorship-general of Lublin, but also from the German military administration in Belgium and from the Warsaw governorship-general. These features indicate that *Land Oberost* had been assigned a special part in Germany's *Ostpolitik*.

The number of studies treating problems of Baltic and Lithuanian history of this or closely related periods is considerable.[4] Some have appeared in the Socialist countries of Europe and are valuable chiefly for their materials drawn from archives to which Western students have no access. Many more research works have appeared in the West. Though doubtlessly very informative in factual description, they deal only with Lithuania or its neighbors and not with the history of the *Land Oberost* as a whole and its place in the complex of Germany's *Ostpolitik*, 1914–1918. Historian Fritz Epstein has noted that in some of these generally valuable works the Baltic problems are placed into a vacuum.[5] Further investigations should attempt to fill this vacuum.

A study of evidence in accessible sources[6] allows the following characterization of the German policies toward the *Land Oberost* in 1914–1918.

Germany's Territorial Objectives in the Baltic Region

Since the closing decades of the nineteenth century the Germans had markedly intensified activities aimed at an enhancement of the German influence and an increase of German settlement in the Baltic lands, primarily in Courland. These activities bore more fruit after the Russian revolution of 1905. German barons from Russia's Baltic provinces, who had previously served the Tsar, became convinced that the Tsarist government had grown too weak to defend their interests, and so they turned to Germany.[7] The cultural activities of German associations (*Deutsche Vereine*) in the Baltic lands camouflaged this pro-German political orientation and effort of colonization. With money obtained from Germany these associations managed to settle in Courland many thousands of German peasants and farmworkers from the Volga and Volynian areas.[8] Factories and plants were founded, often with the capital owned by high German officials. For example, the cellulose plant of the incorporated Russian company Waldhof in Pärnu (Pernau) was a purely German firm, managed from Mannheim, with capital invested by the Kaiser. It was built to be easily converted into a repair shop for German battleships on the entrance of German forces. Armed German units of self-defense, organized during the revolution of 1905–1907, continued to operate up to the very outbreak of the war. The extremely large fire brigades and groups of guards in the German enterprises were chiefly manned by Germans from the Reich. Having studied this situation, the deputy commander of the Daugavpils (Dünaburg) military district, General Kurlov—he was known as a German sympathizer—wrote in his account of October 30, 1914: "There is no doubt that before the outbreak of the war the Baltic provinces had been covered by a serious network of espionage."[9]

Furthermore, several Russian schools of higher learning that were staffed with a considerable number of German scholars—for instance, the Historical-Philological Institute of Nezhin (Director Joseph Lezius, Professor Friedrich Wiedemann, and others)—had become centers of pro-German propaganda. The well-known university of Dorpat retained its nationalistic German character despite the fact that on the eve of the war Germans constituted fewer than 1000 of its 2255 students.

The Tsarist government, seeing the German nobility as a bulwark against revolution, hesitated to take measures against the growing German influence. Suggestions by the commander of the northern front, General Nikolai Vladimirovich Ruzski, and later by General Pavel Adamovich Pleve and General Michail Vasilevich Alekseev that the University of Dorpat be transferred farther inland were declined by the Tsar.[10] In this light, it becomes clear why the commander of the Liepāja (Libau) fortress was confused when the German cruiser *Augsburg* began to shell the town as early as August 1914.[11]

Similar activities were taking place in Lithuania,[12] though the German population there was smaller. Before the war the Germans constituted only 1.41% of the population in the Kovno (Kaunas) province and 0.24% in the Vilnius province. Only in the province of Suvalki, in relation to which, as it is known, Germany had special intentions, did their number reach 5.2% (with 15.92% of the population living in the district of Vil-kaviškis).[13] Nor was the number of Germans in Courland exceedingly large (7.57%), but there, as a result of old privileges, the German aristocrats and burghers held key positions in the local administration and economy.

Such activities were supported by German Balts who lived in Germany and occupied high positions there (Theodor Schiedemann, Adolf von Harnack, August von Oettingen, E. Bergmann, and many others).[14] After the German occupation of Courland many sons of eminent local families, serving in the German armed forces, returned home at the head of their German military units (Osten-Saken, Moltret, and others).

These developments showed that long before the outbreak of Russian-German hostilities in 1914 the Germans had considered the idea of pushing Germany's eastern border at least up to Courland, thus cutting Lithuania off from Russia.

Even though in June 1915 *Reichskanzler* Theobald von Bethmann Hollweg adopted a negative attitude toward the Baltic plans of Schiede-mann and Ludendorff on the grounds that Bismarck had treated the question of the Baltic province as a *noli me tangere*, he was not against borderline corrections that included Lithuania and Courland rather than Livonia and Estonia. After the events of late 1914, it became "obvious" to the "German educated society"[15] that Germany must demand a borderline in Poland that would bring the strongly fortified Narev-Neman(Nemunas) line into German hands. But the fortifications were on both sides of the Neman! Where, then, was to be the ultimate line of Germany's aspirations on the eastern bank of the Neman?

As quoted by Gerhard Ritter, Bethmann Hollweg spoke about the "only open access to the sea" of which Russia should not be deprived in order to avoid long-term animosity. The allusion was to Riga, which even after its German occupation in the autumn of 1917 remained outside the borders of *Land Oberost*. The *Reichskanzler* also considered the Latvians (but not the Lithuanians) to be anti-German, hence not to be incorporated into Germany. But, as far as *Land Oberost* was concerned, first, there never was any question of an ordinary incorporation and, second, it was hard to believe that anybody in Germany would have been afraid of the 224,000 Latvians who remained in Courland after its occupation. True, in his letter to Hindenburg of January 20, 1916, the *Reichskanzler* mentions the possibility of returning a part of the occupied territory to Russia; however, it must be borne in mind that in this letter Bethmann Hollweg emphasizes the necessity of preventing Lithuanian nationalistic propaganda. Had he really meant a return of the greater part of Lithuania to Russia, why would he have expressed such touching solicitude for Russia's interests? Relevant in this connection is the fact that at the very beginning of the war Lithuania was excluded from the revolutionizing policy of the German Foreign Office. Furthermore, it was not only the Lithuanians whose ambitions of national freedom and struggle against Russia's rule were not to be encouraged; even the Lithuanian Jews were to be kept under German control. The Zionist leader of the German Jewry, Max Bodenheimer, was greatly astonished to learn, after his negotiations with the Foreign Office and General Staff Commissioner Bohdan von Hutten-Czapski, who was in charge of the policy of revolutionizing the nationalities of Russia, that the September 1914 appeal concerned only the Jews of Poland and not those of Lithuania.[16]

It was definitely not solicitude for the unity of the Russian multinational state that preoccupied the leaders of the Reich and the army. While there existed some difference of opinion in Germany's ruling circles on the annexation of Livonia and Estonia, the "attachment" (*Angliederung*), not incorporation (*Einverleibung*), of Lithuania and Courland to Germany was viewed by almost everybody as the minimum that should be brought about. Yet this attachment, as we shall see, was to be such as to prevent a strong Lithuanian national movement. The "rapid change" in Bethmann Hollweg's attitude toward the Baltic question, leading him in April 1916 to speak of the annexation of Suvalki, Courland, Kovno, Grodno, and Vilnius, turned out to be no change at all. It was merely Germany's minimal goal in the east, now stated by the *Reichskanzler* more loudly.

German Nationality Policy in the *Land Oberost*

The history of Ludendorff's "private province"[17]—the *Land Oberost*—reveals a noteworthy continuity in the German annexation plans. The many attempts to achieve a separate peace with Russia inevitably fell through because of the German government's unyielding demand that Russia relinquish the territory of Lithuania and Courland. The acquisition of Lithuania and Courland remained a *conditio sine qua non* also in the negotiations of war aims with Austria-Hungary during the rule of Bethmann Hollweg, Michaelis, and Hertling. The grim and tragic picture of Austria-Hungary, drawn by its Minister of Foreign Affairs Ottokar Czernin during his conference with Bethmann Hollweg in Vienna on March 16, 1917, did not discourage the Germans. To facilitate Russia's compliance with this demand, the German government exerted pressure on the tottering Hapsburg monarchy to force it "to sacrifice a part of eastern Galicia"[18] to Russia, although Czernin had indicated the great danger of such a concession to Austria-Hungary's internal political situation.

The political and military intelligence services of Russia kept a vigilant eye on all that was taking place in occupied Lithuania and Courland, then regarded as Russia's defense gates in the west. For the Germans, this territory, with its northern part sharply jutting out to the northeast and its southern forming a bridge to the Ukraine, was merely a base of operations.

Whatever Bethmann Hollweg's personal views, whatever the mist in which he wanted to shroud his real intentions—hinting, for instance, that in the case of a less successful outcome of the war Vilnius might be returned to Russia—the territory of the *Oberost* was seen as an indivisible whole not only by the military command but also by the German diplomats. No sooner had the occupation taken place than the German embassies in neutral states dropped hints that Lithuania might consist of "the provinces of Suvalki, Kovno, Grodno, Vilna and Courland."[19]

The *Land Oberost* was not established based on ethnographic boundaries. It was a multinational area of Lithuanians, Latvians, and large groups of other nationalities. The provisions of the 1916 German census reveal a strong tendency to downplay the actual number of Lithuanians. Much of the population, particularly the Lithuanians, was excluded from the census. The census showed a total population of 2,881,396 (as compared to 5 million before the war), including 1,269,448 Lithuanians, 806,674 Poles, 322,411 Jews, 224,845 Latvians, 159,473 Belorussians, and 61,633 Germans. The fact that even the Lithuanians did not constitute an absolute majority in the region was used by the German authorities as an excuse to ignore the national aspirations of the entire population. At the same time the proclaimed equality of all nationalities meant in fact a neutralization of all national forces. Well-calculated and subtly implemented instigations of one national group against another ensured the policy of divide and conquer.

All political activity, particularly "that of the national groups," was strictly forbidden. Since the Lithuanians constituted the largest nationality in the *Oberost*, their national movement was suppressed the most. The Poles and the Jews were allowed to publish their own daily newspapers. The Lithuanians were denied this right and had to make do with the official newspaper *Dabartis* (The Present), published three times a week,[20] whose contents and linguistic culture were viewed as anti-Luthuanian.

The Poles and especially the Jews, however, were robbed of their means of subsistence by the military administration, which monopolized all trade and industry and sequestered about 1700 estates,[21] mostly in former Polish possessions. The Poles and the Jews were compelled to resort to black marketing, while the Lithuanians were given to understand that after the war they might be able to buy these sequestered enterprises at a low cost. Thus the new rulers both created an economic basis for antisemitism and further aggravated the old Lithuanian-Polish hostility.

Organization and Influence of Military Administration

The occupation regime[22] of the *Land Oberost* had the following characteristics:

(*a*) The administration was exclusively military and exclusively German. No civilian was employed in the occupation apparatus. Army officials were strictly forbidden to fraternize with the civilians.

(*b*) Every salaried position in the administration, even the lowest, was reserved exclusively for the Reichs Germans. Local Germans could not be employed, not to speak of Lithuanians and Latvians. Only specific tasks that paid no remuneration were entrusted to the natives, both German and non-German.

(*c*) District commanders (*Kreishauptleute*) were vested with unlimited power over the population. Only the Reich Germans had the right to appeal.

(*d*) The district commanders also had broad judicial powers, since the military courts could not cope with the extra work made necessary by the administration's system of terror. By order of the *Ost* commander in chief, death sentences were to be carried out secretly. Only a few were to be announced for purposes of intimidation, along with those cases in which, the order stated, the accused was expected to be pardoned.

Court documents and prison books found in the Vilnius State Archives, which contain files on every prisoner and his or her sentence, give testimony that contradicts Ludendorff's in his memoirs about military justice. Court practices also violated international agreements, ignored Russian laws, and pronounced sentences that would conform with the orders and instructions of the commander in chief and the district military administration. Yet most of the legal orders, instructions, and listings of various duties and prohibitions remained unknown to the population. Instead of justice, the courts seemed to practice an arbitrary squaring of accounts with the oppressed population.[23]

The Prussian system, notorious for its strict direction of every step of the population, in *Land Oberost* was reinforced and rendered unbearable by the added imposition of hunger, terror, and insults. The population was forbidden to cross the boundaries of districts and precincts and, in a somewhat milder form, even to change place of residence.

The outline of the administrative system was published only in June 1916—almost nine months after the formal announcement of the administration for this territory.[24] The thorough and precise elaboration of the *Verwaltungsordnung* indicates (an indication confirmed by statements in Germany)[25] that the German military administration *Oberost* was not established for the war period only. The plan *Neuland* (Lithuania and Courland), painstakingly accomplished by the end of October 1917— its documentation is housed in the Lithuanian Historical State Archives— contains calculations based on the intention to retain the area's administrative and exploitative system after the war.[26]

The question whether it was only in April 1916 that Bethmann Hollweg agreed to the annexation of Lithuania and Courland within *Land Oberost* is answered by documents located in the various German state offices. All the preparatory and consultation work for the occupation regime points to the active participation of state offices (*Reichsämter*) in the drafting of the administrative design for the region. The relationship between these governmental offices and the German Military Administration *Oberost* gives good reason to believe Ludendorff when he says that on questions of the *Land Oberost* there was full agreement between the military Command and the *Reichskanzler*.

In this respect it is important to note that the Germans gradually abolished all local administrative institutions that had existed under Tsarist rule as well as the new administrative units that were—remarkably—set up in numerous towns on a democratic basis within days during the change of power in Lithuania. According to German reports from Raseiniai, Biržai, Kupiškis, and other towns, local military commanders were displeased by this action because they thereby lost knowledgeable native personnel.[27] But Ludendorff pursued completely different aims. In his memoirs the general has justified the creation of a special administration on grounds that, on entering into Lithuania, the German army found complete chaos.

It is remarkable that the *Reichskanzler* spoke in almost the same terms when addressing the *Reichstag* on December 9, 1915. Besides, as Erwin Direnberger has already proved, up to 1917 there had been no disagreements between Bethmann Hollweg and Ludendorff. In this connection, Direnberger recalled what great pains the *Reichskanzler* had taken to place Hindenburg and Ludendorff at the head of Germany's armed forces.[28]

The close collaboration of the governmental apparatus in the setting up of the *Oberost* military administration is further evident in the selection of its cadres. Though Bethmann Hollweg disagreed with the leaders of the All-German Alliance (*Alldeutscher Verband*) on some tactical questions, it was nevertheless with the help of his government that an administration of a purely Pan-Germanistic character was set up in *Land Oberost*. It included men who had good knowledge of the colonial order in Africa and experience in intelligence work.

The position of the chief of the "Lithuania" district, which at first consisted only of the former Kovno province, was given to Prince Joseph Isenburg-Birstein, a cousin of the Saxonian King Friedrich August III, who was a Pan-Germanist of the highest order. In Lithuania he was called the "German Muravev the Hangman" because his policy, conducted in the "strict spirit of Pan-Germanism,"[29] was accompanied by cruel repressions. All the warnings that Bethmann Hollweg received from the deputies of the Center party and the Social Democrats—even their hints that Isenburg's activities might lead to an uprising of the population[30]— remained unheeded until January 1918.

Chief of the "Vilno-Suvalki" district (which was joined to Lithuania in early 1917) was Ludwig Count Yorck von Wartenburg, the grandson of the "Iron Yorck." He belonged to the decisive majority in the almighty Prussian House of Lords and was an ardent defender of the anti-Polish *Ostmarkpolitik*. Incidentally, it was just in this district that the greater part of *Land Oberost*'s Polish population lived. He was among the most reactionary members of the Conservative party, "on whom none of the violent events of the world war . . . produced any impression."[31]

Courland's dictator was Alfred von Gossler, Conservative party deputy in the *Reichstag* and also a member of the *Reichstag*'s chief parliamentary commission.

A major role in *Oberost* was played by the head of the Department for Interior Affairs, Baron Wilhelm von Gayl, who some twenty years later became notorious as minister of the interior in von Papen's government.[32] He made plans for a quick and cheap settlement of Reichs Germans in the *Oberost* territory, deporting segments of the local population and preventing hundreds of thousands of the area's refugees to return from Russia.[33]

Lesser officials, too, were selected from similar circles. Baron Ernst von Merck, for example, had had military and diplomatic experience in Guatemala and had rendered valuable intelligence services to Germany. On the personal recommendation of Germany's Foreign Minister Arthur Zimmermann, the military administration also employed the Bavarian captain Dr. Georg Escherich, an expert in forestry who had extensive experience in intelligence work. He had been a forestry expert in Ethiopia and a colonial administrator in the German Cameroons. As head of the *Orgesch* (*Organisation Escherich*) he later became known for crushing the Bavarian Communist government in Munich in 1919. Captain Escherich's political adviser was the chairman of the All-German Alliance, Heinrich Class.

This cohort of the German war machine, planted in the *Land Oberost* with the approval and aid of the Reich government, could not have had any task other than that of carrying out a policy fully in keeping with Pan-Germanistic aims and with Ludendorff's will. This policy was pursued with an astonishing tenacity.

Economic Policies of the Occupation Regime

The government of the Reich and the military High Command allowed the German Military Administration *Oberost* a great measure of independence. The government could thus evade criticism for the regime of terror that this military administration had introduced, though the latter's staff, financial status, and the nature of its relations with government agencies were determined at a military-government consultation in Berlin on April 17–18, 1916. It was jointly decided that the Ministry of the Interior was not to interfere with the administration's activities.[34] Its income, not to be administered by the Ministry of Finance, consisted of "booty funds" (old and new customs duties, taxes, and others), revenues from the police and court proceedings, and profits from "its own" factories and enterprises, from the timber industry, and other sources. While the German government had financial difficulties in maintaining the household of the Warsaw governorship-general and the government of Austria-Hungary was forced to subsidize the administration of the Lublin governor-ship-general, the general military administration *Oberost* soon turned into a multimillionaire.

The growth of the administration's revenues showed its constantly growing exploitation of the population. In January 1916, for example, its police force collected 50,145.36 marks. By June these collections had increased to 109,908.36 marks. Similarly, income from court proceedings during the six months jumped from 175,305.50 to 418,383.48 marks. The total financial turnover tripled from 1,033,628.28 to 3,652,655.66 marks.[35]

By the end of 1917 the German military administration *Oberost* had 70 million marks in its account with the central war bank (*Generalkriegskasse*), in addition to considerable funds in its own treasury and in local banks. The "investments" of the military administration (wood processing and other enterprises) amounted to 324 million marks; its "own" inventory together with the different stocks in the requisitioned estates came to 110 million marks.

This financial strength rendered the military administration independent and influential. Such groups as the cellulose industry and various trade firms competed for its favors. Even the Free Hansa town Hamburg fought for trade in the area of the *Ost* commander in chief.[36] Obtaining license for commercial activity depended entirely on the good graces of the military administration. Under these conditions, created in 1916 with the help of the Reich government, the German military administration *Oberost* could allow itself not to take too seriously even questions of obedience to the High Command. It was in a position to exercise its influence in such political matters as the proclamation of the Polish state and Austrian-German relations. As a result of this arrangement, the Berlin government, while exercising influence, could evade parliamentary criticism of the occupation policy that was voiced by the Social Democrats and other opposition in the *Reichstag*.

The internal policies of the military administration were later characterized in the Lithuanian National Council (*Taryba*) as a bargain driven according to the formula: "Whatever is profitable to the Germans can be done!"[37] At the same time several members of the *Taryba* expressed their astonishment at the military administration's economic policies, which led to a paralysis of production in the area. It was indeed incomprehensible why the administration should continually hurt Germany's war interests by detrimental requisitions of the peasants' seedcorn, destruction of expensive machinery for the small amount of copper contained, and so on.[38] The dismantling and shipping to Germany of many large and small factories and the banning of the production of cigarettes and matches, items that could only be imported from Germany, in effect stopped the wheels of industry in the occupied land. The few factories that were profitable to the military administration could continue working, but were requisitioned and placed under German military management.[39]

Trade became the monopoly of the military administration's Department for Trade and Raw Materials and was restricted to fourteen items
(spirits, cigarettes, matches, salt, sugar, "war soap," etc.). All privately
owned textile and knitware stocks were registered and requisitioned.
The introduction of 500 million *Ostrubel* (*Ostmarken*) in Lithuania and
400 million in Courland, which replaced Russian currency to the population's disadvantage, further contributed to the destruction of local economy. Gold and other privately owned valuables, in part black marketed
in Scandinavia, were also requisitioned.

Diplomatic Attempts to Separate Lithuania from Russia

An examination of the military administration's activities reveals an in-
credibly purposeful striving to destroy the local economy as quickly as
possible, regardless of political or economic consequences. Since such
behavior obviously damaged Germany's immediate interests, it must
have been motivated by some long-range expectations.

The administration also severely suppressed and terrorized the population. During a meeting of the organizational committee for the convention
of the Lithuanian Conference in Vilnius in August 1917 one of the group's
members, J. Stakauskas, exclaimed that "for a hundred years the people
will not forget what they had to suffer from the Germans."[40] German
political agencies in neutral states nevertheless attempted to steer the
Lithuanian national movement along lines of German interest. Gifted
journalists with considerable influence over public opinion in neutral
countries were used for this purpose. Of special importance was the attitude
of American Lithuanians who claimed a population of 800,000.[41] They
had several strong and influential organizations: Union of Lithuanian
Catholics (100,000 members), Union of Lithuanian Workers (125,000
members), Union of Lithuanian Women Catholics, League of the Lithuanian National Fund, Association of Lithuanian Physicians, and others.
The well-organized Lithuanian population of the United States had become a serious political factor, particularly in the election campaign of
1916. In conformity with a Congressional decision of July 21, 1916,
President Woodrow Wilson proclaimed November 1 the day for a nation-
wide collection of donations for the benefit of war-ravaged Lithuania.[42]

Germany took note of these developments. At a time when Lithuania
was hermetically sealed from the outside world, a delegation of the
American-Lithuanian Council, consisting of Juozas Bielskis and Reverend
Vincas Bartuška, was given permission to visit the country. These men

wanted to establish contact between Lithuanian political figures and their colleagues in neutral countries.[43] On May 2, 1916, these American Lithuanians were officially welcomed by the military administration in Kaunas. The Germans listened to their wishes concerning Lithuania's future, made no promises, and only asked, as the Lithuanian philosopher and public figure Reverend Aleksandras Dambrauskas wrote in his diary, "to state their postulates in writing."[44] Bartuška promised American economic aid. Subsequently, Lithuanian politicians complained, according to Dambrauskas, that the lion's share of the aid "had in fact gone to the Prussian Lithuanians whereas the occupied territory was to satisfy itself with the promises."

In addition to fostering anti-Polish attitudes among Lithuanians, German political agents in neutral countries sought to use Lithuanian political figures for pressuring the Russian government into granting Lithuania an autonomy similar to the one the Tsarist government had promised Poland. This would throw Lithuania into Germany's lap and enable it to decide Lithuania's future more easily than that of Poland, half of which was under Austrian occupation. For this purpose the German minister in Switzerland, Gisbert Freiherr von Romberg, contacted a well-known Lithuanian journalist, Juozas Gabrys, an adventurer who loved to boast of his personal relationships with eminent politicians in the Entente countries and who had written a number of articles sharply critical of the German military administration in occupied Lithuania.[45]

In the United States 250 representatives of Lithuanian organizations convened in Chicago on September 21–22. The convention adopted a resolution demanding that Russia immediately grant Lithuania wide autonomy and stressed that the Lithuanian question, like the Polish question, had international significance. This thesis was supported by the demand to reunite Lithuania Minor with Lithuania proper, that is, to join the Lithuanian district of the German-ruled Eastern Prussia to Lithuania.[46] Similar Lithuanian activities kept the Lithuanian question alive in the West and forced the Russian government to continue to discuss it. The Tsarist government, however, was not willing to repeat the Polish variant in the case of Lithuania. It allocated large sums of money for the support of the 300,000 Lithuanian refugees and their institutions in Russia, but refused to make any declaration by which the Lithuanians would be singled out for political treatment.

To extort the coveted declaration from the Tsar, Germany used methods of political blackmail. In 1916 it staged negotiations with Lithuanian politicians on the establishment of an independent Lithuanian state, though at that time neither political nor military leaders in Germany had any intention of promoting a free Lithuanian state. In December 1916 a representative of the Swiss Lithuanian Center, Reverend Antanas Steponaitis, arrived in Lithuania to take part in such "negotiations" with the Oberost military administration and local Lithuanian notables. Once he had arrived in occupied Lithuania, he realized that the negotiations were merely "a comedy."[47]

On January 15, 1917, as a result of diplomatic activity aroused by the German peace proposal of December 1916 and by Steponaitis' mission, The Permanent Delegation of Lithuania's National Council (the Bern Lithuanian Committee) headed by Gabrys—such a council did not exist in reality—addressed a memorandum to the governments of Russia and the Entente countries. The Council suggested that the German government planned to issue a manifesto on Lithuania soon, similar to that issued by both the German and Austro-Hungarian Kaisers in relation to Poland on November 5, 1916. The memorandum further proposed that the initiative be immediately taken out of German hands and that the Tsarist government officially give Lithuania the same promises it had given Poland. It listed the provinces and regions to be included in the territory of Lithuania (the provinces of Vilnius, Kovno, Suvalki, and Courland, one district of the Minsk province, and a part of Lomzha province up to the rivers Lyk and Narev).[48]

These "negotiations" of the unofficial German representatives with the Lithuanian politicians deluded the Russian intelligence service. In January they sent to their government reports about the existence of a project in Germany to create a "pseudo-independent Lithuanian monarchy including the province of Suvalki as well as Courland."[49]

To pressure Russia, the Germans again used the press in neutral countries. The Gazette de Lausanne, whose pages often carried Gabrys' writings, on February 1, 1917, suggested that Germany would proclaim a Lithuanian state within a month. The Russian chargé d'affaires, Bibikoff, informed the Russian government, which did not swallow the bait, however. In his 1917 memorandum on the Polish question Minister of Foreign Affairs N. N. Pokrovskii concluded that "the liberation of the Lithuanians is not in our interest" and suggested that all measures be taken to hinder the growth "of the political consciousness of the Lithuanians."[50]

The February Revolution in Russia aroused new hopes for a separate peace, and the German government remained interested in those Lithuanian politicians whose aim was to obtain a Russian declaration that would weaken Russia's bonds with Lithuania. At the beginning of April, as Russian Foreign Ministry archives show, Gabrys sent the Provisional

Government a telegram of congratulations, expressing the hope that the principles of the "Great French Revolution" would also be applied to the Lithuanian people. The Permanent Delegation, in turn, handed a memorandum to the Russian chargé d'affaires signed by Bartuška and dated April 10, 1917. In this document the Lithuanians again tried to induce the Russians to compete for Lithuanian loyalties with the Germans by proposing that Russia outrun the Germans in granting Lithuania the same freedoms it had granted to its "old ally"—Poland. The territory of the proposed Lithuanian state covered the *Land Oberost*.

A promise of wide autonomy, sought also by the Lithuanian politicians in Russia, would single out the Lithuanians and bring the Lithuanian question, like the Polish question, into the international arena, thus taking it out of exclusive Russian jurisdiction, which could doubtlessly justify a change in Lithuania's political status. This could occur only according to Germany's prescriptions. The extraordinary efforts of the Lithuanian politicians in Switzerland may have made the Provisional Government suspicious and confirmed its decision to avoid binding declarations, despite the assurances of the Lithuanian politicians in Russia that the internationalization of the Lithuanian question "would not be a concession to the enemy."[51]

Lithuania had to beware not only of Germany's, but also of Poland's annexationist ambitions. Polish politicians, such as Roman Dmowski and Erasmus Piltz, who enjoyed "the full trust" of Russia's Provisional Government,[52] sought the annexation of Lithuania and Courland. So did the Austrian Poles—even more vigorously.

Early in the summer of 1917 Gabrys tried to persuade the legations of the Entente states in Switzerland to bring up the question of Lithuania at the inter-Allied conference in Paris in July. He was advised to appeal to the Russian mission, where, as before, he received a point-blank refusal. A secret memorandum, written under Foreign Minister M. I. Tereshchenko's direction, said that "the Lithuanian question is entirely a Russian question."

So in deciding the *Land Oberost*'s future the German government had to do without the desired Russian declaration.

Solution of the Lithuanian Question

Deportations, compulsory work, requisitions, and personal maltreatment roused the population to passive and active resistance. Armed peasant revolts broke out. During a requisitioning in Girkalnis peasant resistance was crushed by a punitive expedition that, according to the report of the Raseiniai district commander, left the place bare.[53] Armed groups began to appear in the woods of Lithuania, at first composed almost entirely of selected Russian Cossack servicemen. This so-called gang movement had started in the summer of 1915, when the Russian Supreme Command decided to launch a "guerrilla movement" in the German rear.[54]

Since the "guerrillas" were gaining sympathy and support from the population on both sides of the front, the Tsarist Supreme Command disbanded them to avoid a popular war. The "guerrilla" units that got stuck behind the German front lines, however, soon were augmented by Russian fugitives and prisoners of war and later also by local inhabitants.[55] As both German archives and Lithuanian sources show, the military administration combated the gangs in two ways. It cruelly punished villagers who extended support to the gangs. And it used the gangs as a pretext for depopulating rural districts and turning them, as the Polish deputy to the *Reichstag*, Wojciech Korfanty, charged, into regions ready for German colonization. The newspapers of the Central Powers, which otherwise had little knowledge of the misery reigning in the *Oberost* area, reported that "a systematic policy of removing local population" was being implemented.[56] Noteworthy in this connection is the remarkable buildup of forces in the autumn of 1917 in the *Oberost*, specifically in Lithuania, that occurred despite the tension on the western front. An executive order dated October 26, 1917, reveals that sixty-four permanent infantry companies and five rifle and six dragoon squadrons were stationed in Lithuania proper. Moreover, the military governor of Kaunas had the right to make use of all military units temporarily quartered in the town to fight "rebellion."[57] These units were to collaborate with the local German police and gendarme corps. On top of this, large special detachments were always on hand to fight the "gangs."

In late October the *Oberost* commanders received new reinforcements— the 41st Cavalry Division and a regiment of guards—all of which were intended to be used against the "gang movement."

New political developments in the spring of 1917 compelled the Reich government to adopt new tactics toward the *Land Oberost*. Besides the political and social changes brought about by the February Revolution in Russia, there were also Polish activities following Poland's proclamation as an independent state as well as the crisis in the relationships among the nationalities of Russia.

The Polish State Council lost no time in claiming Poland's "historical borders" and intensified its criticism of German politics. The concession made on September 12, 1917, as a result of which the Polish State Council was enlarged and a Regency Council was formed, did not diminish Poland's expansionist appetites, nor did it increase sympathies for Germany.[58]

A Pole-hating Lithuania in the Polish rear, firmly retained in German hands, could well serve the German interests. This is exactly what Rudolf Nadolni later suggested in his memorandum to the Foreign Office, which also mentioned the necessity of finding seven "reasonable Lithuanians" who could establish a Lithuanian government.[59]

The February Revolution in Russia had also created conditions for an impetuous growth of autonomist national movements. These movements were encouraged by the Council of Workers' and Soldiers' Deputies, which in disagreement with the policy of the Provisional Government proclaimed the principle of the self-determination of nations. The Ukrainians and other nationalities started a struggle for the implementation of this principle. Having failed to obtain from the Russian government a declaration that singled out the Lithuanians by a promise of national autonomy, the Germans now turned to the use of the slogan of self-determination, though this in no way tallied with their annexationist intentions toward *Land Oberost*.

While preparing for the armistice negotiations with the Russians in May 1917, the German Foreign Office and military command decided to make no concessions concerning the intended annexation of Lithuania and Courland.[60] The same documents reveal, however, that in his instructions to the German negotiating team Ludendorff spoke of an "attachment" (*Angliederung*) of these areas in such a way as to take into account "the national claims of the Lithuanians and Courlanders." He also directed that expressions like "annexation" and "border rectifications" be avoided by all means. These instructions were endorsed by Baron Kurt von Grünau, the representative of the Foreign Office at the General Headquarters. Thus began a period during which the German authorities adopted the formula "make annexations without calling them annexations," in conformity with a corresponding plan devised by the state secretary for foreign affairs, Arthur Zimmermann.[61] The German government was to demonstrate to the nationalities of Russia its positive attitude toward their national aspirations and to drive the states emerging from the wreckage of Russia into Germany's arms. Russia's political agents informed their government that this plan was first and foremost intended as an attraction for Finland, Estonia, and the Ukraine.[62]

In May 1917 Bethmann Hollweg personally gave instructions to "dress up" Lithuania and Courland as independent states without in any way impairing Germany's rule in this area.[63]

Even the Peace Note of the Pope played a role in the tactically changed competition for these regions. In the spring of 1917 the Pope began preparations to launch mediation activities and later enumerated in his note all the conditions that should create a basis for peace negotiations. These included the creation of an independent state of Poland in the "areas which constitute parts of the old Polish kingdom." The press of the Vatican interpreted these words as a proposal to join Lithuania and Courland to Poland.[64] Yet since the note also spoke of the hopes of the nationalities living in the area, which had to be protected "insofar as it was rightful and possible," the Germans found it necessary to make haste and produce a resolution to the effect that Lithuania and Courland demanded the establishment of independent national states that would maintain "eternal" relations of friendship with Germany.

The new developments forced the government of the Reich to embark upon a "Baltic policy" in Courland and a "Lithuanian policy" in the rest of the *Land Oberost*. That the Lithuanians did not constitute the majority in the *Oberost* area (even without Courland) was no longer important. The German authorities selected a group of German sympathizers (e.g., landowners in Courland) who brought into existence the *Landesrat* (a Land Council) in Courland. In Lithuania the Germans allowed the election of a Council (*Taryba*) at a conference in Vilnius. These bodies were to impersonate the "self-determination" according to German will. How seriously the German authorities took this matter becomes evident from the already-mentioned plan *Neuland*, which provided for the *Land Oberost* a colonial status under a military administration.[65]

Even after the peace of Brest-Litovsk and the Kaiser's recognition of the nonexisting states of Courland and Lithuania, no change in Germany's policy with respect to this territory occurred. There was much talk about the *Taryba* in the German press and in the *Reichstag* in connection with the following events. On February 16, 1918, the *Taryba* proclaimed an independent Lithuanian state, separate from Russia and with no ties to Germany. Berlin refused to recognize a Lithuanian state without permanent economic, military, and diplomatic ties to Germany. Notwithstanding this rejection, with the support of the German Catholic Center (*Zentrum*) party, the *Taryba* declared itself State Council and on July 11 invited the Catholic duke Wilhelm von Urach to be king of Lithuania and to assume the name of Mindaugas II.[66] However, this ploy was not acceptable to the Germans either. It merely caused the withdrawal from the Council of Social Democratic representatives who returned only after the controversial decision was repudiated. These independent stirrings of the Council deluded world public opinion as to the actual role and importance of the *Taryba*. In reality, the conditions under which it had been created, under which it worked, and into which the military administration had placed it made it impossible for the *Taryba* to carry any weight. It possessed neither formal legitimacy nor power based on popular support, nor did the Germans allow it to organize an administrative apparatus. Although by its numerous protests it tried to defend the population from total exploitation by the occupants, it failed to gain popularity. The military administration resorted to various devices to isolate the *Taryba* from the people and to check any growth of its influence. Members of the *Taryba* were not permitted to travel even in Lithuania.[67]

The future relations between the Reich and the still nonexistent states of Lithuania and Courland were decided at the Berlin conference of political and military representatives (*Kommissarische Beratung*) in May 1918. This conference accepted in principle the drafts of conventions, written by Professor Johann Victor Bredt, that proposed to give the *Land Oberost* a colonial status. Lithuania and Courland were to be "attached" (*angegliedert*—a new term invented by Bredt) to Germany. Severance of the "attachment" was to be impossible for all times. Bredt explained that the agreements were so formulated that the "attachment" would constitute a basis without which the very existence of Lithuania and Courland would be impossible.[68] The *Taryba*, kept in the dark about this conference, was only to sign the "convention" and then be replaced by a more obedient body.

German Occupation Policy in Perspective

In conclusion, it may be said that the aim of the German policy in the *Land Oberost* was indeed to create an entity resembling the medieval "East Elbe military colony," as Eduard David defined it in the *Reichstag*.[69]

Ludendorff regarded *Land Oberost* as a deployment area against Russia and insisted that it be treated as an indivisible whole.[70] According to him, "all the efforts of the High Command were directed toward an achievement of a peace that would secure the best possible position for a future war."[71] These thoughts matured into the idea of an "interrupted and resumed war,"[72] an idea of a "permanent war" for world power, which meant that after attaining a preliminary peace on one front and a decisive victory on the other, war on the first front should be resumed. In the west, this meant at least bases for the German navy in Belgium. In the east, it meant the annexation of the Baltic provinces or at least of Lithuania and Courland. This was the essence of the idea of "the Belgians and the Balts" (implying the Flemings and Baltic Germans), popular in diplomatic circles, for which even the very influential Hamburg shipping magnate Albert Ballin expressed his admiration in a letter to the Prussian chargé d'affaires in Hamburg (October 1915).[73]

Reacting to the German peace proposals in his statement of December 18, 1916, Lloyd George exposed the German plans. He compared German tactics with those of Napoleon, who knew how to play the role of a peace angel in similar circumstances. The reply came in the form of Gustav Stresemann's lecture "Napoleon and We" delivered in the Prussian House of Representatives on January 29, 1917. Stresemann praised Napoleon's "progressiveness," his strategic and "administrative" genius.[74]

Land Oberost was, in addition, very valuable for its strategic political importance not only against Russia, but also against the Poles, whose hostility toward the Germans kept growing. One of the most influential German diplomats, Botho von Wedel, emphasized that a weakening of Germany's rule in this part of the Baltic would lead to the reestablishment of Russia's power. Should Russia again arise, Germany must "be prepared for 'a second Punic war' and then probably fight once more against the Anglo-Russian coalition."[75]

To serve as a Baltic base of operations, *Land Oberost* was to remain in the firm clutch of Prussia and in the shortest possible time be converted into a military colony. Any other solution, such as the Kaiser's promise to give Lithuania to the king of Saxony,[76] could only serve as camouflage.

In this way, the "modest" aim of the annexation of "Vilna, Kovno, Grodno...with a population of 2–3 million" was integrated into a far-reaching objective—the "Leap to World Power" (*Griff nach der Welt-macht*).

II

Baltic Political and Constitutional Development

The Rise of Authoritarian Rule in the Baltic States

V. STANLEY VARDYS

By choosing independence, the Baltic peoples in 1918 rejected Lenin's Bolshevik system of government and instead decided to subscribe to West European political theories and institutions. In the aftermath of World War I democracy was the dominant political philosophy in Europe. It inspired the constitutional systems of all newly emerging Central and East European nations. In less than a generation, however, most European democracies succumbed either to their own social burdens or to the Great Depression and evolved into varieties of authoritarian regime. The Baltic republics were no exception. After the initial experimentation with democracy, they, too, were inundated by the waves of authoritarianism that swept the entire European continent from the Baltic to the Mediterranean.

The political development of the independent Baltic States, therefore, can be divided into the democratic and the authoritarian periods. Neither period has been very extensively researched, but both Western and Soviet scholars have recently developed greater interest in the study of authoritarian systems. In the Soviet Union such interest has produced unusual results. The late Lithuanian party secretary Antanas Sniečkus, for example, strongly reprimanded Communist historians for depicting Lithuania's authoritarian period as democratic—no doubt, many view it as democratic in comparison to the totalitarianism of the Communist system.[1]

This chapter focuses on the transition from the democratic to the authoritarian type of government, attempting to find the causes for the eclipse of Baltic democracy and describing the government systems that emerged afterward.

Assembly-Type Democracies in the Baltic

The roots of Baltic authoritarianism can be found largely in Baltic disenchantment with the workings of their democratic systems.

Though Communist victory in Russia caused Estonia, Latvia, and Lithuania to seek independent statehood and thus a nationalist rather than a Leninist road of development, Russia's revolutionary democratic ideas of 1917 immensely influenced the emergence of Baltic political systems. The Balts who shaped early constitutions and reforms were of radically democratic and egalitarian convictions assimilated from Russian liberals. Of Western countries, Germany had the greatest impact, and its Weimar constitution won out over others as the basic constitutional model. All three Baltic nations adopted constitutions that read as if they had been lifted from a textbook on egalitarian-participatory democratic theory. There was the usual bill of rights, though in Latvia this matter was handled somewhat differently. In Estonia a detailed provision even guaranteed "freedom of expression of personal ideas in words, print, letters, pictures and sculpture" (Article 13). All three republics, furthermore, secured generous rights for ethnic minorities, though Lithuania and Latvia failed to completely live up to the guarantee of complete cultural autonomy. Nevertheless, minorities freely participated in political life and maintained their religious, educational, and cultural institutions.

These egalitarian constitutions, in the fashion of the day, prescribed assembly-type political systems. Also known as the French or Weimar method of democratic organization, this type of system exalted in the supremacy of the parliament. The executive branch was completely dependent on unqualified legislative decisions, better described as whims. The Estonian constitution so magnified the powers of the parliament (*Riigikögu* in Estonia, *Saeima* in Latvia, *Seimas* in Lithuania) that the institution itself formed the government and accepted its resignation (Article 59).

Furthermore, the Baltic assembly-type governments were shaped by the system of proportional representation, which was buttressed by liberally granted rights of political participation and legislative initiative. As a result, the number of political parties proliferated, especially in Estonia and Latvia. In 1923, twenty-six political parties ran for the parliament in Estonia and fourteen were elected. In 1925, twenty-six parties were elected in Latvia.[2] Lithuania generally had only twelve parties. Among them were a host of ethnic minority parties, such as Jewish, Polish, and German parties. Minorities frequently played an important part in electoral and parliamentary politics, most crucially in Lithuania in 1926. But even without minorities the political spectrum became too finely divided, with parties often differing not on economic or social, but on personal or ideological grounds, both of which became very important. The main political wings in the parliaments of Estonia and Latvia were occupied by the Agrarian and Socialist parties. In Lithuania the Socialist party was third in importance—though it included influential individuals—because of Lithuania's conspicuously rural character. The dominant group in Lithuania was the Christian Democratic bloc, which often won absolute majority in the parliament and competed not only with the Socialists but with the mildly socialistic Populists, who were the second-ranking political power.

Such a politically divided parliament made for a very unstable executive. Estonia had seventeen cabinets in fourteen years. Latvia had sixteen. Lithuania had eleven cabinets in seven years. The average life span of a cabinet thus was only eight to ten months. The rule by elected representatives actually became a rule by political parties. Procedural regulations further strengthened the importance of the parties and demeaned that of the parliament. Democracy turned into partocracy.

It must be said that such partisan division and cabinet instability did not necessarily impair the states' stability, though at times—in Lithuania in 1926, in Estonia and Latvia in 1934—it seemed that the little republics might be torn asunder by their failure to organize political consensus. In times of external danger, such as the Communist putsch of 1924 in Estonia, the parties closed ranks in defense of common statehood. Communist parties, since they had opposed Baltic independence, were generally outlawed or had to function under assumed names. They continued to lose strength in Estonia and Latvia, but gained some in the 1930s in Lithuania. In 1940 the Communist party of Lithuania had a clandestine membership between 1305 and 1780. In Latvia at this time the party had 967 members; in Estonia, only 133.[3]

Also, it must be said that the "happy anarchy" existing in the Baltic democracies, especially in the early years of enthusiasm inspired by nationalist feelings, did not impair their capacity for handling the difficult tasks of nation building.[4] The most creative period of Baltic statehood, including the epochal agricultural reforms, the reconstruction and reorientation of industries, and the reorganization of education, was during the political domination of legislative assemblies. Popular democracies released the latent creative energies needed for a socially progressive molding of the economic and social framework of the Baltic States.

The Collapse of Democracy in Lithuania: Military *coup d'état*

However, in the democracy that the Balts established mass participation and consensus were not balanced by strong executive authority. Societies that had for centuries been ruled by the iron hand of foreigners were not ready for such a system of self-governance. As a result there was a shift to less participatory governmental systems, which have been variously called dictatorial, fascist, or authoritarian. Especially short-lived was the democratic system in Lithuania, which perished just seven years after the declaration of independence. The Estonian and Latvian democracies were swept away with the new wave of European authoritarianism that sank Germany.

The Lithuanian *coup d'état* of December 1926 and the Estonian and Latvian takeovers in 1934 represented Nationalist Agrarian reaction to economic difficulties and to the perceived deficiencies of democratic performance. However, the changeover and the resulting dictatorships also showed important differences. Furthermore, while the Estonian and Latvian situation smoldered for three or four years before exploding, the Lithuanian *coup* was a result of quick and possibly rash decisions reached within two or three months.

The differences that distinguish the transition in Lithuania from that of its northern neighbors require a separate discussion of the Lithuanian case. There the *coup* was staged on December 17, 1926, the birthday of the Lithuanian President, Dr. Kazys Grinius. It coincided with the fall of the coalition government of Chancellor Wilhelm Marx in Germany, but apparently had nothing to do with either Soviet or German manipulations as alleged by Poland's Josef Piłsudski, who claimed that he had foreseen the overthrow of President Grinius (1866–1950). It is possible that Piłsudski's own *coup* in Warsaw in June served as an example for the Lithuanian putschists. It was engineered by a committee of young military officers of the Kaunas garrison for the benefit of the small Nationalist party, which had succeeded in electing only three representatives to the Diet in May 1926. At first, these Nationalists tacitly supported the Populist–Social Democratic coalition cabinet—they were able to win seats as a result of an electoral coalition with the Populists—but after thus paying the political debt, they turned against the government. The Nationalists were not numerous, nor were their sympathizers, but their leaders, Antanas Smetona (1874–1944) and Augustinas Voldemaras (1883–1942), were highly respected, prestigious men who were associated with the founding of the

Lithuanian state and preached the ideology of "national unity." They were therefore trusted by the conspiring nationalist officers. To conduct the operations, the conspirators freed from prison two colleagues. One of them, a major of the General Staff, Povilas Plechavičius (1890–1973), who had by coincidence been arrested on disciplinary charges, was elected "the dictator" for the changeover.[5]

Nationalist leaders supported the *coup d'état* because they had nothing to lose and the most to gain. They had decided that the democratic system was inefficient for the nation and unfavorable for the Nationalists. It offered virtually no advancement for either the talented and ambitious Smetona and Voldemaras or the Nationalist party. The *coup* thus promised the only road to power.

The military overthrow was further aided by segments of the Christian Democratic bloc. Its leaders apparently accepted the changeover as a corrective measure that would lead to new elections in which the Christian Democrats could again hope to win a majority. Their real reason for the support of the *coup* and of Smetona, however, has remained a mystery. One of the Christian Democratic leaders, Reverend Mykolas Krupavičius (1885–1970), has emphatically denied the party's participation in the conspiracy. He has asserted that individual Christian Democrats and their sympathizers aided the overthrow without the approval of the party's Central Committee. The party was invited by Smetona to participate in the government after the *fait accompli*, and the Christian Democrats agreed "for fear of a civil war. Civil war would have meant the death of independence." Reflecting on the events some thirty years later, Krupavičius further wrote that "if the eventuality of such war was real, we acted correctly. If it was not true, we were misled and committed an error."[6] The victim of the *coup*, President Kazys Grinius, secured from Voldemaras a pledge to preserve the constitution of 1922, and the Christian Democrats received a similar promise from Smetona. Grinius resigned after Voldemaras' assurances, and the Christian Democrats took over two ministries in the Voldemaras cabinet. A rump session of the Diet, with the leftist coalition boycotting the meeting, elected Smetona president. They expected Smetona to order new parliamentary elections. Smetona reneged on the promise, however, by dissolving the existing parliament in 1927 and promulgating a new constitution that clipped the wings of the parliament and provided for an independent election of a strong president (shades of Gaullism thirty years before de Gaulle!). The Christian Democrats resigned from the coalition with the Nationalists, and authoritarian rule began in earnest.

The origins of the idea of the *coup d'état* are obscure, but the list of grievances against the government offers a reasonable explanation of why it occurred.

Economic difficulties, that is, the slowing pace of economic activity and disappointment in the expected economic upturn under independent rule, apparently played a role, but in Lithuania economic conditions were not of decisive influence. Far more important was the early collapse of communications between the ideologically hostile major political parties and the consequent instability of the executive.

Shortly after achieving international recognition and security guarantees for Lithuania, the Populists lost confidence in Christian Democrats as partners in government. The parties nevertheless needed each other for the formation of cabinets and for the enactment of domestic reform policies. The Populists and the Socialists had abstained from voting for the rather liberal constitution of 1922, and later the Populists abstained from, while the Social Democrats opposed, the legislation of agrarian reform. The dividing issues were religious and clerical. Neither the Populists nor the Socialists approved of compulsory religious education as outlined in the constitution, and both opposed the principle of compensation for expropriated estate lands as provided by the land reform. Furthermore, they strongly objected to the Christian Democratic allotment of land to churches and monasteries.[7] The Christian Democrats and the Populists, not to speak of the Socialists, refused to compromise. The president of the Republic, the Christian Democrat Aleksandras Stulginskis, too, was chosen under a cloud, the Populists and Social Democrats maintaining that he could be elected only by an absolute majority of the entire Diet membership. The constitution did not specify the kind of absolute majority needed.

The Christian Democratic–Populist coalition broke up in 1922, and the relations so much deteriorated during the years of Christian Democratic rule that the parliamentary campaign of the spring of 1926 became a struggle of "backwoodsmen"[8] which not only destroyed the vestiges of trust, but threw the Populists into the arms of the Social Democrats. The Christian Democrats lost this viciously fought election, but with indecisive results. The Populists now turned to the Socialist party, which had doubled representation; their combined total, however, was still short of parliamentary majority. To allow a coalition cabinet to be formed, these parties solicited the votes of ethnic minorities. Thus the minorities facilitated what was widely perceived as a dangerously leftist alliance. At first, however, the cabinet of Mykolas Sleževičius (1882–1939) scored international successes and remained sufficiently popular. Difficulties arose when his cabinet turned to domestic affairs.

Under Socialist pressure, the Diet, by only a bare majority, passed some very unpopular economic measures that had inadequate support in the country and strongly upset influential political forces. First, as if to punish the clergy for electoral opposition, the Sleževičius government refused to accept the legality of the newly established Catholic Church province of Lithuania. Too, the Socialist minister of the interior refused to honor baptismal certificates issued by the chanceries of the newly established dioceses, and the Socialist minister of education disqualified teachers of religion appointed by these institutions.[9] Furthermore, the government cut the budget for religious teaching while its supporters proposed that clergymen be directly paid by the government instead of through the newly appointed bishops.

Turning to another important anti-Socialist group, the new government threatened to reorganize the army and to reduce the size of the officer corps. This suggestion may have ignited the spark of rebellion, as it was in the officer corps that the *coup* was hatched. In addition, the government started judicial proceedings against some prominent opposition politicians, charging corruption, and imprisoned some military officers on other charges.

Furthermore, the coalition government made itself unpopular by supporting the Polish minority. As repayment for votes in the Diet, the minister of education had licensed a further expansion of the network of Polish private schools. The timing of this concession was absolutely disastrous; almost at the very moment—as if purposefully further to incite the "Kaunas' Lithuania"—Polish authorities in the Vilnius region closed the doors of a number of Lithuanian schools. The issue of Polish schools in Lithuania therefore became exceedingly emotional and fed the fires of the already-excited nationalist sentiments.

To compound the difficulties, the government terminated the limited martial law that had existed since an attempted *coup* by Polish conspirators and had been used primarily against the Communists, though the Nationalist Smetona, too, had fallen victim to it. As a result, Communist agitators emerged, even if under different names. Police confrontations with students occurred, followed by street incidents involving military officers. Neither helped the situation.[10]

All of this, in view of the newly signed nonagression pact with the Soviet Union—though the pact was negotiated by the previous Christian Democratic administration—gave the government an undeserved pro-

Communist and antinationalist reputation. The authors of the takeover even alleged that their action had saved the country from the already-scheduled Communist *coup*. Voldemaras claimed that the Communists had been incited by Poland to provide Pilsudski with a pretext for intervening in Lithuanian affairs.[11]

The military, therefore, had much support in the country. Lithuania's electorate had become impatient with the assembly-type partocracy that neither the country's actual divisions nor its social structure could support without a strong political axis between the Christian Democrats and the Populists. With this alliance destroyed, the assembly system of democracy was overwhelmed by both its hotheads and its enemies.

The Fall of the Assembly System in Estonia: Preventive Intervention against the Extreme Right

The fall of the Estonian and Latvian democracies was more protracted, the battle lines between the parliamentarian and antiparliamentarian forces more clearly drawn, economic factors of more import, and the role of the military much less direct.

The Estonian changeover was caused by two factors: the economic depression and, especially, attempts at constitutional reform. The depression engulfed Estonia in 1931. The unemployed numbered 45,000 during the winter of 1932–1933.[12] Since most of Estonia's exchange reserves were in British pounds, the devaluation of the pound cut the Estonian foreign exchange assets by one third. Foreign trade began to show a deficit; as farm prices dropped, loss of markets further hurt the farmer. The Depression, in other words, endangered the prosperity of very large and diverse sections of the electorate. Furthermore, the Estonians had begun to doubt that assembly-type democratic institutions could solve their problems. The scales finally tilted against the system when both the rural leaders and the urban leaders of the middle class despaired of being able to repair the system so that it could continue to serve the nation's economic needs.

Estonian politicians began proposing constitutional reforms after the Communist *coup d'état* of 1924. Essentially, the proposals provided for the office of a president and a stronger, stabler executive, the need for which had been conspicuously demonstrated by the Communists in 1924—in part, their attempted *coup* had been provoked by the disarray in the parliament. In November 1924 the ruling cabinet was made up of a minority coalition, resting on the support of only one third of parliamentary membership. To the Communists it must have seemed that the Estonian assembly system was just a pushover. However, the subsequent proposals for reform—beginning with the ministerial declaration of Dr. Jüri Jaakson in December 1924—brought about only adjustments, rather than real changes. The cabinet merged some executive offices. In 1926 the Assembly modified the electoral law to require candidates to make a deposit and to qualify a political group for seating in the parliament as a faction only if two of its candidates had been elected. Mergers of political parties in 1931 and 1932 further reduced the number of candidates and parties in the *Riigikõgu*.

These changes, initiated by supporters of the assembly system, seemed to be glaringly insufficient to meet the requirements of the times, however. Since parliamentary parties of the Right were incapable of making further progress, initiative was seized by the extraparliamentary radical Right, which demanded not just legislative changes, but a constitutional reform.

Extreme Nationalist groups, which first surfaced in 1923, began to grow in the 1930s. They resembled the Finnish "Lapuan" movement and were spearheaded by the Central League of the Veterans of the War of Independence (*Vabadussojalaste Keskliit*) founded in 1929. This group wore uniforms, used Nazi-type salutes, and held parades; some of its leaders corresponded with the German Foreign Ministry.[13] In 1931 it proposed a revision of the constitution. Not to be outdone, in August 1932 the parliament submitted its own revised constitution to a referendum, which failed to pass, though by less than 1% of the vote. Had the Socialists voted for it, the draft would have carried the day. The paramilitary Veterans then put forth their draft, which called for an independent chief executive, who would be elected separately from the parliament, who would choose his own cabinet, and could rule by decree. Instead of submitting this proposal to a referendum vote, as required, however, the Assembly revised its own defeated proposal, which merely strengthened the executive branch. In June 1933 this proposal was decisively defeated, with the Socialists again voting against it. In the meantime the Agrarian party leader Konstantin Päts had endorsed the Veterans' proposal, leading to rumors of an impending *coup d'état* by the Veterans. As a result, Prime Minister Jaan Tõnisson (1868–?) declared a state of emergency and with the Assembly's approval ordered the closing of the Veterans' organizations. A limited press censorship and restrictions on organizations and the right of assembly were also imposed.

The Veterans, however, kept up their pressure, forcing the Assembly to put the Veterans' constitutional proposal to a referendum. On October 14–16 it was approved by 73% of those voting.[14] The Veterans now opened an overt campaign against the existing democratic system. To everyone's surprise, in January 1934 they won many municipal elections and, thus encouraged, sought to elect one of their own as the chief executive in the elections scheduled for April 22–23.

In the meantime, on January 1, 1934, when the newly approved constitution went into effect, Konstantin Päts became acting president. On March 12, that is, more than a month before the election, Päts invoked emergency powers granted him under the new constitution, dissolved the Veterans, who had introduced these emergency powers, and arrested at least 100 of their leaders.[15] Päts claimed that the Veterans had planned a *coup d'état*, though this is doubtful in view of the general expectation that their candidate for chief executive, General Andres Larka, would win the upcoming election. Thus Päts forestalled the extremist victory. To destroy extremism, however, he had to resort to his own authoritarianism. On March 16 the Assembly endorsed Päts' actions, and he began to rule by decree. He postponed the scheduled elections, annulled the municipal victories of the Veterans, and permanently closed the Veterans' organization. Five weeks later he also dismissed the Assembly. Reconvened in the fall, the Assembly had turned so overwhelmingly critical of Päts that he dissolved it permanently. The takeover was complete.

Latvia: The Sacrifice of Democracy to Civic Peace

The eclipse of democracy in Latvia occurred barely two months after that in Estonia. In Latvia, too, the Depression was harsh, and dissatisfaction with the workings of the assembly system had accumulated through the years. The Nazi method of solving difficulties in Germany served as an example in Latvia as well, though Latvian political life was both more pulverized and more polarized than the Estonian.

The Estonian Socialists, that is, the Left, opposed to all attempts at reform, finally acquiesced in the takeover by Päts as the lesser of two evils. They probably felt at least partially responsible for the failure of a democratic revision of the constitution, which was indeed true. The Latvian Socialists also opposed the strengthening of the executive, but they were more doctrinaire and they noisily fought the fascists. As early as 1923 a clash between Socialist and fascist youth on the streets of Riga precipitated a cabinet crisis and caused the Socialists to withdraw from the coalition.[16] In 1926 a mass meeting of Nationalists in the capital city was staged to denounce the "demagoguery of the Leftists" and speeches sympathetic to Mussolini were made.[17] Later a small but vociferous National Socialist party, not connected to the Nazis in Germany but "anti-semitic in tendency," was formed.[18] Several other pro-Nazi organizations emerged as well.

In 1933, in the depth of the Depression, there arose a party known as Fire Cross (*Ugunskrusts*). Immediately banned by the government, it returned under the name of Thunder Cross (*Pērkoņkrusts*). This group represented Latvian right-wing extremism. Its members wore gray shirts and black berets, used a Nazi-style salute, rallied to the slogan "Latvia for Latvians," and propagandized against minorities, especially the Germans and the Jews. This extremist group, pro-fascist or outrightly Nazist, though anti-German and anti-Semitic, lumped together the Socialists and Communists as enemies of Latvia. For fear of an anti-Communist *coup* by Latvian fascists, the Left-of-Center coalition government of 1927 had allowed the organization of a Socialist Workers Sports League, which in effect became a paramilitary Socialist organization.[19] The Agrarian party of Kārlis Ulmanis (1877–1942) in turn could rely on paramilitary support from the Latvian *Aizsargi*, the national militia. Thus political groups had their own armed organizations, as had been the case in Weimar Germany.

As in Estonia, the Latvian Diet did not reflect all the social tensions in the country. Since the extreme rightists had hardly any representation, the warring parliamentary parties were the Agrarian-Rightist coalition on the one side and the Socialists on the other. Very serious tensions between these blocs developed in 1933, when Latvia's Supreme Court convicted seven crypto-Communist (Communist front group) members of the *Saeima* of collusion with a foreign power. This conviction was later submitted as proof of Communist preparations for a *coup*.

After this incident, the Socialists introduced a bill demanding the dissolution of all fascist organizations, the dismissal of fascists from government positions, and the expulsion of German Nazis from the country.[20] At the same time, the Socialists refused to support yet one more—and this time the final—draft of constitutional reform proposed by Ulmanis' Farmers Union, which would have strengthened the presidency. Thus the situation was stalemated, and the government fell again, this time because of the withdrawal of Ulmanis' party. This maneuver—though ostensibly caused by policy disagreements—may have been executed to bring Ulmanis to the position of prime minister. Indeed, it was Ulmanis who formed the new cabinet, which was supported, in addition to the Farmers Union, by the parties of the Right and Center and by almost all ethnic minority parties.

From this position Ulmanis moved against both the fascists and the Socialists. On May 15, shortly after becoming prime minister, he invoked constitutional emergency powers, disbanded the Diet, outlawed political parties, and organized a new cabinet. He did it with the agreement of General Jānis Balodis and the right-wing Socialist leader Marǵers Sku-jenieks (1886–?).[21] Scores of Social Democrats and extreme rightists were incarcerated, though quickly released. The leader of the Socialist Workers Sports League remained in prison, however. The prime minister claimed that his actions were intended as preventive measures against domestic clash and anarchy and were "not aimed against Latvian democracy."[22] Whatever Ulmanis' intentions, his *coup d'état* did destroy the assembly-type democracy without a definite promise of its restoration.

The Profile of Authoritarianism

In Latvia ideological contradictions between the Left and the Right played a large role in undermining democratic consensus, and in this respect the Latvian *coup d'état* resembled its Lithuanian precursor. In both cases the *coup* leaders claimed that they had saved the country from Communism. In Estonia, the Communist issue did not exist, nor was it used as a pretext. It may be said, however, that in Estonia democracy was outvoted by the people—the new constitution of 1933 was largely authoritarian—and that Päts saved the country for the moderates by refusing to deliver it to the extremist Veterans. In Latvia party divisions could have led to conflict and possibly chaos, and thus Ulmanis sought what he must have considered to be the best possible solution, namely, the collapse of both of the opposing wings. To do this, he had to veer still further to the Right and to resort to arbitrary action. In Lithuania, on the other hand, a groundless or at least premature belief by some Christian Democrats and the army that a military *coup* can remedy the ills of a democratic system played into the hands of ambitious Nationalist leaders of the Right.

The ascendancy and containment of the extreme pro-fascist Right, which in the other Baltic republics predated the collapse of democratic power, occurred after the *coup d'état* in Lithuania. The leader of this extreme movement and its secret paramilitary adjunct known as the Iron Wolf (*Geležinis vilkas*) was Professor Augustinas Voldemaras, Smetona's prime minister. He was a diplomat, well known in Europe for his sharp confrontations with Polish and Western statesmen in the League of Nations. While Smetona, except for some words of praise for Mussolini's Fascism had generally very little use for it, Voldemaras' group harbored more than a tinge of fascist sympathies and later, when working in the underground against Smetona, developed pro-Nazi tendencies and received some financial support from Nazi Germany.[23]

Voldemaras, who later became alienated from his movement, acted the dictator and concentrated on developing the organization of the Iron Wolf, his base of power. In 1929, after an unsuccessful assassination attempt on him, Voldemaras developed irreconcilable personal differences with Smetona, who for some time had anxiously watched Voldemaras' growing power and ambition. In February 1929 Smetona succeeded in quietly pensioning off "the dictator" Major Plechavičius, now a colonel, who after the *coup* had served as the army's chief of staff. On September 19 the new president dismissed his chief competitor, Voldemaras. At the same time, Smetona appointed a new leader for Voldemaras' organization and ultimately disbanded it altogether. Voldemaras' attempts to return to power by repeated military *coups* failed, as did Socialist and other attempts to overthrow Smetona. With Voldemaras' dismissal, the power now fully rested in the hands of the mild-mannered but clever and stubborn Smetona, a dictator of moderation like the other Baltic presidents.

These three men—Smetona, Ulmanis, and Päts—governed the Baltic States until their occupation by the Soviet Union. As dictatorships go, however, their rule was the mildest in Europe. Whatever the reasons, the vigor and oppressive character of a dictatorship on the European scene seemed to be related to the size of the country where it reigned. The question of whether this relationship was causal or coincidental—though important for comparative politics in general and for prognosticating Baltic development in particular—must unfortunately yield to the characterization of the systems that the three autocrats introduced.

In the context of European dictatorships, which ranged from the ideological Communist and Nazi regimes to Antonescu and Horthy in southeast Europe, it is fair to designate the Baltic regimes as authoritarian. That is, they were largely nonideological arbitrary governments of predominantly rural, conservative nationalist character, restrained by the leaders' self-imposed limitations and by the old social pluralism, which the rulers merely contained rather than destroyed. The distinction that von Rauch has made between Estonian and Latvian "authoritarian democracy" and the Lithuanian "presidential regime" is not real.[24] Päts and Ulmanis were every bit as "presidential" as Smetona, and the "democratic" features in Lithuania just before the outbreak of World War II were probably even more pronounced than in Latvia, though not in Estonia. Of the differences that existed some were the result of cultural and social traditions and others rested in different tactical and organizational arrangements for exercising supreme power. In all three cases, the presidents basically relied on the military. In addition, Ulmanis and Smetona had harnessed the support of the old paramilitary "Riflemen's" associations, the *Aizsargi* in Latvia and *Šauliai* in Lithuania. Finally, Smetona and Päts—though not Ulmanis—refined their own political parties or movements into presidential instruments. Smetona even organized his party on the principle of "the leader." These political parties had no competition. Communist parties were completely suppressed and their leaders imprisoned. Other parties, though outlawed, were not denied individual personal initiative. The press had some freedom to influence public affairs, especially on the municipal level and in the field of culture. The "Left" made full use of this limited right of publication, censored as it was, and a number of leftist writers, such as the future Stalin prize winner Vilis Lācis in Latvia and Salomėja Neris in Lithuania, gained national recognition.

The court system remained independent. Private enterprises dominated the economy, as before, coexisting with cooperative organizations. However, the governments now more actively and directly entered into industrial development, ownership, and management. The result was economic prosperity and a higher standard of living (less so in Lithuania than in the other two republics) than in Stalin's Russia and in Poland.[25] While tinges of fascist corporatism and ideological influence can be discovered—labor unions, for example, were put under central state control—only the Latvian economic and cultural life was, in a rudimentary way, organized into professional corporations.[26]

A government's attitudes toward churches and minorities usually are a fair measure of its liberalism. In the Baltic countries the new authoritarian governments held similar views about the freedom of religion. There was freedom for religion as well as for atheist propaganda. In Lithuania, however, while the Catholic Church flourished, relations between the state and the Church were strained and frequently hostile over the issue of freedom for organizations of Catholic Action.

The Latvian and Lithuanian policies of "Latvianization" and "Lithuanization," respectively, caused some friction with minorities, which was absent in Estonia. Ulmanis, to decrease German domination in Latvia's financial affairs, created an uproar in Germany by abolishing ethnic German economic organizations in Latvia.[27] This also naturally affected other minorities. Nevertheless, there were 400 primary schools in Latvia being taught in minority languages, the largest number of them in Russian, German, and Yiddish.[28]

In Lithuania Smetona especially attempted to "Lithuanize" the Klaipėda district, where the German influence was overwhelming, and, as long as he could defy Hitler, restrained the activities of German National Socialists. In 1934 the Lithuanian government dissolved two pro-Nazi organizations and charged scores of their members with conspiracy against the state. The court convicted 82 persons, including Dr. Ernst Neumann, the Nazi leader of the German minority in Klaipėda district, who had served as a leader of the dissolved Socialist National Community (*Sozialistische Volksgemeinschaft*), and Theodor Freiherr von Sass, the leader of the banned Christian-Socialist Labor Community (*Christlich Sozialistische Arbeitsgemeinschaft*).[29] Minority-language schools were partly or wholly supported by the government. Yiddish and Hebrew schools were in the majority.[30] Unlike the Poles and Russians, whose cultural activities were modest, Lithuanian Jewish organizations published a number of newspapers, maintained some theaters, and supported at least one world-famous rabbinical school. All religious groups, including the Jewish, received annual state subsidies for religious affairs.[31]

In 1937 Päts and in 1938 Smetona sought to legalize their rule by promulgating new, essentially authoritarian, constitutions.[32] Ulmanis still governed under the constitution of 1922, though he had subverted its provisions. Smetona's decision to adopt the constitution of January 1938 was prompted by political unrest at home, indicating a decline of his power and his ability to control events. Furthermore, after the Polish ultimatum in March 1938 demanding diplomatic relations, President Smetona had to make additional political concessions to his opponents. As a result, the unofficially existing Christian Democratic and Populist parties joined the Cabinet of "national unity." The mainstay of Smetona's regime, the army, was still loyal, but military leaders appeared to be unreliable. Though the new *Seimas,* elected in February of 1938, was a completely Nationalist rubber stamp, political collaboration with the two opposition groups in the cabinet eased Smetona's long-standing and ascerbic conflict with the Catholic Church, decreased enforcement of restrictive laws on organizations and the press, and softened press censorship. Contemporary observers thought they saw a move toward democracy.

In Estonia Päts sought to find a *modus vivendi* with his opposition in a semidemocratic fashion. His constitution of 1938 provided for direct presidential election and for a parliamentary role in the nomination of the candidates. In parliamentary elections individuals were allowed to compete against Päts' Patriotic Front, and though freedom to campaign was limited, officially unendorsed candidates contested the elections in almost all electoral districts. As a result, the president's Patriotic Front elected only two thirds of the parliamentary membership of 80.[33] Among the competitors were the old party parliamentarians Ants Piip and Jaan Tõnisson. Thus Päts allowed the opposition to participate through the parliament, as Smetona had done through the cabinet.

These Estonian and Lithuanian developments suggested a slow return to democratic foundations though certainly not to the assembly-type of partocracy. Historians, however, disagree on the meaning of this clearly perceptible shift.[34] Today what the Baltic political evolution would have been can only be conjectured. The Baltic States did not have another chance to work out either their domestic problems or their ultimate destiny. Their independence was snuffed out by Stalin, in collaboration with Adolf Hitler, the other leading ideological tyrant of the day.

Ethnic Minorities in the Estonian and Latvian Parliaments: The Politics of Coalition

MICHAEL GARLEFF

Though the Estonians and Latvians constituted the majority in the newly established republics of Estonia and Latvia, they introduced a democratic order that allowed for the participation of minorities in their parliamentary life.[1] In Latvia minorities made up 26.6% of the population in 1925. The largest was the Russian group (12.6%), followed by the Jews (5.2%). The Germans, though historically the most important minority, were only 3.8% of the population; Poles, 2.8%; Lithuanians, 1.3%. Estonians constituted only 0.4%, while the category of "others" covered 0.6%. By 1935 these percentages had changed, though rather inconsequentially. The percentage of Latvians grew to 75.5%, with the minorities registering a very slight loss. Russians now had 12%, Jews—4.8%, Germans—3.2%, Poles—2.5%, Lithuanians—1.2%, Estonians—0.3%, and "others"—0.5%.

In Estonia 87.6% were Estonian in 1922, 8.2%—Russian, 1.7%—German, 0.7%—Swedish, 0.4%—Jewish, and 1.4%—"others." In 1934 the percentages were 88.1% for the Estonians, 8.2% for the Russians, 1.5% for the Germans, 0.7% for the Swedes, 0.4% for the Jews, and 1.1% for the "others."

This chapter examines the participation of these groups in Estonian and Latvian parliaments—the *Riigikogu* and the *Saeima*, respectively.

Minorities in Political Life

The percentage of minorities in the Latvian parliament usually reached 16–19%; in Estonia it stayed between 4 and 7%.[2] The Russians formed the largest minority in both countries, though not necessarily the largest minority group in their parliaments. Deep divisions caused by differentiated social structures hindered the political development and concentration of power of the Russian minority. In Estonia the Russian National Union did represent the political interests of the Estonian Russians, but no carefully constructed organization existed to coordinate their various social and professional organizations.

In Latvia there were tensions between the large body of Russian farmers and the small elite of Russian officials and merchants. The mostly upper-class Russian politicians could neither rally all the Russian votes with a program appealing to all social groups nor form a common front by themselves, not to speak of uniting in a manner comparable to the Baltic German parties. The Latvian Russian political disunity was so great that in 1931 the delegate M. Kalistratov supported an attempted vote of no confidence by the Social Democrats against the fourth cabinet of Kārlis Ulmanis (March 27, 1931–December 5, 1931) in which a Russian, Dr. V. Trofimov, had just been named minister without portfolio.[3]

The Russian minorities in Estonia and Latvia never achieved political representation corresponding to their numerical strength. The main reason for this was the large number of splinter parties. Six different groups competed for the votes of the Russian minority: the Christian Union of the Latvian Orthodox, with the politicians M. Kalistratov, Iu. Iupatov, M. Sinitsin, and V. Korelov; the party of the Orthodox, led by their archbishop Jānis Pommers; the Union of Russian Officials (Party for Communal Activities), led by its founder Leontin Shpolianskii; the Russian National Workers' party, with the attorney Peter Koretskii; the Russian Workers' Union, led by A. Bochagov; and the Russian National Union, with P. Iacobi. Seven Russian groups ran in the elections to the third *Saeima* in Latvia in 1928.[4] The number of elected Russian representatives in Estonia never reached its theoretically attainable level, though one Russian who had previously run as an Estonian Socialist was a candidate for the Russian faction during the last legislative period (1932–1934).[5] In contrast, the Baltic Germans of Latvia, utilizing all possible voting technicalities, consistently achieved an overrepresentation for their 3.5% of the population by successfully winning five or six seats in the parliament.

The Jewish population of the Baltic region can be divided basically into Zionist and non-Zionist factions, a differentiation carried over to their political parties. Further, the Latvian Jews fell into four groups: those living mainly in Courland, who considered themselves a part of the German culture; those associating themselves with the Russian culture; those orientated toward a Hebrew-speaking Zionist culture; and the Yiddish-speaking Jews.

The resulting language barrier did not contribute to unity within the Jewish minority. The Jewish educational administration, for example, had to deal with four languages in its schools. Political divisions were even stronger. The five Jewish parties participating in the 1928 *Saeima* elections ranged from the extreme Right to the Social Democrats (Jewish Workers' League). These were: the party of the orthodox Jews, *Agudas Isroel*, led by Morduch Dubin; the bourgeois party, *Zeire Agudas Isroel*, under J. Baranchik; the Zionist Organization, *Misrachi*, led by the delegate Markus Nuroks; the Ethnic Socialist party, *Zeire Zion*, with Professor Max Lazerson as the best-known member; the Socialist Workers' party, the Jewish *Bund*, to which Dr. N. Maisel belonged and which joined the Latvian Social Democrats in 1923 as an autonomous faction; and the Socialist party of the Zionists, also with a Marxist program (with J. Kron and J. Meierson).

This proliferation of parties split the Jewish vote, decreasing Jewish representation in the *Saeima*. While five Jews were delegates to the second and third *Saeimas*, splinter parties reduced Jewish representation to three in the 1931 elections to the fourth *Saeima*. Almost half of the Jewish votes in this election were wasted.

Two other minority parties were the Swedish Ethnic party in the Estonian *Riigikögu* and the Polish Association in the Latvian *Saeima*. The latter found support mainly in Latgale. This Eastern region of Latvia had become differentiated from the rest of the country by its historical development. Because of its long association with the Polish-Lithuanian Commonwealth, Latgale was mainly Catholic. Its administrative separation from the other Baltic provinces lasted until 1917. With independence, various particularist Latgalian parties developed, thus increasing the proliferation of political parties in the Latvian *Saeima*.

Latvian educational legislation of December 8, 1919, granted independent educational administration also to the Belorussian minority, a step that in effect recognized them as an "official minority." By this legislation the Latvians may have sought to dilute the strength of the Russian and Polish minorities whom the Belorussians had been supporting.[6]

The position of the Baltic German minority in the early 1920s has perhaps been best expressed by Paul Schiemann, for many years the leader of the German parliamentary group in the *Saeima*. Commenting in the *Rigasche Rundschau* of June 21, 1921, on the inaugural address of Zigfrīds Meierovics' first cabinet (June 19, 1921–January 26, 1923), he stated: "We have to declare that we, like the majority of the population, have a historical right to our homeland and that we are called to cooperate with the government, as is every Latvian." No longer did it base its national and political rights "on some privilege of culture, wealth or tradition, but solely on the right of a minority, on the right to self-determination."

Practically the only common goal shared by all the minority parties was that of cultural autonomy. They did cooperate in this area and occasionally made some gains. Still, rarely did the minorities take advantage of the opportunities that the size of their parliamentary representation offered (16–19% in the Latvian *Saeima*, 5–8% in the Estonian *Riigikögu*). Resistance to minority-party cooperation was most pronounced among the Germans of Latvia, particularly within their conservative wing, whose speaker, Baron Wilhelm von Fircks, espoused the opinion that the Latvians and Baltic Germans, because of their attachment to the soil, had more in common with each other than with the other minorities. Considered in historical perspective, such an opinion was not unreasonable. The Baltic Germans demanded a favored status among the minorities and objected to being termed a "minority."[7]

As a result, of the numerous bills dealing with cultural autonomy introduced in the *Saeima* at the beginning of the 1920s only the first one was concerned with "general autonomy." All the others aimed at the enactment of a special law "with regard to the German National Community in Latvia." It was assumed that the right-wing Latvian parties, especially the Peasants' League, would be inclined to grant more to the German ethnic group than to the other minorities.[8] When Schiemann, at the end of 1925, advocated a general minorities law rather than an exclusive one, he faced strong resistance. Karl Keller declared that the Baltic Germans would act politically "only as people of this country . . . not as pioneers for rights which we share with the Jews and the Russians."[9] Schiemann failed to sway the conservative wing even by arguing that there would be no support for abandoning a position based on minority rights in favor of a new law "based on our historical positions." The principal opponent of a general law was Baron Fircks, who considered it disadvantageous to the Baltic Germans in view of their historical role in the country. Five years later economic reasons forced him to agree to a general law, though he still found it annoying for the Germans "to be treated like all other nationalities."[10] A lack of unity among the other minorities also helped to prevent the creation of a minority coalition. Furthermore, the general splintering of political forces made effective cooperation of minorities more difficult in Latvia than in Estonia. Baltic German parties in Latvia, however, were united under Schiemann and Fircks. Though this unity was shaky, it gave the Latvian Germans a political image, distinguishing them from the other minorities.

The political organizational structure of the Baltic Germans in Latvia, dating from the early days of the republic, could have served as an example to the other minorities. An attempt to unite all Baltic German parties first came during the summer of 1919.[11] In early 1920 the Baltic German Democratic party succeeded in forming a single list of German candidates for all of Latvia. The aims were obvious: to represent politically all Latvian Germans, instead of a "National Committee" representing the estates; to consolidate the Baltic Germans from within; and to increase the influence of the democratic parties on Baltic German politics.

The "Directions of the Committee of the Baltic German Parties"[12] dated February 13, 1920, emphasized the two main concerns of the organization: the correlation of the parties' ideas on the political questions of the day and the formulation of a common approach to all cultural questions pertaining to the Baltic Germans. A revised program of December 1924 also listed the prevention of splintering of the German vote in municipal and state elections. In the new statutes the Committee was considered to be a "League of Baltic German political organizations registered in Latvia." All essential political questions came to be discussed and decided not by the parliamentary group, but by the Committee of Baltic German Parties. Though tactics were worked out in the meetings of the parliamentary group, the discussion of the political line took place in the Committee. The success of this unification is shown by the decreasing importance of the individual Baltic German parties until 1934. The official Latvian roster of the members of the Latvian National Council and Constituent Assembly listed the Baltic German members according to their separate parties. From 1922 on, however, only the designation "Baltic German Party of Latvia" appeared. In reality such a party did not exist and was merely a designation for the Committee of Baltic German Parties.[13]

Not all minorities were able to achieve such unity. The only parallel can be found in the organization of the Russian minority in Estonia, which also was not limited to Russian political parties. In 1923 a committee to decide the tactics of the faction was formed consisting of two members each from the Russian welfare organization, the teachers' organization, and the Russian Workers' party.[14] That year the *Revaler Bote* noted that the Russians, based on their proportion of the population, could actually have six to seven delegates. This was considered unlikely, however, because of their "well-known lack of ability to organize," the crankiness of the groups, and their negligible interest in the fate of the Estonian state.[15] In Latvia the diversity of political views among the Russian and Jewish minority groups made effective cooperation even more difficult.

Coalition Making in Latvia

A minority faction or party that wanted to form a coalition with another political group for the purpose of greater parliamentary power had two choices. It could either join a party of the ethnic majority, as did the Estonian Swedes in joining forces with the Christian People's party or the Latvian Jewish League in collaborating with the Social Democrats, or it could cooperate with other minority parliamentarians. Of the several possible levels of cooperation the highest one would have been a coalition of all the minority parties in the parliament.

Before the April 1920 elections to the Constituent Assembly Paul Schiemann appealed to a "natural alliance with the other ethnic minorities,"[16] which had been established on all essential questions during the negotiations in the National Council. He called for a unified political ticket and the formation of a large minority faction that would "take up a certain and fixed position toward the nationality questions in Latvia. This is the attitude of justice." While the formation of a bloc for this election was unsuccessful, the "guidelines for the political activities of the minorities' representatives in the Constituent Assembly," written by Schiemann, were eventually accepted by the representatives of all ethnic groups. The basic minority demands in this nine-point agenda were the following: national autonomy with the right of self-taxation protected by the government; free use of one's mother tongue; and constitutional protection of minority school autonomy. On May 8, 1920, seven Baltic German, six Jewish, and one Russian representative, led by Schiemann, founded the Committee of Latvia's Minorities and its Office of Information, which was to supply the representatives with material, particularly translations of Latvian documents. On May 13 Schiemann was elected chairman by a vote of 9 to 2; Bochagov and Moritz Mintz were elected vice-chairmen.[17]

At the first meeting the seats on parliamentary committees were distributed among united minorities according to their relative size. It was decided, furthermore, that minorities would participate in the government only after reaching consensus on a common policy.

With the establishment of working subcommittees within the minority bloc, a diligent and initially promising activity began. The Office of Information started to assemble a newspaper archive,[18] and the Economic Council of the Minority Committee conferred weekly about proposed economic laws.[19] Another activity was the documentation of illegal requisitions by the government, which the minority factions desired to bring before parliament. The minorities were more effective in parliament after first agreeing among themselves in their own committee sessions.[20]

The summer of 1920 saw an increase of anti-Semitic feelings in the Latvian military and bourgeois circles.[21] On July 2 the government decreed that all foreign residents who had not yet applied for naturalization leave the country. This decree weighed particularly harshly against the Jews who had fled Soviet Russia. On June 22 the Jewish delegate moved that the Minority Committee adopt a common stand as an expression of the "solidarity of minorities." Schiemann, together with the Russian representative, interceded with the prime minister, who explained that the expulsion decree was necessary as a measure against Bolshevik agitators' entering Latvia as refugees.[22] There followed a slackening of the expulsions, however.

Nevertheless, it soon became obvious that the heterogeneous minority "bloc" held conflicting opinions. A Baltic German–Russian conflict arose when several Russian groups asked the government to replace the chairman of the Russian minority educational system. Schiemann forestalled the move, since it would have undermined minority school autonomy.[23] In late May 1920 basic differences between Schiemann and the Jewish representative Jacob Hellmann also became evident. The Social Democrats, supported by Hellmann, proposed a constitutional article guaranteeing the right to strike. Schiemann, opposing this, suggested that the Minority Committee withhold its votes on this question in the Constituent Assembly so as to present a unified minority front, "because the members of the Constituent Assembly will watch with close attention."[24] Though the chairman did manage to maintain unity within the minority faction for a while, by the end of the year the conflict had broken wide open. Based on Schiemann's proposal at the beginning of January 1921, the Committee requested that the Jewish faction withdraw Hellmann "as the representative of the minorities from the committees of the Constituent Assembly because of his attacks on German delegates and that he be replaced by another personality."[25] Schiemann refused to call a meeting of the Minority Committee until Hellmann had resigned, thus forcing Hellmann out of the minority bloc.

Because of nonpayment of membership dues, the financial situation of the Minority Committee deteriorated. On April 20, 1921, the head of its office, Oskar Grosberg, notified the minority parties that as of May 1 the office would be closed, though it would continue to serve the German parties. The actual dissolution of the Minority Committee was brought about by the attitude of the Jewish faction, which on September 20 did not vote against a proposal in the Constituent Assembly that June 22, the anniversary of the battle of Cēsis, be made a national holiday.[26] Even though the Committee did not consider a total break with the Jewish parties desirable, it declared on October 11 that "the decision to cancel the former close alliance with the other minorities is correct."

In spite of this, in October 1926 minority factions closed their ranks for the second time. After long negotiations Schiemann succeeded in uniting all sixteen representatives of the minority bloc on certain minimum demands in school and nationality questions. The Arturs Alberings cabinet, which was looking for coalition partners, was notified about this newly formed faction. A bare fourteen days later, however, this bloc became split when the Russian representative Leontin Shpolianskii included in the protocol a request for an appointment to a post in the State Bank that had not been authorized by the bloc. With the benefit of hindsight, Schiemann later wrote about the failure to stabilize the political situation: "Even from the beginning it had not been intended that a lasting political bloc could be created out of the strongly dissenting minority groups."[27] Such a bloc could function only in times of common danger to minority political positions when all other issues could be ignored. "Yet there was the possibility of forming a temporary alliance in the face of compelling needs to satisfy certain urgent demands, such as the ability of a free avowal of one's nationality."

Election Alliance in Estonia

The most important event during the elections to the Fourth Assembly on May 11 and 12, 1929, in Estonia was the formation of a coalition between the Baltic German party and the Swedish Ethnic party.[28] After their electoral successes during the first years of Estonian independence (in 1920 they cast 18,000 votes and gained four seats) the Baltic Germans became overconfident of their political unity. This led to negligence in electoral preparations, which caused a large loss of votes in the 1923 and 1926 elections, when the Baltic Germans won only about 16,000 and 13,000 votes, losing one seat in each election. In 1926 many votes were lost to the Houseowners' and Workers' parties.

With only two seats the German ethnic group no longer qualified as a faction, that is, it could not cast votes as a unit in electing parliamentary committees. In the fall of 1928 the group therefore approached the Swedish minority about the possibility of forming an electoral coalition. On the German side the talks were conducted by Werner Hasselblatt, a member of parliament, and Hermann Koch, a lawyer. Koch's participation was particularly appropriate, since he had previously worked in the Estonian Provisional Government of 1918 as a German "People's minister" and had established close connections with the Swedish "People's minister" Hans Poehl. These ministries were later replaced by German and Swedish "People's secretariats," to which a Russian Secretariat was added on July 1, 1922. They were affiliated with the Ministry of Education. In 1926 Poehl ran for the Estonian Christian People's party, and two years later stepped into a vacant seat in the Assembly.

Successful negotiations led to the formation of a German-Swedish ticket that increased the combined German-Swedish vote by 20.9%. With the election of Hasselblatt, Schilling, and Poehl the coalition gained sufficient strength to be admitted as a parliamentary faction. The three politicians represented their ethnic groups in seven parliamentary commissions. Hasselblatt was on the Committee of Finance and Election Law and on the General Committee; Baron Schilling was seated on the Committee of Agriculture and Education; Poehl worked on the Rules Committee and in the Committee of Budget and Accounting. When Hans Poehl died on January 22, 1930, he was succeeded by Matthias Westerblom, a merchant from Tallinn, who for many years had been prominent in Swedish ethnic activities.

Representatives of each of the two minorities participated in the meetings of the other minority.[29] However, they did not merge into a single German-Swedish party or a single "Party of the Ethnic Minorities"[30] for all the assemblies and the Constituent Assembly.

Minority Activities in Parliaments

The political cooperation of the minorities at the beginning of the Fourth Assembly in Estonia was not limited to the formation of the German-Swedish election "bloc" and the resulting parliamentary faction. A coalition with Russian representatives was formed in the Assembly itself for the purpose of influencing appointments to parliamentary committees. The minority Russian party in Estonia, the Russian National Union, had suffered a severe defeat in the 1929 parliamentary election—from 19,000 votes in 1923 to 17,500 in 1926 and then further to slightly less than 14,000 in 1929.[31] The Russian National Union then lost 5000 votes to the Estonian Social Democrats, whose two Russian candidates, Kov and Grechanov, had won in the predominantly Russian-populated areas. The Russian National Union thus gained only two seats, which were won by Joann Bulin, the Archimandrite of the Pechora Monastery, and Smirnov, a priest. Together with the German-Swedish parliamentary and the House-owners' factions they formed a bloc, thus placing the Russian minority on the parliamentary Committee for Self-Administration.

This German-Russian cooperation had a precedent in the Third Assembly. Having won only two seats, the Baltic German party had lost the right to form a faction and thus to nominate candidates to committees. To preserve their influence on committees, the Baltic German representatives formed a coalition with the three Russian members of parliament. Hasselblatt worked in the General Committee and the Russian representatives participated in five other committees.

In Latvia, too, the minorities nominated coalition lists of candidates for parliamentary committees. For tactical purposes these arrangements continued even after the collapse of the minority bloc, though the large number of minority representatives made such *ad hoc* agreements very tenuous. Minority individualism and mutual jealousies led to disagreements that in the end only damaged their common cause.

Both the Jewish and Russian ethnic groups nominated candidates to the Committee on the Constitution of the Latvian Constituent Assembly instead of agreeing on joint support for a common candidate. Both lost.[32] As a result, ethnic minority representation on this committee decreased by one. Ten years later three minority representatives separated themselves from the joint ticket and ran independently, with the result that none of them was elected.[33] The remaining minority parliamentarians, united in elections, were able to capture a total of twenty-five seats on sixteen committees.

The minorities maintained close contact whenever their autonomy was at stake. In the spring of 1921 the German, Swedish, and Russian representatives jointly introduced a bill in the Estonian Assembly dealing with the cultural autonomy of ethnic minorities.[34] This project was advocated in parliament and in the committees primarily by the Baltic German delegates "on behalf of all minority parliamentary parties." When the second reading of the proposal was voted down at the beginning of March 1923, minority delegates issued "for the first time in the history of the Estonian Parliament" an extraordinary joint declaration. The group condemned the intention of the Estonian "People's Party" and of some

Social Democrats "to stoke the national contrasts in long speeches, the purpose of which is the delay of the bill." After the Swedish Ethnic party had lost its representative, Hans Poehl of the Christian People's party also came to support this bill.

In 1923, when the Estonian government was negotiating with the League of Nations a document on the protection of minorities, the minority delegates asked to be admitted to the negotiating sessions. Furthermore, the Baltic German delegate, Gerhard Kress, in the name of all three minority parties handed the state elder (president) a memorandum in which he energetically asked for an international guarantee.

In Estonia declarations and memoranda signed by all minorities were common, as were speeches by delegates "in the name of all minorities." They continued even after the passage of the "Law on the Cultural Autonomy of the Ethnic Minorities" on February 5, 1925.

No such joint measures could be found in Latvia. In May 1921 the Committee of Baltic German Parties refused to band together with the other ethnic groups, since the Germans wanted to maintain a free hand in the shaping of the law as well as in the formulation of tactics and strategies. This, however, did not hinder negotiations,[35] in particular with the Jewish lawyer Professor Mintz, and the exchange of proposals among the separate ethnic groups. It was agreed, for example, that "every minority group submit its own project on autonomy; every project, however, must be signed by all delegates of the minorities." This action failed when the Russian minority submitted two proposals to the Constituent Assembly, of which the German faction signed only one. For the sake of appearance Germans formed a coalition with other minorities, since an overly separatist stance would have roused Latvian mistrust of German proposals.

Minorities, furthermore, occasionally concluded agreements for joint *ad hoc* measures. According to Schiemann, the ethnic groups supported one another in cultural demands, while maintaining a free hand on political issues.[36] This situation existed after the failure to establish closer minority ties and the dissolution of the minority bloc in Latvia in 1921. An example of the occasional *ad hoc* cooperation is the minority reaction in late 1923 to the obligatory Latvian-language examinations for minority teachers and educational administrators established by the Latvian minister of education Hugo Celmiņš. Keller complained about the lack of consistency among the Poles, the Jews, and the Belorussians. In early 1924 he further complained that "in the end the other minorities had again shown their usual passivity."[37] However, later three Russian and two Zionist Jewish delegates who supported the Valdemārs Zāmuels cabinet (January 27–

December 18, 1924), kept the cabinet's decision on language examinations out of the government bulletin by threatening to disrupt the coalition.[38] Concern for continued minority school autonomy often led to negotiations and joint action by the minorities.

Finally, as early as the spring of 1924 Russian and Jewish representatives supported the Zāmuels cabinet in accord with the other minority groups. A year later the German action supported the Celmiņš cabinet (December 19, 1924–December 3, 1925). Russians, Jews, and Poles remained neutral by not voting in matters that directly concerned the government. After the second German attempt to create a joint minority bloc failed, a portion of the minority parliamentarians began to cooperate more closely. Two Jewish, two Polish, and three Russian delegates formed a faction with the somewhat misleading name "Democratic Bloc of Minorities," which leaned toward Left-of-Center Latvian parties. The three other Jewish delegates, together with the German faction, though also "democratically" inclined, tended to support the bourgeois coalition.[39] The "Democratic Bloc of Minorities" declared its intention to cooperate with other minority representatives in cultural matters. Its leader, the Jewish delegate Markus Nuroks, was asked in December 1926 to form a government after Alberings' cabinet had been overthrown on December 7 with the support of the German faction. Following fruitless negotiations with the leftist Social Democrats and a part of the Center, he declined; together with the "Democratic Bloc of Minorities," however, he aligned himself with the cabinet of the rightist Social Democrat, Marģers Skujenieks. The German parliamentary group and the bourgeois Jewish delegates adopted a wait-and-see attitude toward this government. They did not participate in the vote of confidence. The same sort of friendly neutrality was shown by the German faction in May 1927 when offered the post of minister of justice in a future government by the right-wing "Peasants' League" in return for help in overthrowing the Skujenieks cabinet.

Minority Conferences

Besides parliamentary cooperation, Baltic minority politicians in the 1920s made several attempts to discuss mutual problems. On cultural autonomy, which was one topic of basic importance to all minorities, there was general agreement, but differences of opinion on specifics. Estonia's law of 1925 provided a model for this autonomy, but, as Karl Keller has emphasized, the actual school organization was influenced by ethnic peculiarities.

In 1921 a so-called Journalists' conference in Kaunas brought together German, Russian, and Jewish representatives from Estonia, Latvia, and Lithuania. The editor-in-chief of the *Revaler Bote*, Axel de Vries, expressed hope that the Baltic peoples, having won their own freedom, would support free cultural development of the minorities as well.[40] Another Baltic press conference took place in Kaunas at the end of January 1935. Here ground for a "Baltic Entente of the Press" was prepared.[41]

On January 16 and 17, 1926, Schiemann summoned a conference of the Baltic States minority representatives in Riga. Nine German, four Jewish, two Russian, and two Polish politicians from Estonia, Latvia, and Lithuania participated. The discussions concentrated on Baltic economic problems (the creation of a customs union) and minority autonomy. When Max Lazerson, a Jewish professor, stressed the lack of irredentism in the Baltic States, de Vries pointed out that "our movement is not a movement of minorities but a movement of nationalities."[42] The proposed Estonian autonomy law, he said, would establish Estonian rights over minorities in areas of mostly non-Estonian population. Thus a step would be taken away from minority rights toward international nationality rights, which proclaimed equality for all nationalities, including the majority population. Schiemann demanded that state functions be transferred to the minorities in the form of self-administration. Critical among them, he said, were state and community revenues, the tax law, and the freedom of national identification. The conference unanimously agreed on "all important questions discussed, particularly those that concerned the elimination of national discrimination from the economic life, the implementation of cultural autonomy and the protection of civil rights." The participants also resolved to increase cooperation.

Though the meeting strengthened the minority position vis-à-vis the majority, it did not bring about lasting cooperation among the minorities. The Baltic German representatives from Estonia and Latvia did establish closer contact, but the intended organizational alliance, with monthly sessions taking place, did not materialize.[43]

The *coups d'état* of March 12, 1934, in Estonia and May 15, 1934, in Latvia terminated all parliamentary and political party activities of the minorities.[44] During the last six years of Baltic independence there developed considerable differences in their political life. In Latvia the authoritarian measures were never legalized by a parliament which was dissolved and never recalled. In Estonia a new parliament came into being in 1938, albeit on a changed foundation. A new voting law allowed only the Russian ethnic group, which was larger and had settled in a contiguous area, to participate in the Chamber of Representatives. According to the constitution, only one delegate of the two existing cultural administrations—German and Jewish—could be sent to the upper house. Dr. Hellmuth Weiss represented the Baltic German ethnic group in the National Assembly for the purpose of drafting a new constitution. From 1938 on Baron Wilhelm Wrangell performed the same function in the Council of State. But when it was realized that the interests of the Jewish and German minorities were not always parallel, President Konstantin Päts appointed, in addition to Dr. Weiss, the Jewish lawyer Dr. Gutkin as an official minority representative.

Estonian minorities suffered a certain denigration of their status as a result of the authoritarian measures of 1934 and the new constitution that became effective on January 1, 1938. The constitution limitated the scope of their self-administration and the right of minority schools to conduct classes in minority languages. Closer cooperation among the leaders of the Baltic German, Russian, and Jewish groups developed as a result of their futile attempts to oppose these measures. In Latvia, furthermore, minority parliamentarians could not defeat the much harsher measures of Ulmanis' authoritarian government, which abolished school autonomy as well as the so-called New Year laws. Ulmanis' "Latvianization" could not be countered on a parliamentary level, as had been done in *Saeima* days, since the parliament had been dissolved.

III

Baltic States in Europe between the Wars

The Baltic States between Nazi Germany and Soviet Russia

ALEXANDER DALLIN

The historian seeking to reconstruct the relationship between the Baltic States and their neighboring powers would have a simpler task if a single paramount dichotomy had governed their international situation—say, between the successor states (which included the Baltic republics) and the victims of the Versailles system (which included both Germany and Russia). What obtained in reality, however, was a combination of several simultaneous cross-cutting cleavages.

The Baltic States themselves were of course not politically homogeneous. Nor did they always agree in their assessment of friend and foe. They were divided by traditional rivalries and resentments and by their differences in ethnic and cultural background, some of which tended to align Estonians against Lithuanians and Latvians and, more importantly, others that tended to separate Lithuania from Latvia and Estonia. Above all, Lithuania, being closer to Germany and farther away from Russia, was more prone to lean on the Soviet Union than were Latvia and Estonia, which had Russia at their gates (as well as sizable *Volksdeutsche* minorities —another source of tension).

There had been interest in the various projects of Baltic Union. Its widest version—a union from Warsaw to Helsinki—had in the early postwar years been promoted by Baltic statesmen to whom a cohesive barrier between Russia and Germany seemed to be a precondition for a stable equilibrium in Eastern Europe. But by 1923 it was clear that such efforts were doomed to failure. And just as the broader Baltic Union proved to be a mirage, so even the narrower Entente among the three Baltic states remained more token than real, despite the Treaty of Friendship and Cooperation concluded by them in 1934. In part this was due to Lithuania's distinct position, shaped in large measure by its continued friction with Poland.[1]

Here was a primary instance of the disharmony between the Baltic States and their neighbors who shared membership in that "world between" Germans and eastern Slavs. Poland and Lithuania were troubled not only by memories of earlier greatness and glory and by the Jagellonian aspirations of some of Warsaw's statesmen, but more directly by the Polish incorporation of Vilnius, which the Lithuanian authorities considered not only theirs but even their capital. The resulting tension provided an added stimulus for the conclusion of the Soviet-Lithuanian treaty of 1926. More generally, in the 1920s the Soviet Union—out of weakness, and cognizant of the fact that its Baltic neighbors had been among the first to accord Soviet Russia diplomatic recognition—had assumed a posture of "ostentatious benevolence" (to use Reddaway's phrase), despite—or perhaps because of—Soviet fears that Latvia and Estonia were centers of anti-Soviet activity.

While Aristide Briand, recasting Clemenceau's notion of a *cordon sanitaire*, explored the possibility of an "Eastern Locarno," Germany refused to accept her eastern boundaries as final; and Britain was disinclined to make any commitments in regard to Eastern Europe. It remained for Maksim Litvinov in 1929 to include the Baltic States among the parties with which the Soviet Union concluded protocols bringing the Kellogg-Briand Pact into immediate force.[2]

To the Baltic States themselves the League of Nations must have appeared as the logical protector of their integrity, a proposition that was not seriously tested until the mid-1930s. By then of course the impotence of the League had become only too manifest. And by then Germany, under Hitler, had begun to gather strength and to seek new means to pursue an expansionist course—by pressure and threats, and if necessary by force of arms.

The interwar years thus witnessed a precarious and deceptive calm, thanks in large measure to the exceptional weakness of both Germany and Russia. Once that anomaly disappeared, the architects of the earlier peace settlement proved to be unwilling to make sure that it would last. It was then essentially the destabilization of the international system, due largely to Hitler's initiatives, that set the stage for the crisis of which unexpectedly the Soviet Union was to be the primary beneficiary in the end.

In the 1930s Moscow was in the throes of internal exertions and upheavals. Stalin clearly preferred not to face serious threats and crises abroad. But once he became aware of the rising menace of a resurgent Germany (and, analogously, of Japan in the East), a new phase of Soviet foreign policy was launched. The "revisionist" pro-German line toward the European system was abandoned, instead aligning the Soviet Union with France and Czechoslovakia and the Kremlin now joining the League and reverting to traditional Russian national appeals and symbols. One of the early manifestations of the new course was a Soviet proposal, in March 1934, that Germany and the Soviet Union guarantee the independence and territorial integrity of the Baltic States and Finland. Berlin rejected the proposal. Still, Moscow had no serious cause to be concerned about the Baltic States.[3]

From the mid-1930s on the three small republics were caught in the crossfire of that earlier German-Soviet cold war. Poland, whose leadership alternately found itself repelled by and drawn to Germany, in the end wound up eager to accept Western guarantees when—after the Austrian *Anschluss* and the dismemberment of Czechoslovakia—Danzig and the Polish Corridor loomed as obvious German targets. Latvia and Estonia, by contrast, chose *not* to solicit—and to make clear that they would not accept—Western (let alone Soviet) assurances of support against foreign encroachments. Indeed, the Baltic States deemed it axiomatic that their best prospects of remaining aloof from future great-power conflicts lay in staying uninvolved and uncommitted. If this formula was a truism, the policy it invited could be either astute or suicidal.

Soviet policy, from 1935 on, comprised efforts to extend the "collective security" system and to pressure weaker partners into closer cooperation. Thus Kaunas, Riga, and Tallinn were among the capitals to which Foreign Commissar Litvinov addressed offers of bilateral mutual-assistance pacts, which the Baltic States declined. But after 1936 there was also some greater nervousness along the frontiers. Incidents on the Soviet border multiplied. And there were occasional verbal outbursts such as Andrei Zhdanov's well-publicized speech of November 29, 1936, in which he referred to the possible danger to the Leningrad area—his fief—if neighboring states such as Finland permitted their territory to be used by other powers—presumably Germany. Some of the foreign press reports including those in the Baltic States sensationalized, or overreacted to, his speech; there are manifest discrepancies between the published Soviet version and some of its reports abroad, which had Zhdanov threatening Estonia, Latvia, and Finland with the prospect of enlarging Russia's "window on the Baltic."[4] Given his later role, it is not inconceivable that Zhdanov used the occasion to apply pressure within the Soviet leadership on behalf of a more militant line. But he was probably only a little ahead of others in Moscow in his alarm at the prospect of German utilization of the eastern Baltic. In 1937–1938 Moscow was again busy trying to mend fences and increase its leverage in the Baltic States, though mutual suspicion remained profound.

Polish conduct contributed to the breakdown of the existing order. Just as it was to benefit from the Czech crisis in regard to Cieszyn (Teschen), so at the time of the *Anschluss*, in March 1938, Warsaw gave Kaunas an ultimatum to "normalize" relations, which implied bowing to Polish pressure and accepting the *status quo* in regard to Vilnius. The other Baltic capitals failed to react, apparently feeling closer to Warsaw than to Kaunas. Germany, too, refused to intervene; as we now know, Hitler was prepared to occupy parts of Lithuania if the Poles marched in.[5] Warsaw had reason to assume that there was no danger of Soviet intervention on Lithuania's behalf. Indeed, Litvinov urged the Lithuanians to yield so as to avoid a showdown. Later Soviet accounts were to assert that it was only a Soviet threat to denounce the Polish-Soviet nonaggression pact of 1932 that led Warsaw to moderate its demands (such as dropping the demand for a change in the Lithuanian constitution to delete the identification of Vilnius as the capital) or in fact to cancel a military advance. Though Litvinov's concern is not in doubt, the available documents fail to bear out this Soviet claim.[6]

If the United States ambassador Joseph E. Davies can be trusted, Lithuania's assessment again differed from that of its northern neighbors. Lithuanian envoy Jurgis Baltrušaitis believed that Soviet protection was Lithuania's only hope. At root, Davies reported to Washington, there was the fear that

> Poland had some secret agreement with Germany whereunder Germany would support a Polish [effort] to absorb Lithuania and find an outlet to the sea, in consideration for which Poland would relinquish the Polish Corridor to Germany. . . . If such were the actual facts of the situation, there was a general conviction [among observers in Moscow] that the Soviet Union would be compelled to come to the aid of Lithuania and that war would result.[7]

An unlikely contingency; but in the event no such conflict occurred. It was Hitler's further endeavors that precipitated the next crisis. The Polish-Lithuanian incident reinforced the belief that Kaunas could count on no foreign support in the face of German demands for the cession of Klaipėda. When in December 1938 the *Volksdeutsche Liste* scored a clear electoral victory there, the British ambassador to Berlin cabled home: "It is too late to save Klaipėda for Lithuania."[8]

Indeed, when in March 1939, after the German occupation of Prague, Lithuanian Foreign Minister Juozas Urbšys stopped over in Berlin on his way home, von Ribbentrop demanded of him the cession of the *Memelland,* threatening military action in case of refusal. The Kaunas government yielded, losing its only port of consequence. Having anticipated such a possibility in an escape clause of the Baltic treaty of 1934, the Latvian and Estonian authorities rationalized their inaction by expressing the hope that this removed the last territorial issue jeopardizing the sovereignty and integrity of the Baltic States. In effect, Lithuania now found herself isolated and vulnerable to German pressure. Moreover, having no common border with the Soviet Union, it scarcely figured in the international negotiations that followed, in which the fates of Latvia and Estonia were important issues.

As for the Soviet Union, during the Klaipėda crisis Litvinov was not available. But a few days later he warned that Moscow would consider it intolerable if a third power succeeded in imposing terms infringing Latvian or Estonian independence and freedom of action.[9] The recipients of his *note verbale* replied, in effect, that they could take care of themselves and would not recognize the right of any other party to intervene, directly or indirectly, in their affairs.

Moscow now argued that neutrality—which it had earlier welcomed among its western neighbors—was no longer enough: it was a form of escapism, if not appeasement, which "does not assure the small states safety from danger in the event of a war among the great powers."[10] As Soviet Foreign Minister V. M. Molotov was to tell Latvian Foreign Minister Vilhelms Munters a few months later, a neutral Baltic States— that was too *nenadiozhno* (insecure, unreliable).[11] Moreover, Moscow also opposed, as it always did, all attempts at alliances and coalitions among its neighbors so long as it was not a party to them.

Litvinov continued his efforts to break out of the diplomatic isolation in which the Soviet Union found itself. The Munich accord served to dramatize its predicament. But Stalin soon turned to explore alternative courses of action, and Litvinov himself was to become a victim of this reorientation. What did Stalin want? Abstractly of course, at some future point, the adherence of the Baltic States to the Soviet Union—which after all had been explicitly designed as an incipient "world state"—and their communization were taken for granted. But this assumption had no operational significance, at least since the failure of the communist *coup d'état* in Estonia in December 1924 and more generally during the era of interwar "coexistence." No timetable was attached to this prospect, which, in regard to the Baltic as to any other states, was ultimately an article of faith. In terms of specific political initiatives or the balance of power, there had been neither opportunity for, nor any urgency to, any attempt to gain control. Once the German danger seemed paramount, Stalin had additional reasons to avoid any move that would have aroused other powers against him—and any attempt at takeover or subversion assuredly would have.[12] There were no doubt some genuine Soviet security concerns here, as foreign observers and diplomats recognized from time to time. As the British Foreign Office cabled its envoy in Moscow, "His Majesty's Government fully appreciate . . . that the military occupation of one of the Soviet Union's northwest neighbors, whose resistance might be quickly overborne or who might even acquiesce in the occupation, might be regarded by the Soviet Union as a menace to the security of the Soviet Union."[13] As late as July 1939 the key German negotiator with the Russians, Dr. Karl Schnurre, reported on the basis of his talks with the Soviet chargé that "our assumption that the Baltic countries and Finland, as well as Romania, were in [the German] sphere of interest completed for the Soviet Government the feeling of being menaced."[14]

But, then, Moscow had always looked upon the pursuit of security as offering a variety of options, from armaments to alliances and from defense to offense. Complete security, and the complete denial of an area to a potential enemy, could come about only with complete control. In practice, of course, partial solutions were typically the order of the day. But it is understandable that some students of the problem should have concluded that until 1939 Soviet political objectives in this area were unclear. To promote Soviet control took not only a desire, which may well have been latent, but also a propitious, low-risk situation, which did not exist.

By contrast, there can be little doubt of Hitler's objectives. Ever since writing *Mein Kampf*, he had identified the Baltic republics as part of the German *Lebensraum* and a historical locus of German settlement. Baltic Germans played a prominent part in the Nazi leadership. Hitler had spoken repeatedly of the Baltic as a German sea. In April 1938 he told one of his ambassadors that he did not want to rule over any non-Germans; but "*wenn schon, dann über die Randstaaten.*" The protocol of the Führer conference of May 23, 1939, contains Hitler's pledge to "widen the *Lebensraum*" at the expense of Poland as well as to proceed to the "*Lösung des Baltikumproblems.*"[15] Still, compared to Poland and the Soviet Union, the Baltic States were in 1939 fairly incidental among Hitler's concerns and objectives —as was indeed shown by his willingness to trade them away to Stalin by the secret protocol concluded with Moscow later that year.

When in April 1939 President Roosevelt called on Hitler to issue a nonaggression pledge to neighboring states that might feel threatened by Germany, Hitler asked who among them felt menaced by the Reich. With some equivocation the Baltic States could not but reply in the negative. But the political differences among them were again on the increase. While there were prominent dissenters, the Estonian elite, in particular, was decidedly more fearful of Soviet than of German intentions.[16] In Riga and Kaunas opinions seemed to be divided, but on balance the Latvian authorities evidently suspected Hitler's purposes at least as much as Stalin's, especially after Germany rebuffed Munters' effort to secure an assurance that it would respect Latvian neutrality (much as Belgium's) in case of war. Still, as if in protest against the prospect of an unsolicited Soviet pledge of help against Germany, Estonia and Latvia in June 1939 signed nonaggression pacts with the Reich; a rather futile endeavor, given the great-power negotiations being conducted over their heads at the time.

Great Britain, having given guarantees to Poland and Romania, made it clear in April 1939 that it would offer no such assurances to the Baltic States. Yet a guarantee by the three powers—Britain, France, and Russia —to the countries lying between the Baltic and Black seas was a major point of the Soviet proposals to the Western democracies on April 18. Moscow wanted the belt of states from Finland to Turkey to become part of the contemplated security system regardless of whether they wanted or refused such a commitment. Moscow objected to the French and British proposals, among other things, because they failed to provide for a symmetrical British and French undertaking to come to the defense of Finland, Estonia, and Latvia. As London indeed instructed its ambassador to Moscow, "Our object is, of course, to prevent our being dragged into war by Russia over a Baltic state without our having any voice in the matter."[17] Moscow also objected because the Western terms called for help to targets of German aggression only "if desired" by the victim states. Whether viewed as reflecting a position of greater integrity or as evidence of shortsighted procrastination, the British position is likely to have reinforced Stalin's eagerness to explore alternative arrangements with Berlin.

The course of negotiations between Moscow and the Western powers is a matter of familiar record.[18] By the end of June Britain and France were willing to conclude a secret protocol accompanying the planned tripartite security pact, which would list, among others, Latvia and Estonia as objects of assistance in case of aggression. (Lithuania was omitted because the earlier drafts spoke of "neighbor" states "bordering" on the

Soviet Union.) The two Baltic governments concerned had meanwhile raised insistent objections to what they understood to be the likely terms of the treaty: if faced with the choice, some elements in Tallinn and Riga would clearly have preferred German to Soviet rule; others argued that to identify certain countries in such a fashion was to heighten the likelihood of hostile action on the part of Germany.

But even as policymakers in London and Paris reluctantly reached the conclusion that they needed to ignore such concerns for the sake of the treaty with Moscow, two other major obstacles remained. One was the Soviet insistence on the right to station troops on the territory of some of the countries: while Poland was the major stumbling block here, the Baltic States would have resisted the prospect with equal firmness. Another was the Soviet insistence that the accord cover "indirect aggression" as well as a direct German attack. In the words of a recent Soviet account, the British and French governments

> refused to act against Germany if she resorted to indirect aggression—the organization of a coup in the Baltic States or the adoption by these states of a pro-Hitler orientation, despite the fact that this was precisely the most probable manner of subordinating the Baltic to Nazi Germany.[19]

In the end, Sir William Strang urged the British Foreign Office to recognize that this dealt indeed with "aggressive action undertaken according to the new technique with which the Axis powers have made us familiar. If we wish to understand how [the Soviet leaders] feel about the Baltic States, we have only to imagine what our own attitude would be to the establishment of German influence over Holland or Belgium."[20] But even when on July 23 agreement was reached in principle (a definition of indirect aggression remained to be worked out), negotiations shifted to the coordination of joint military action, since Moscow insisted that this was an essential condition for conclusion of the tripartite pact. Delay was only likely to enhance the Soviet bargaining position. Thus the unsigned and unratified treaty remained in limbo, including the provision that the three powers would come to each other's assistance if any one of them was involved in defending against aggression a state "whose independence or neutrality the contracting party feels obliged to defend"—a strangely loose formulation. The secret draft protocol enumerating the countries to which this was to apply included Latvia and Estonia.

All this of course turned out to be a quixotic exercise. In the Soviet-German talks being conducted simultaneously, without the knowledge of the British and French, the Baltic States figured as objects of bargaining only toward the very end. Both sides initially assumed that any German-Soviet accord would simply reaffirm the integrity of the Baltic States. As late as July 26 the two key officials, Schnurre and Counselor Georgi Astakhov, seemed agreed on this point.[21] But now Hitler was getting nervous. Time was running out before the attack on Poland was due to be launched. Ambassador Werner Schulenburg was instructed to make clear to Molotov that Germany was prepared to respect "vital Soviet interests" in the Baltic area, and Molotov was so informed. What these Soviet interests amounted to was not yet spelled out. When in the course of exploring the terms of possible agreement, Minister of Foreign Affairs Joachim von Ribbentrop on August 16 proposed a joint Soviet and German guarantee to the Baltic States, it became clear that this no longer satisfied the Soviet leadership, who sensed the opportunity to hold out for more tangible advantage. Moscow's reply suggested a special protocol that would define their mutual spheres of influence; Berlin agreed.[22]

Ribbentrop left for Moscow with instructions to propose a partition of the Baltic area, with the river Daugava as the dividing line between the German and Soviet spheres. But in their first meeting in the Kremlin, on August 23, Stalin insisted that Soviet Russia also needed access to the major Latvian ports, Liepāja and Ventspils. Ribbentrop secured Hitler's consent by telephone, thus making possible the conclusion of the famous secret protocol to the nonaggression pact, which gave Finland, Estonia, and Latvia (among others) to the Soviet sphere and placed Lithuania in the German orbit.[23]

A month later, Germany had defeated Poland and occupied the major part of the country, and the Soviet Union took over the rest. On his second visit to Moscow, at the end of September, Ribbentrop agreed to transfer Lithuania to the Soviet sphere in return for a slice of Polish territory.[24] Moscow thus had a free hand in the Baltic States.

It is curious that no effort was made to specify the form or scope of Soviet "interest" in the area. However, neither side had any doubt as to what was intended. As early as October 3, 1939, Ambassador Schulenburg in a report to the German Foreign Office took it for granted that "incorporation" of the Baltic republics would result.[25] Though the precise terms of the protocol remained secret, Stalin himself made their substance clear to the Baltic diplomats summoned to Moscow in the following weeks, if only to indicate that they could expect no backing from Germany if they sought to resist Soviet demands.[26] Similarly, Ribbentrop secretly informed the German envoys in the Baltic States of the terms of the deal.

For all intents and purposes, the signing of the Nazi-Soviet Pact with its definition of spheres of influence sealed the fate of the Baltic States. What followed was largely a matter of mechanics and timing, pretense and form. In substance, Hitler paid a price for which he expected a *quid pro quo* from Stalin. True, Moscow could not fully cash in on the German promissory notes immediately, though in effect the "mutual assistance pacts" signed with the Baltic States gave the Soviet Union the crucial foothold that, within less than a year, enabled it to transform the Baltic republics into constituent republics of the Soviet Union.

It remains an open question to what extent the collapse of the Western front—the German victory over France—in June 1940 triggered the final phase of the incorporation of the Baltic States into the Soviet Union. There is no clear evidence to conclude, as some observers have, that the fall of France brought home to Stalin his earlier miscalculation and prompted him to change course by the outright annexation of the three states. On the other hand, the timing of their absorption—and of the analogous Soviet moves in Bessarabia and Northern Bukovina—was probably determined by German preoccupation elsewhere and by a Soviet effort to offset somewhat the accretion in the power position of the Reich.

It has been argued that in August 1939 Britain and France had been similarly prepared to make the Baltic States the pawns they might have traded for agreement with Stalin. In the end, they were indeed prepared to recognize Soviet "special rights" and legitimate security concerns there and elsewhere in Eastern Europe. Winston Churchill had even earlier acknowledged that "for Russia it is of vital interest that these states not fall into the hands of Nazi Germany." But this is a far cry from sanctioning their annexation. Moreover, there is no reason to think that either side was thinking of such terms of a trade. And Britain and France, ignorant of the imminence of Stalin's German option, lacked all sense of urgency in the frustrating talks.

What choices had the Baltic States had in pursuit of their own security and independence? Essentially, they had sought refuge in neutrality. At times they had sought to balance Soviet and German influences and interests. Neither of these approaches carried any assurance of lasting success; it certainly did not once Moscow and Berlin made common cause—something that was beyond the power of the Baltic States to prevent.

They could seek guarantees from Germany against Russia, and vice versa. This meant choosing up sides and acknowledging a measure of outside hegemony. All three governments sought to avoid this, but they leaned in different directions, to different degrees, at different times. In the end, the Pact rendered this an impracticable option, too: the choice was no longer theirs. Plans for a regional alliance were stillborn: the Baltic-Polish was out of the question because of the Polish-Lithuanian problem; the Scandinavian-Baltic had failed (and the Scandinavian countries themselves were eager to stay out of the conflict); and the Baltic Entente was no more effective or promising in 1939 than it had been during the preceding two decades. Joint military coordination and resistance might have forced a change in the circumstances, the time, and the methods of Soviet takeover; they could not have affected the outcome. Finally, the Baltic States could have tied themselves to the Western powers—above all Britain, whose influence in the area was not inconsiderable. But London was disinclined to assume obligations here, even if the countries concerned had been prepared to accept them (as in fact they were not).

The question remains whether agreement over the status and defense of the Baltic area, in the tripartite negotiations in the summer of 1939, might have speeded the conclusion of an accord among the three powers and thus forestalled the Nazi-German pact, which spelled the end of the three Baltic States' independence. On balance, it must be concluded that other obstacles—such as Polish objections to the passage and stationing of Soviet troops, and British-Soviet military coordination—were even more serious and fundamental obstacles to such an accord, obstacles that would have remained even if the Baltic question had been "solved."

With the benefit of hindsight, the foreign policies—and assuredly the domestic policies—of each of the three Baltic nations can be subjected to severe critique. No doubt, more representative, responsive, and responsible regimes might have been able to mobilize popular support far more effectively.[27] But the fact remains that whatever these countries did or failed to do was ultimately immaterial. As one writer puts it, "Whether or not they concluded nonaggression pacts with their great neighbors; whether or not they pursued a policy of neutrality; whether or not they treated their ethnic minorities well; whether they banned or allowed Communist parties—all this was of no consequence for the final result."[28] More perfect democratic systems, however desirable, would scarcely have saved them from absorption in 1939–1940.

In the last analysis, their broader setting made no crucial difference either—neither the imperatives of geography, which had placed them between hammer and anvil; nor the imperatives of smallness, which had put them at the mercy of stronger aggressors; nor the overlapping cleavages and their alignment in competing international subsystems. In the course of World War II big states were victimized much as the small ones were. Countries that remained neutral (Norway, Denmark, Netherlands) were occupied as were those that committed themselves. Those that had ties with the Soviet Union (Czechoslovakia), with the West (Greece), and with Germany (Romania) were equally victims of foreign rule and abuse. Those that had accepted Western guarantees (Poland) suffered as much as those that had not. The one country that, under more favorable geographic and political conditions, chose to fight—Finland—acquired a record of heroism but in the end, too, was obliged to yield to superior force. It was soon back in the war on the Axis side; but it did insure its survival as an independent nation after World War II.

On the other hand, the ensuing events hardly validated the one serious Soviet argument—security concerns (the other Soviet claims, access to warm water ports and economic considerations, being palpably more contrived and less substantial). Soviet defense needs were real if they sought to anticipate a German invasion, though surely they did not warrant territorial annexation. True, the German attack did indeed come through the Baltic as well as adjacent areas in 1941. But Stalin's own behavior—his unwillingness to believe that a German attack was coming—more than undid whatever defensive benefits control of the Baltic States had brought the Red Army. We will never know whether or not Leningrad might have surrendered had it not been for the Baltic annexations. But for all intents and purposes the German Army cut across the area in a matter of weeks after it struck on June 22, 1941, opening another chapter of tragedies.

Along with the strategic and economic arguments, Soviet spokesmen at times made reference to historical precedent. Molotov, for instance, told the Latvian foreign minister Munters in October 1939 that some countries had already disappeared from the map of Europe. What was established in 1920 could not last for eternity. "Peter the Great saw to it that an outlet to the sea was gained. We are now without an exit, and the situation in which we are now cannot remain."[29] And when Lithuanian vice-premier Vincas Krėvė-Mickevičius saw Molotov in June 1940, he was told—or so he later related—that for reasons of state Russian tsars sought to reach the Baltic Sea ever since Ivan the Terrible. While no doubt the patriotic card in Stalin's deck could be an effective trump, at home and abroad, it remains very doubtful whether this was indeed the motivation behind Soviet moves. National-historical rationales could be, and often were, manipulated at will. Molotov may have come closer to the true impulse when he commented (in the same exchange): "It would have been unforgivable if the Soviet government had failed to take advantage of this opportunity, which may never recur."[30]

Stalin's desire to acquire and reshape the Baltic States in the Soviet image had been there, dormant but real nonetheless. To implement it required a set of circumstances in which Moscow could successfully pursue such an objective with relatively low risk. The breakdown of the international order in 1939–1940 permitted Stalin to shed such inhibitions as might earlier have restrained Soviet behavior. For creating the conditions in which the absorption could be carried out, by commission or by omission, all the other actors bear some share of responsibility—be it by their naiveté and shortsightedness; by their indifference, wishful thinking, or misguided priorities; or finally, in the Nazi case, their direct complicity. And of course Germany was soon to conquer the Baltic States until driven out by the Soviet forces in the course of World War II.

Great Britain and the Baltic States, 1938–1939

DAVID M. CROWE, JR.

Great Britain was the Baltic States' principal supporter during their brief period of independence. The basis of England's ties with Estonia, Latvia, and Lithuania lay in its diplomatic, economic, and cultural relations with them, which in turn opened up other avenues of influence and friendship.

British-Baltic ties developed during the Russian Civil War. The British government granted Estonia and Latvia *de facto* recognition in 1918 and recognized them *de jure* on January 21, 1921. Lithuania was recognized on December 20, 1921. The British government based its future relationship with the Baltic States on this move and on the "general obligations involved in Membership of the League of Nations," which the Baltic States joined in September 1922.[1]

As early as 1918 Great Britain and the Baltic republics established unofficial diplomatic ties and by 1920 London had a vice-consul in Pärnu to handle its interests in the "Baltic Provinces." A year later Whitehall appointed a consul-general at Kaunas to oversee matters in the Baltic States. It upgraded this mission in 1922 and appointed a minister at Kaunas to all the Baltic States, assisted by consuls in Tallinn and Riga. The British minister for the Baltic nations moved to Riga in 1923. London appointed a consul to Kaunas at this time, and established a consulate in Klaipėda a year later. This remained the basis of British representation in the Baltic States during the interwar period.[2]

The Baltic States did not send official representatives to Great Britain until 1922, when Latvia appointed a minister to London and Estonia a chargé d'affaires. Tallinn upgraded this position in 1923 when it named a minister to England. Lithuania sent a minister to the British capital in 1925. The size of the Baltic missions to Great Britain grew throughout the interwar period, and by 1939 the Baltic States had diplomatic and trade representatives throughout the British Empire.[3]

Economic relations played an extremely important role in British-Baltic affairs between 1918 and 1940. British trade with the Baltic States had grown steadily since 1920. England, Germany's principal trade rival in the Baltic, found the three countries quite receptive to its economic overtures because of the convertibility of British sterling vis-à-vis the Reichsmark. This, combined with the desire of the Baltic States to avoid building an export surplus with Germany through the Reich's clearing system, made Great Britain an attractive trading partner.[4] The British also kept cultural relations with the Baltic States.

Overall, Great Britain and the Baltic States maintained friendly relations between 1922 and 1940. The advent of Hitler's administration, however, produced some problems that affected ties between England and the three Baltic countries, particularly when Germany successfully began to use the clearing agreement system to weaken British economic influence. The British government formally protested these efforts in the Baltic capitals, which strained British-Baltic ties. The Baltic States, in turn, were upset over the potential threat of Germany because of Chamberlain's appeasement policy. Consequently, by 1938 conflicting national interests affected relations among Great Britain, Estonia, Latvia, and Lithuania. The Klaipèda crisis and the British-Soviet negotiations became the acid test of the British-Baltic friendship.

Klaipèda

One of the most sensitive territorial issues in Eastern Europe after World War I involved Klaipèda (Memel), an important Baltic trade center influenced by Lithuanian and German culture. The Allied Powers recognized Lithuania's claim to the district as early as 1919, but maintained international control of Klaipèda until 1923, when Lithuania annexed it. Lithuania agreed to accept the Klaipèda Statute of March 15, 1924, sponsored by Great Britain, France, Italy, and Japan. This organ, unfortunately, served only to complicate Lithuania's administration of Klaipèda, since the Statute's provision for governing the district soon found local Germans controlling the Diet and Lithuanians dominating the Directory.[5]

In spite of these differences, Klaipèda prospered under Lithuanian control. The advent of Hitler's administration in Germany in 1933, however, produced Nazi-sponsored unrest that threatened its economic and political stability. The Nazis hoped to bring the district completely under their control so that Germany could annex it. Between 1933 and 1938 more important territorial issues confronted Hitler. Germany, however, began to take more interest in Klaipėda after the threat to Lithuania during the Polish-Lithuanian crisis of March 1938. Consequently, Berlin presented Lithuania with a series of demands that, if accepted, would have placed the district under complete Nazi control. At the same time Berlin directed Klaipėda's Nazis to intensify their efforts to acquire control of the district. The situation in Klaipėda became particularly acute after the Munich crisis. This prompted Great Britain to review its position as a sponsor of the Klaipėda Statute.[6]

An important factor in understanding Great Britain's position vis-à-vis Lithuania and the Klaipėda question was Chamberlain's appeasement policy, which sought to avoid conflict with Germany. This explains, for example, the efforts of the British Foreign Office consistently to minimize Lithuanian reports regarding the severity of the Nazi threat to the district. London advised Kaunas to distinguish between those German demands that were efforts to reinterpret the Klaipėda Statute and those that were unfriendly, though not illegal.[7]

It is to the credit of His Majesty's government, however, that it did take a stand on the situation in Klaipėda when it became apparent that the Nazis might seize it after the December 11, 1938, district election. On December 7, 1938, Laurence Collier, the head of the Northern Department of the British Foreign Office, initiated an effort to convince the French government to intercede with von Ribbentrop, who was in Paris, regarding the German threat to Klaipėda. Paris hesitated to make any move that would harm its new relationship with Germany. At the insistence of British Prime Minister Neville Chamberlain, however, the French finally agreed to make a representation to Berlin about the Klaipėda matter. The French, however, sabotaged British efforts to meet with Germany over the situation in the district. This resulted in the British-French *démarche* of December 12, which dealt with German respect of the *status quo* in the region.[8]

The English had concluded before this time that Lithuania would ultimately return Klaipėda to Germany. Edward Viscount Halifax, the secretary of state for foreign affairs, stated on December 10, 1938, that even if Berlin agreed to discuss the Klaipėda question, it was probable that it would still insist that Kaunas cede the district to the Reich, something that the Smetona government would probably accept only under protest. Therefore, the idea of a proposed meeting with Hitler would be to get the Führer to agree to make no further demands upon Lithuania.[9] Later

Halifax told Count Edward Raczynski, the Polish ambassador to Great Britain, that while the Lithuanian Government might be constrained to surrender Memel, a threat to the independence of Lithuania itself would be a matter that would "affect us all."[10]

The real question, then, was the status of Lithuania itself. At the time, the Nazi threat to the district masked British intentions. When the December election crisis passed, members of both the Chamberlain and the Smetona governments viewed the British-French *démarche* as the source of Hitler's failure to retake Klaipėda, even though he had decided before the elections to wait for a more propitious moment to acquire this region.[11]

What, then, was the purpose of the December 12 *démarche*? The British, unlike the French, felt that Lithuania and the Klaipėda question were part of the "bigger issues" in Eastern Europe. Collier stated that Lithuania was a segment of Hitler's greater plan for dealing with Poland and the Soviet Union. London, however, made it clear that while it was willing to protest Nazi moves against Klaipėda or Lithuania, it would not go to war if Germany attacked Lithuania or the other Baltic countries.[12]

In light of this position, His Majesty's government continued to downplay news from Kaunas that the Nazis were attempting to create a new series of incidents that would ultimately result in the reunion of Klaipėda with Germany.[13] When Bronius K. Balutis, the Lithuanian minister to Great Britain, told Collier of these new violations, the British official questioned the report. This attitude was part of an overall mood in the Foreign Office that resulted, for example, in a denial by Halifax's spokesman in the House of Commons that the Bertuleit directorate in the Klaipėda district allowed the Nazis to violate the Klaipėda Statute, and that Whitehall had received no reports regarding these moves from the Smetona government.[14]

On January 30, 1939, Halifax learned from what Collier considered a very reliable source in the German Embassy in Moscow that Hitler planned to seize Klaipėda sometime after March 15. Yet the Foreign Office continued to minimize these reports because of its current economic discussions with Germany.[15] The British, who controlled the largest percentage of the Lithuanian import-export market, denied Lithuanian rumors that the talks involved the "delimitation of economic spheres of influence." Collier did tell Balutis, however, that while London had no intention of surrendering its economic position in the Baltic, its discussions with the Germans would involve price fixing and the division of markets.[16]

On March 16 the Smetona administration formally warned England of the imminent German threat to Klaipėda and asked London about its position in light of such a move. Halifax conducted a series of talks with the French and within the Foreign Office in response to this query. This resulted, however, in the decision that another *démarche* would do no good.[17]

The conversations within the Foreign Office lasted from March 16 through March 21. Halifax agreed with Alexander Cadogan that it would be useless to protest the German seizure of Klaipėda unless Great Britain was "going to fight for the maintenance of the Memel region." If not, then the less said about the district, the better. Cadogan stated that the British had "bigger fish to fry."[18] In a meeting on March 21, Halifax, Cadogan, and Collier agreed that if the Lithuanian government requested British aid, they would be told to "acquiesce under protest." If Germany's demands, however, went beyond the control of Klaipėda and resulted in an attempt to establish an economic protectorate over Lithuania, then Kaunas could justifiably consult with its neighbors.[19]

Once they had decided not to take a stand on the Klaipėda issue, the three British officials discussed how they would explain their position to the British public. At Halifax's instigation, Collier suggested the defense of British inaction on grounds that this particular question was similar to the Sudeten issue, "in that it is not physically possible, even with the aid of Lithuania's neighbors, if that could be obtained in time, to prevent a German seizure of the territory in dispute." In addition, Collier noted that Germany could make as strong a case for Klaipėda on the basis of "self determination" as it had with the Sudetenland. He realized that the Foreign Office had to be careful with the issue of self-determination, because used too liberally, it could affect every frontier region in Europe. Consequently, Collier concluded that the physical impossibility of preventing the Nazi takeover of the region, combined with the obvious German strength there, should make up one aspect of London's defense of its Klaipėda policy. He thought that His Majesty's government was merely a signator of the Klaipėda Convention, not a guarantor of it. In other words, he suggested that England was not "obliged to take any particular action to uphold it." Finally, Collier felt that it was important for his country to emphasize that Hitler's takeover of Klaipėda was "a breach of faith," particularly in light of the Nazi leader's pledge to Chamberlain at Berchtesgaden, that all he required of Lithuania in regard to Klaipėda was the strict observance of the district's governing Statute. Halifax and Cadogan approved Collier's defense statement and passed it on to the Foreign Office's News Department.[20]

The principal difficulty now facing Chamberlain and the matter of

British relations with Lithuania centered in the question of recognition of the German acquisition of Klaipėda. London, under pressure from Berlin, had to consider this step to keep its consulate there and to protect its commercial interests in the district. As the recognition proposal circulated through the Foreign Office, almost all interested department officials agreed that England had undertaken "no special guarantee to protect Lithuania in her enjoyment of sovereignty over Memel." Halifax's department concluded that Lithuania's cession of Klaipėda made the territory German "*de facto* and *de jure*." One official noted that if London failed to recognize Germany's latest territorial gain, it would be admitting that it had failed to carry out a "special responsibility for maintaining Lithuanian sovereignty in Memel." On May 10, 1939, the Chamberlain government accepted this rationale and informed Berlin of its decision to grant *de jure* recognition of Germany's annexation of Klaipėda.[21]

The British-Soviet Talks and the Baltic States

Rumors of German designs on Romania and Poland stimulated the formulation of a plan known as the Four Power Declaration, which proposed that Great Britain, France, the Soviet Union, and Poland immediately consult one another about steps to take regarding threats to the independence of any European nation. Poland, suspicious of the Soviet Union, rejected the plan.[22] However, a series of discussions among the remaining three states that dealt with the future security of Europe emerged.

The Baltic States became part of these talks after Estonia and Latvia rejected an independent Soviet guarantee of their independence on April 7, 1939. Moscow, determined to secure the Baltic States as a buffer zone against a potential German invasion, then proposed that Great Britain, France, and the Soviet Union offer to render assistance to any country subject to an act of aggression that shared a border with the Soviet Union.[23]

Tallinn and Riga immediately informed Chamberlain they were not interested.[24] The Päts administration became so concerned over this matter that on May 13 Foreign Minister Karl Selter asked William Gallienne, the British consul in Estonia, about the possibility of a four-power guarantee of Estonia's neutrality. After Gallienne had indicated that the proposal would not interest his government, Selter asked him if Whitehall would consider interceding with the Soviet Union in an effort to keep it from invading Estonia in time of war.[25] Selter's query prompted a mixed reaction in the Foreign Office. William Strang, the head of the Central Department, stated that Selter's remarks surprised him, particularly in light of Tallinn's previous requests not to have the British discuss Estonian matters with the Soviet Union without the approval of the Estonian government. Collier, however, defended Selter, and noted that rumors of an imminent Soviet invasion of Estonia had prompted Selter's remarks.[26]

The Soviet position vis-à-vis the territorial integrity of Estonia and Latvia so concerned these countries that they gave serious consideration to Germany's offer of nonaggression pacts on April 28–29. On May 15 the Estonian government asked the British for their opinion of the proposed treaty between Estonia and Germany. London replied three days later that although His Majesty's government questioned the value of this type of bilateral agreement, its only objection would arise over any clause in such a treaty that had "express or implied conditions of any sort," a reference to that part of the pact that dealt with aid to enemies of Germany. Whitehall applauded Estonia's efforts to keep Germany from interpreting the agreement along these lines. In the same message, the British suggested to Selter that a British-Soviet pact would reduce the Soviet danger to Estonia. If the situation, however, ever arose in which the British government felt that the Soviet Union threatened to take aggressive action against Estonia, Great Britain "would naturally be interested in dissuading [the] Soviet Government from it."[27] This would be London's strongest word of support regarding Estonian security.

On May 24 Halifax sought to reassure the Päts and the Ulmanis governments of his country's position vis-à-vis an unwanted guarantee. As a gesture of sympathy for the Baltic States, the British foreign minister supported a proposal by Vilhelms Munters, the Latvian foreign minster, that individual Baltic states could request the aid of the British, the French, or the Soviets, if another country violated their neutrality. Halifax attached considerable importance to this formula, since he opposed any action that did not allow for previous consultation with the Baltic States.[28]

Halifax and Chamberlain were the two strongest proponents of the position of Estonia and Latvia during this period. The British foreign minister felt that his country should point out to Stalin that the proposed guarantee of the Soviet Union only "covered German *direct* aggression" against the Soviet Union.[29]

Soviet insistence that Estonia and Latvia receive the same type of pledge given to Poland and Romania sabotaged efforts to obtain the Kremlin's approval of this plan.[30] It became increasingly apparent to London that the Soviet Union would accept nothing less than complete freedom of action in the Baltic States.

Regardless of the British position, Whitehall's talks with Moscow created considerable unrest in Estonia and Latvia and produced a rising chorus of anti-British propaganda in both countries. The Ulmanis government lifted its press ban on attacks on British foreign policy and allowed newspapers such as the Baltic German *Rigasche Rundschau* to level criticisms against the British which some Latvian officials felt unwise to express publicly. An anti-British whispering campaign in Estonia betrayed similar fears. These stories prompted a number of official British complaints in Tallinn and Riga, particularly in light of the fact that some of the information came from German sources. Yet, even after the two Baltic governments became convinced of London's sincerity in defending their neutral status in its talks with the Soviet Union, there was very little that they could do to counter this propaganda without antagonizing Germany or the Soviet Union.[31]

In the meantime, Britain's refusal to include the Baltic States in an unwanted guarantee system produced an interesting development which caused a mild stir within the Foreign Office. On June 23 M. Valters, the Latvian minister to Belgium, met with Sir Robert Clive, the British ambassador in Brussels. Valters began the conversation by telling Clive that the nonaggression pact was not popular in Latvia. Valters went on to explain that his country's recent agreement with Germany had forced Riga to refuse to accept the British-French-Soviet offer for fear of offending Hitler. It was Valters' next statement that was startling. He indicated that if London decided to accept the Soviet proposal to assure the territorial integrity of Latvia, "this would be welcomed in Latvia even though there might be, for the sake of form, an official protest." The Latvian minister then added that he felt that this was also true of Estonia. He emphasized the fact that "a very dangerous situation would arise" if the British-French negotiations with the Soviet Union collapsed. At the end of the conversation, Valters reëmphasized this point. While he admitted that his opinions were personal, he felt that it was important for the British government to learn of these views.[32]

The Foreign Office, however, found the Latvians and the Estonians still unalterably opposed to any guarantee from the Soviet Union. One British official, Frank K. Roberts, reported that a number of Latvian diplomats took every opportunity while he was in Moscow to convince him of "the insufferable Latvian objections to being included in any Soviet guarantee." On his way home from the Soviet capital, Roberts met with Charles W. Orde, the British minister to Estonia, Latvia, and Lithuania in Riga on June 22, where Orde told him that the Latvian Foreign Ministry had not changed its attitude about the proposed Soviet guarantee. Orde informed Whitehall in a telegram on June 29 that the Latvians disliked the nonaggression pact with Germany. He stated that he had not found the agreement popular in Latvia, but neither did the Latvians resent it. They tolerated it because it was an alternative to an unwanted guarantee from the Soviet Union. Orde felt that an unsolicited declaration of support from the Soviet Union would evoke more than a formal protest from the Ulmanis government. Orde reported, however, that the Päts and Ulmanis administrations did not want to object too loudly to the proposal for fear of throwing "themselves into the arms of Germany."[33]

Valters' conversation with Clive did nothing to alter London's position vis-à-vis the Soviet Union, particularly in light of Molotov's formal introduction of the question of indirect aggression in the discussions on July 1. Three days later Molotov insisted that the proposed treaty include a statement on indirect aggression, which he specifically defined as "an internal *coup d'état* or reversal of policy in the interests of the aggressor." This interpretation would apply to Estonia and Latvia.[34]

The ramifications of the new Soviet proposals specifically dealt with the very fears that had caused Estonia and Latvia to reject any consideration of a Soviet guarantee of their territorial integrity. The British, of course, realized that their acceptance of the new terms would have been an immediate and open invitation to Soviet intervention in the Baltic States.

As the British-Soviet talks continued throughout July, it became apparent that Great Britain and the Soviet Union could not come to terms on the question of indirect aggression and the Baltic States, even though Whitehall announced that it intended to continue to discuss this matter with the Soviet Union in the upcoming military talks in Moscow.[35] For all practical purposes, the Baltic question ended any hope of a strong British-Soviet front against Hitler.

Conclusion

Great Britain was the closest ally the Baltic States had in the West, but London would not risk war to defend Baltic independence. Its stand on the Klaipéda issue fit neatly into Chamberlain's appeasement package.

Annexation of Czechoslovakia sobered him up, and England then attempted to organize an anti-Nazi coalition to stop Germany.

Soviet insistence on a free hand in the southeastern Baltic, however, forced London to choose between a British-Soviet front against Hitler that would in effect allow the Soviet Union to commit the same type of aggression that Hitler had and a moral stance that would prevent a coalition with the Soviets but at least temporarily preserve Baltic independence. Such a British decision was made too late to be of use to the Baltic States or generally to Eastern Europe.

General Hans von Seeckt and the Baltic Question

JULIUS P. SLAVENAS

Though cursorily the destruction of the Baltic States can be viewed in terms of the totalitarian Hitler-Stalin collusion of 1939, the independence of Estonia, Latvia, and Lithuania had been questioned by many powerful persons and groups ever since the Balts proclaimed their sovereign statehood at the end of World War I. It is the thesis of this chapter that an important spiritual mentor of the Nazi-Soviet nonaggression pact of 1939 and the gravedigger of Polish and Baltic independence was General Hans von Seeckt, the commander of Germany's armed forces after World War I.

The son of a Prussian military officer, von Seeckt was commissioned a second lieutenant at the age of 21. When World War I broke out, he held a rank of lieutenant colonel and served as chief of staff with the Third Brandenburg Military Corps. During the war he had no influence on German policies in the Baltic region and did not belong to the group of military politicians who clamored for the absorption of the *Baltikum* and Lithuania by the Reich in one form or another. Von Seeckt considered their annexation detrimental to Germany's geographic position.

After the defeat of Germany in 1918 von Seeckt rapidly evolved as the most influential general officer. By the same token, he came to play an active role in Baltic affairs. At first interested in the possibility of establishing a Baltic bridge between Germany and (a future non-Communist) Russia, he was not opposed to retaining German military units, including the Free Corps, in the Baltic region to fend off Bolshevism. Eventually he discarded this notion. He envisioned no long-run gains for Germany in maintaining troops in the Baltic States. Above all, he did not want German troops to get involved in local wars. Early in 1919 he criticized General Magnus von Eberhardt, the military commander in Lithuania, for assisting the infant Lithuanian Army in an attempt to regain the city of Vilnius, which had succumbed to the Red Army and a Lithuanian Communist regime.[1] In Seeckt's view, such support of

Lithuania was unrealistic, and he favored cessation of German military activities in the area. For this reason he had no personal difficulties in carrying out the orders by Allied Powers to evacuate all German military from the Baltic States.

The most important phase of the general's military career began in 1920 when he assumed command over the German armed forces. It should be pointed out that as chief of the Weimar *Reichswehr* von Seeckt enjoyed influence and authority never accorded to a military commander in a democratic state. The term "a state within a state," a cliché that is commonly applied to Imperial German armed forces, can be extended to the *Reichswehr* as well. With the support of sympathetic parliamentarians and the tacit agreement of the Weimar government, Seeckt, whose main object was to restore Germany as a strong power, proceeded to circumvent the restrictions that had been imposed on the German military establishment by the Treaty of Versailles. To beef up the truncated German Army and secure advanced training for German military personnel, Seeckt became an ardent champion of close ties between Russia and Germany, who temporarily shared the status of outcast nations.[2] Thus the Eastern policy in the early years of the Weimar Republic was largely generated by Seeckt, who displayed great ability to comprehend political issues in realistic terms.

Though there is no indication that Seeckt was particularly troubled by the loss of the Baltic "bridge," he shared the deep concern of many Germans who envisioned a Polish threat. In January 1920, when a Russian-Polish war appeared imminent, Seeckt observed to a military colleague that Russia should not be prevented from regaining her frontiers of 1914,[3] a point to be reiterated by Seeckt in the future. Seeckt thus put himself in the Bismarckian tradition. Otto von Bismarck, when presiding over the unification of Germany, took it for granted that the German-Russian frontier would remain at the river Nemunas,[4] and Bismarck never showed any interest in absorbing the Baltic provinces, even though many of his friends were Baltic German nobles.[5] On the contrary, after his ouster from the chancellorship in 1890, Bismarck feared that the Russians might display an appetite for expanding westward at Germany's expense. Bismarck, one may say, attempted to formulate a policy of containment. He expressed the hope that the Russians, confronted by the German minorities in Latvia and Estonia, would be reluctant to help themselves to even more territory inhabited by the Germans and also by the Poles.[6]

Seeckt shared such views. The territorial clauses of the Treaty of Versailles affecting East Germany particularly infuriated Seeckt. Viewing France as the chief culprit in the West and Poland as her client state, Seeckt's opinion prior to the Polish–Russian war of 1920 was that under no circumstances was the *Reichswehr* to give any assistance to Poland, even if it meant abetting the complete annihilation of that country. For it was precisely Seeckt's view that Poland should be destroyed. By the same token he argued that Russia should not be prevented from absorbing Lithuania and Latvia as well. Seeckt's views, expressed in 1920, subsequently were fully endorsed by many politicians, among them Joseph Wirth, the future chancellor, who agreed with the general that Poland should be destroyed.[7]

The unexpected defeat of the Bolshevik forces by the Poles and the occupation of the Vilnius territory in the fall of 1920 merely strengthened Seeckt's conviction that Poland was a major threat to Germany in the east. Polish attempts to secure a foothold in Lithuania were a development that Seeckt deplored. At all costs he wanted to prevent the expansion of Polish hegemony in the Baltic region. Thus, as one of the protruding Baltic *Randstaaten*, Lithuania came to play an increasingly important role in Seeckt's diplomatic machinations.

When in the spring of 1921 Wojciech Korfanti launched a revolt in Upper Silesia to secure for Poland the whole plebiscite area, the Allies were apathetic. As a result, irregular German troops moved in and were soon at war with the Poles.[8] The Allies finally intervened to separate the belligerents. This and other Polish initiatives merely reinforced Seeckt's belief that accommodations with Russia were a crucial necessity. Himself a staunch anti-Communist, Seeckt was of the opinion that in the long run the interests of the Russian state would prevail over ideology. He did not view Bolshevism as a threat to the internal order of Germany. Being steeped in the Hegelian notion of the state, Seeckt saw the state as a permanent phenomenon, with ideologies being merely temporary manifestations. Thus he took it for granted that in both Germany and Russia, while the state grew stronger, different political and ideological commitments might well manifest themselves in the future.

Writing to Count Ulrich von Brockdorff-Rantzau in 1922, Seeckt repeated the point that the destruction of Poland would be tantamount to the elimination of France as a major force in European affairs. Moreover, as far as Seeckt was concerned, Russia shared with Germany the desire to prevent the rise of a strong Poland. He stressed to Brockdorff-Rantzau, who was to serve as the German ambassador to Moscow, that the frontier of 1914 should be the basis for a Russian-German understanding.[9]

While it was not yet possible to destroy Poland, the Russians agreed with the Germans that Poland should be prevented from exerting more influence in the Baltic region. After the Polish occupation of the Vilnius territory, the relations between Poland and Lithuania became poisoned.

Lithuania severed diplomatic relations with Warsaw. Seeckt liked this tension, for now Lithuania could be played off against the Poles.

Next to Vilnius, it was the disputed Klaipėda Territory that generated discord between Lithuania and Poland, and the personality of Seeckt had a crucial bearing on the Lithuanian insurrection in Klaipėda in January of 1923.

Having lost Vilnius, the Lithuanians grew increasingly concerned that the Klaipėda Territory might never be awarded to Lithuania by the Allies. By virtue of the Treaty of Versailles, this area had been detached from the German Reich and put under the control of a French High Commissioner who administered the Territory on behalf of the Allied and Associated Powers. What type of an ultimate disposition of the area the Allies had in mind is not clear. At the Paris Peace Conference in 1919, lip service was paid to Lithuanian interests, but it appears that, at least to the French, a Lithuanian solution in Klaipėda would be equal to a Polish solution, assuming that Lithuania would become a province or junior partner of Poland. Nobody could have been more concerned than Seeckt about any future Polish encroachments in the Baltic area, and such concerns were shared by German government circles.

In discreet statements made early in 1922, German government representatives indicated to Lithuania that no issue would be made if Lithuania were to help itself to the Klaipėda Territory.[10] Assurances of this type were of great importance to Lithuania at the end of 1922. The government received alarming news from the Lithuanian envoy in Paris—because of French and Polish pressures, the Council of Ambassadors was about to award to Poland special privileges in the port of Klaipėda. Lithuanian Prime Minister Ernestas Galvanauskas interpreted this development as a Polish attempt not only to encircle Lithuania, but to reduce Latvia and Estonia to the status of Polish client states.[11]

This development induced the Lithuanians to shop around for reactions among the major powers to a possible Lithuanian insurrection in the Klaipėda Territory. Though a Lithuanian *coup d'état* was not officially endorsed, it appeared that no opposition would be forthcoming from Britain, Italy, and Japan.[12] Soviet diplomatic overtures were also of significance. Deputy Foreign Commissar Maksim Litvinov expressed great concern about a forthcoming Klaipėda solution as contemplated by the Allies and dispatched notes to the British, French, and Italian foreign ministers indicating that Russia and Belorussia had to be included as participants in any negotiations affecting the status of Klaipėda and that no unilateral decisions would be recognized by Moscow.[13]

All in all, it appeared that no major obstacles to a Lithuanian *coup* in

Klaipėda would arise. Thus, at the end of 1922, the leadership of the Lithuanian Riflemen's Association (*Šauliai*) proceeded to organize an insurrection with the idea that the rebels, mostly members of the Riflemen's Association, would penetrate the Territory in civilian clothing. But before implementing the insurrection, the leaders of the Riflemen's Association wanted to make sure that no opposition to the *coup* would emanate from East Prussia and the German armed forces there. Too, they wanted to be certain that local German officials, above all the police of the Klaipėda Territory, would refrain from resisting the Lithuanians.[14]

To find out exactly what the German reaction to a Lithuanian *coup* in Klaipėda might be, three prominent leaders of the Riflemen's Association, among them the famous writer and professor Vincas Krėvė-Mickevičius, traveled discreetly to Germany to meet with General von Seeckt and obtain his reaction. Seeckt assured the Lithuanians that there would be no German resistance to a Lithuanian initiative in Klaipėda.[15]

He advised the Lithuanians to move quickly and to resist Polish overtures for a union between the two states. Seeckt also predicted, correctly, that the tiny contingent of French forces in the Territory would not offer any resistance. These French soldiers, according to Seeckt, would not be interested in "dying for Poland." By the same token, Seeckt, the superb diplomat, pointed out that if, in the future, Lithuania should make any deals with the Allied powers over the status of Klaipėda without German participation, such agreements would be null and void. Seeckt even assisted the leaders of the Riflemen's Association in purchasing weapons in Germany.[16]

Professor Romuald Misiunas, who examined the Seeckt Papers, did not discover any statements that would corroborate the Lithuanian sources on the above-mentioned meeting.[17] By the same token, it would have been very unusual for Seeckt to have made statements on record that might incriminate him for posterity. Needless to say, no German general or politician could have gone on record to support such insurrection in a territory that the Germans claimed as German, the Treaty of Versailles notwithstanding. What Seeckt had in mind was to thwart any possible Polish encroachments; a Lithuanian solution in Klaipėda appeared to him as the lesser of two evils. Moreover, this was clearly the position of Russia as well, a point of utmost importance to Seeckt.

If Seeckt hoped that the Lithuanian insurrection in Klaipėda would constitute a defeat of Polish interests in Eastern Europe, he was only partly correct. While failing to penetrate Klaipėda, the Poles achieved a diplomatic victory on a different front. On March 15, 1923, the Conference of Ambassadors recognized the *de facto* Polish-Lithuanian frontier, and the Vilnius territory was put under Polish jurisdiction.

Even though Seeckt was determined to check Poland in all possible ways, he did not want to get overly involved with a *Randstaat* (border state) such as Lithuania. When in October 1923 representatives of the Lithuanian Riflemen's Association visited with the officers of *Wehr-kreiskommando I* at Königsberg for the purpose of exploring the possibility of closer ties with Germany, such as a military alliance, Seeckt expressed his opposition to the idea of alliances with the Baltic countries without Russian participation. Once again, the point was observed that the interests of Russia and Germany were running parallel in relation to the *Rand-staaten*.[18]

After his dismissal as chief of the *Reichswehr* in 1926, Seeckt's influence began to decline. In speeches and in writing he continued to consider Poland as the foremost enemy of the Reich. In his books, when referring to the dangers of Bolshevism, he pointed out that Germany was much more immune to Bolshevization than were the Western powers of France, Britain, and, ultimately, the United States.[19] Seeckt was very critical of the foreign policy of Gustav Stresemann, whom he regarded as an appeaser and pro-French.[20] In particular, Seeckt was disturbed by the possibility that many Germans had given up hope of revising the eastern borders of Germany,[21] that is, bringing about the destruction of Poland.

Ultimately, however, Germany moved in the direction advocated by von Seeckt—the destruction of Poland and the Baltic States, as Seeckt had hoped, though it is most likely that he would have been horrified by the German attack on the Soviet Union in 1941. Such an attack was utterly out of tune with his objectives. Unlike Seeckt, Hitler had no intentions at all of accepting the Russian-German frontier of 1914 or anything close to it on a permanent basis. While posing as a conventional statesman with limited objectives, Hitler was awaiting the opportunity to implement the objectives that he had set out in *Mein Kampf*. Among them the annexation and Germanization of the Baltic lands were promi-nent. Out of tune with the Bismarckian tradition, Hitler was in accord with numerous influential persons and forces in Germany that had an appetite for devouring the Baltic lands and many parts of Slavic Eastern Europe as well. Even though the Nazi concepts of *Lebensraum* differed significantly from von Seeckt's more limited objectives in Eastern Europe, in the long run they shared a common denominator: either approach was detrimental to the independence of the Baltic States.

The Baltic Entente: Phantom or Reality?

EDGAR ANDERSON

Before World War II the facade of the impressive Latvian Ministry of Foreign Affairs in Riga contained an inscription in Latin: *Concordia res parvae crescunt, discordia magnae concidunt* (United they stand, divided they fall). This ancient bit of counsel by Sallust is particularly appropriate when applied to the three Baltic States. Geographic factors and historical development have created strong conditions for the closest possible cooperation among Estonia, Latvia, and Lithuania.

Sallust's advice was not followed, however. Since the security of the Baltic States depended on the balance of power between Germany, Poland, and Russia, it was in the interest of Estonia, Latvia, and Lithuania that this balance remain undisturbed. The three nations could have helped to keep it so by consolidating and using their potential strength as buffer states between their three larger neighbors. But Baltic perceptions of their relations with these neighbors differed widely. A sympathetic British observer noted that Baltic attitudes had a certain "lives of the haunted" quality, making it difficult for the Balts to decide whether they feared most the provocative solicitude of the Soviet Union, the clumsy directness of a potentially aggressive Germany, or the devouring overtures of Poland.[1]

During their brief tenure as independent states the Baltic countries tried hard to serve as a pacifying and stabilizing element in the turbulent region of Central and Eastern Europe. They placed great hopes in the League of Nations, not realizing at first that the League would become a vehicle for furthering the conflicting interests of the Great Powers without much regard for those of smaller and weaker countries. By the time Latvia was seated in the Council of the League in 1936 the Baltic nations had already lost their confidence in the international organization and in the support they could count on from the Western democracies that maintained it. In 1938 they therefore proclaimed their absolute neutrality in the struggle between their more powerful and greedy neighbors.

Nevertheless, for a long time the Baltic States had assumed, however unreasonably, that the Western Powers would come to their assistance in case of a grave danger to their independence. They did not know that as early as November 1923 the British government had decided that, apart from obligations arising under the Covenant of the League of Nations, Great Britain would not feel obliged to object to such changes as the federation of the Baltic States or even their absorption by Russia.[2] The British had in fact proposed a Scandinavian-Baltic alliance as early as 1918 and 1920 and were greatly annoyed when such an alliance failed to materialize due to the Scandinavian self-imposed isolation and the Lithuanian-Polish dispute, which prevented closer relations between all the countries bordering Russia in the west.[3]

France, having signed a military alliance with Poland in February 1921, tried several times to encourage the Baltic States and Finland to join Poland in a military alliance, though refusing to guarantee them directly.[4]

As the strongest and largest of all the countries lying between Germany and the Soviet Union, Poland naturally attempted to unite all of them under her leadership. The domineering attitude and even arrogance displayed by some of the Polish leaders annoyed the other states, however. Poland's territorial disputes with almost all of her neighbors further alienated the other countries. The Polish occupation of the ancient Lithuanian capital city of Vilnius on October 9, 1920, caused irreparable damage to relations between Poland and the countries to the north. After a series of conferences Finland and Latvia refused to enter an alliance with Poland, unless a mutually satisfactory settlement of the Polish-Lithuanian conflict was reached. Polish-oriented Estonia, though unwillingly, went along with them. Poland was frequently viewed in the Baltic countries as a security risk rather than a guarantor of peace.[5] Moreover, German and Soviet diplomats often threatened the Baltic leaders with dire consequences if they were to form an alliance with Poland.[6] The Polish-German non-aggression treaty of 1934 and Polish participation in the partition of Czechoslovakia further alienated Poland from Latvia and Lithuania, though not Estonia.[7]

From 1918 to 1920 several plans were advanced for the future cooperation and strengthening of the Baltic States. The boldest of them envisioned a large federation of the Scandinavian countries, Finland, the Baltic States, and possibly Poland. Another scheme called for an alliance between all the countries bordering Russia in the west—Finland, the Baltic States, Poland, possibly Romania, and possibly the Ukraine. The Bulduri Conference of August 1920, which provided the greatest opportunity for forming a regional diplomatic, economic, and military alliance, was destroyed by Poland's subsequent seizure of Vilnius.[8] Among the proposals on a smaller scale were a federation of Finland and Estonia, a federation of Latvia and Lithuania, and a union of Lithuania and Poland. Next in line was the alliance of Estonia, Latvia, and Lithuania and, failing that— an Estonian-Latvian entente.[9]

On July 7, 1921, Latvia and Estonia signed a military and political alliance, which was further extended on November 1, 1923, and February 17, 1934. It was found difficult to attach Lithuania to this alliance.[10] The Estonians and, to a certain extent, also the Latvians were unwilling to become involved in a possible Lithuanian-Polish or Lithuanian-German war over the possession of Vilnius or Klaipėda. Lithuania, for her part, had been lulled into a false sense of security by her treaties with Germany and the Soviet Union, which, she imagined, would protect her from Poland.[11] Fierce nationalism and pride in unadulterated independence, too, were formidable obstacles to the meaningful cooperation of the Baltic States. Each refused to sacrifice any portion of its hard-won sovereignty for the sake of its neighbors and common Baltic interests. Still largely strangers to one another, the Baltic States had no close cultural contacts. For a number of years—to the amusement of German, Russian, and Polish diplomats and to the disappointment of American, British, and French observers—they indulged in mutual jealousies, petty bickering, and almost deliberate obstruction of one another's objectives. German, Polish, and Soviet manipulators did their best to encourage friction among the Baltic governments.[12]

The situation changed in 1934, however. Lithuania suddenly found herself completely isolated. Her former "protectors"—Germany and the Soviet Union—were hostile to each other, and Poland had signed a nonaggression pact with Germany. Hitherto the Soviet Union had been opposed to any sort of alliance between the Baltic States. From 1934 to 1939 the Soviets were no longer opposed to a Baltic entente, if it could be turned against Nazi Germany. They were also willing to sponsor treaties guaranteeing the independence of the Baltic States with or without their acceptance, on condition that the Soviet Union itself decide when and how these states were threatened and that it protect them with or without their permission.[13] The Baltic States were unwilling to allow Soviet troops on their soil, however, for fear that they would never leave again. Poland, Germany, France, and Great Britain also turned down Soviet proposals based on these terms.[14]

In September 1934, though Poland at first was strongly opposed to a Baltic alliance, neither Russia nor Germany tried to prevent it. Apparently they were now more preoccupied with preventing each other from establishing a preponderant influence in the Baltic States than with strengthening their own hold there. Even Germany for a while was anxious to preserve a condition of fluidity in the countries between herself and Russia. A stalemate resulted, which the Baltic States could make use of to draw a little closer together.[15]

The Treaty of Friendship and Cooperation, signed on September 12, 1934, for a period of ten years, did not create a full alliance of the Baltic States. The three governments undertook only to confer on questions of foreign policy of common concern and to afford one another mutual political and diplomatic assistance in their international relations. Article 3, however, excluded some "specific problems," namely, Klaipėda and Vilnius, from the category of questions of common interest. The treaty provided for semiannual conferences of the Baltic ministers of foreign affairs. The three governments were also to instruct their diplomatic and consular representatives abroad and their delegates to international conferences to establish appropriate contact. The texts of treaties concluded between any one party and a third state were to be communicated to the other parties, and the Baltic treaty was to be open for accession by others, with the consent of the contracting parties. The treaty did not cover military cooperation, and the question of a common customs union was left hanging.[16] The purely defensive Estonian-Latvian alliance remained in force. However, narrow nationalism, economic competition, petty ambitions, and personal jealousies continued to mar cooperation of the Baltic States.

Theoretically the Baltic States could muster more than 500,000 soldiers, which could be a force of some significance. The total strength of peacetime armies in the Baltic States amounted to 4660 officers and 58,000 men, with 900 guns, 100 tanks, 30 armored cars, 9 armored trains, 2 railroad batteries, 400 warplanes, engineering troops, and signal battalions. The combined strength of the Baltic navies consisted of 4 submarines, 1 torpedo boat, 8 gunboats, 4 minelayers, 4 trawlers, 11 cutters, and 1 submarine depot ship. The Border Guard units included 6000 men, the police 8300 men, and the Home Guard almost 200,000 men and women, with its own infantry, cavalry, motorized, aviation, and naval units. The military expenditure amounted to one third or one fourth of the total budget of the Baltic States.[17] In practice, however, the Baltic States could arm only 360,000 men (100,000 in Estonia, 130,000 in Latvia, and 130,000 in Lithuania). Their total mobilization theoretically could be effected in 72 hours.

The Estonians would have 8 brigades, the Latvians 8 divisions in 2 army groups, and the Lithuanians 5 divisions and 2 cavalry brigades.[18]

For the sake of comparison, note that Finland with only half of the population of that of the Baltic States had to cover twice as long a boundary with the Soviet Union. The Finnish border formed a natural obstacle, however, and Finland could also rely on Sweden as the hinterland, while the Baltic States, after the fall of Poland and the secret understanding between Germany and the Soviet Union, were completely isolated.

During their Wars of Liberation the Baltic armies had cooperated only sporadically and on a small scale. As early as January 6, 1920, the Baltic military leaders, prompted by their British military advisers, had agreed on the necessity of a military alliance between the Baltic States, but the Baltic political leaders had dropped this proposal.[19] Only once, in 1930, the Estonian and Latvian military leaders had again seriously discussed closer military cooperation, and only once, in 1931, had they held joint maneuvers of the Estonian and Latvian navies and armies.[20] During the next eight years the Baltic States had exchanged only some military information and a few officers.

They had never made an agreement about unified command, unified weapons systems, common armaments industry, or even common command language. The Latvian weapons were mostly of British origin and British ammunition was used, most of the Estonian weapons were of Russian and German origin and Russian ammunition was used, and most of the Lithuanian weapons were of German and French origin and German ammunition was used. During the war Latvia would be completely cut off from British sources of supplies, and the Baltic countries would not be able to help one another with ammunition and spare parts. Only Lithuania had bought some weapons from nearby Swedish armaments factories.[21]

Estonia had relatively well developed shipbuilding and machine industries and an arsenal, and the Estonian soil contained considerable quantities of oil shale, which could produce machine oil and gasoline. Latvia had a highly developed electronics industry, facilities for shipbuilding and repairs, an automobile assembly plant, a budding aircraft industry, an ammunitions factory, and an arsenal that produced light weapons, gas masks, and similar items. Lithuanian industry was in early stage of development, but Lithuania, too, had an ammunitions factory and could produce good, light aircraft; Lithuanian military technology was greatly modernized during the last years before World War II. Most of the Estonian and Latvian weapons were antiquated, but their military training was superior to that of Lithuania, according to Western observers. The same sources considered the high command in all three countries, with some individual exceptions, to be not well suited for the expected duties.[22] The armies were also hampered by the lack of maneuvers on a large scale. The transportation system was the most adequate in Latvia and the least adequate in Lithuania. Latvia and Estonia also contained large, excellent seaports and sizable, though antiquated, merchant fleets.[23]

Immediately following the First Conference of the Baltic Ministers of Foreign Affairs in December 1934, the French and Soviet ministers informed the Estonian government that their countries would look favorably upon a conclusion of a Baltic military alliance, but the Estonians did not want to comment on this suggestion.[24] Several times, in 1934, 1936, and again in 1939, the Lithuanian leaders—Stasys Lozoraitis and General Stasys Raštikis—also suggested a military alliance between all three countries.[25] As early as 1935 the Estonian military leaders officially proclaimed that the Baltic Entente had no military significance and that Estonia would not enter into a military alliance with Lithuania until she had regulated both the Vilnius and Klaipėda questions. Estonia did not wish to become involved with either Poland or Germany. According to the Estonian leaders, there was only one potential enemy—the Soviet Union.[26]

Even after Lithuania had "regulated" her disagreements with Poland and Germany in March 1938 and 1939, respectively, the Estonian military leaders continued to refuse to consider a military alliance with Lithuania. Worse than that—obviously deceived by some high-ranking German (e.g., Field Marshal Werner von Blomberg, Admiral Wilhelm Canaris, and General Franz Halder) and by Polish military visitors to Tallinn they tried to destroy the still existing Estonian-Latvian military alliance as well.[27] The British-German Naval Agreement of June 1935 was regarded in some quarters as virtually handing over control of the Baltic Sea by the British to the German Navy.[28]

At that time Baltic diplomacy appeared to be confronted with a choice between only three possible lines of action. The three states could place their trust in their ability to remain neutral and in the development of closer cooperation among themselves on the basis of the Pact of Baltic Union. Or they could follow Poland's dubious example of rapprochement with Nazi Germany. Or they could engage in an alliance with the Union of Soviet Socialist Republics.

Latvia obviously favored the line of neutrality and went so far as to leave both her eastern and southern boundaries unfortified. Her extremely long coastline also remained unarmed. Her financial situation doubtlessly did not allow her to fortify all of her boundaries, which lacked natural obstacles. However, her relatively short eastern boundary, considered by the Estonians to be the most dangerous and the most exposed one, remained widely open. This aroused grave suspicions and even fear among the Estonian military leaders who viewed the Latvian minister of foreign affairs, Vilhelms Munters, as an outright traitor to the Soviets and were reminded that the Latvian minister of war, General Jānis Balodis, had remained neutral during the Estonian and Northern Latvian life-and-death struggle against the Germans in June of 1919.[29] Personal jealousies were involved, too. The Estonian military leaders confided to the British diplomatic representatives that in their opinion Latvia had assumed an unwarranted role of leadership among the Baltic States. They left an impression that Estonia should be the natural leader of the Baltic States.[30] They also suspected the Lithuanians of being too cozy with the Soviets.[31]

Estonia's leading military men explained to American and British military observers that Soviet Russia would always present a 100% menace to Estonia, but they saw no danger to Estonia from Germany, at least not for the time being. They conjectured that Latvia had a 25% chance of being attacked by Germany, while Lithuania had a 75% chance of being attacked by either Germany or Poland. They reasoned that the "military pact between all border states menaced by Russia is not at all feasible due to the fact that the situation in each one of these countries is quite different from that of the other countries."[32] Therefore some Estonian leaders preferred a military alliance with Germany and/or Poland to military ties with their next-door neighbors. They did not realize, however, that Germany had no intention whatsoever of protecting the Baltic States. The German leaders obviously utilized Estonia as a pawn in breaking up the hated Baltic alliance and creating a power vacuum in this strategically important area.

Lithuania for a while preferred an alliance with the Soviet Union, but Maksim Litvinov, the Soviet commissar for foreign affairs, dashed her hopes early—the Soviet Union did not wish to fight Lithuania's wars for the retention of Klaipėda or the repossession of Vilnius.[33] The Lithuanian military leadership also caused misgivings. Until about 1935, Western observers generally viewed the top Lithuanian military leaders as given to domestic political squabbles—"flighty, egotistical, and opportunist," unfit for their military ranks and duties. Toward the late 1930s, with the advent of young, properly educated, and professionally motivated high-ranking officers, the situation in the Lithuanian armed forces greatly improved, however.[34] The new Lithuanian military leaders pressed for close military cooperation. The Latvians were interested, but, fearing a loss of the existing military alliance with Estonia, did not commit themselves.[35]

As early as May 1936 the Fourth Conference of Baltic Ministers of Foreign Affairs was preceded by some disparaging and belittling remarks made by General Johan Laidoner, the Estonian commander in chief, aimed at Latvia and Lithuania on the occasion of the Polish national holiday.[36] In the summer of 1937 the Estonian High Command no longer visualized military cooperation with Latvia and reorganized its plans of mobilization.[37] On December 5, 1937, Hans Frohwein, the German minister to Estonia, wrote that, in his words, the naive General Laidoner had stated that as far as the Estonian alliance with Latvia was concerned no one would shed any tears if it had never existed.[38] On December 20, 1937, an Estonian diplomat, Nikolai Kaasik, told the British minister that the military alliance was more important to Latvia than to Estonia. In the future Estonia would fight without any assistance from Latvia.[39] In this connection one recalls an article by an American observer with a significant title—"The Self-Extermination of Self-Determination"—which was aimed at the Baltic countries.[40]

On January 24, 1938, the British minister to the Baltic States sadly reported that mutual suspicions had ruined any prospect of a Baltic Entente that could secure respect for the independence and neutrality of all three Baltic countries.[41] The German and Soviet planners were, no doubt, deeply satisfied with the processes of self-destruction that were at work in the Baltic States.

The Baltic military planners had seriously considered the possibility of a Soviet invasion. The Lithuanians also reckoned with German or Polish aggression, but the Latvians had taken into their reckoning a remote possibility of a German attack. The Estonians refused to take part in Latvia's preventive planning against possible German aggression.[42]

Until the collapse of Poland, Lithuania had no common boundary with the Soviet Union, but Estonia and Latvia had a long border with Russia and an even longer unprotected seacoast. Their small armed forces could hope to detain the Soviet troops for only a short time while waiting for Poland and some Western powers to come to their rescue. After the collapse of Poland that hope, too, was gone.

The Estonian defense was based on the line of natural barriers in the east: Narva River–Lake Peipsi–Lake Pskov–the swampy and wooded area of Lida and Vruda. The second line of defense was inside the country

(Piusa–Petseri–Pankjavitsa–Laura), and the last line lay around the Estonian capital Tallinn and on the Estonian islands. The principal defense line was fortified with fifty reinforced concrete bunkers. The Gulf of Finland would be defended by minefields laid in the areas around Suursaar, Tütarsaar, and Lavansaar islands and on the Äigna–Porkkala line.[43]

The Latvian general staff had prepared three war plans: A—defense against the Soviet Union; D—defense against Germany; and K—defense against both the Soviet Union and Germany. Plan K was not seriously considered. Plan A visualized cooperation with the Estonian Army, but Plan D counted on possible cooperation with the Lithuanian Army. Plan A—the most seriously considered one—provided for a slow retreat to the main defense line, Pededze River–Lake Lubāns–Aiviekste River in central Latvia, and possible retreat to the Daugava line, which was also included in Plan D. Sea-lanes to Riga and its vicinity, and possibly to Liepāja and Ventspils, would be mined. Weak land forces would defend the long coastline.[44]

Although the Lithuanian government had repeatedly demanded restoration of the Vilnius territory from Poland, the Lithuanian armed forces had no offensive plans. The Lithuanian general staff had prepared only two defense plans—one against possible Polish or Soviet invasion and another against German attack. In the first case the Lithuanian army would withdraw from the borders to the Kaunas–Nevėžis line and from there to the Dubysa line. In case of a German invasion the Lithuanian Army would also retreat to the same Dubysa line, which formed the principal line of defense and was fortified with reinforced concrete bunkers. Only the Latvian defense lines remained unfortified.[45]

By actualizing its plan of defense, the Latvian Army would create a dangerous gap in the Estonian system of defense, while the Lithuanian Army, retreating to its main line of defense, would open a dangerous gap in the Latvian system. The Baltic military planners had visualized only the temporary defense of their own countries and had not planned common action against foreign intruders.[46] As late as October 5, 1939, John Cooper Wiley, the American minister to Latvia, expressed amazement at the lack of intelligence and communication among the three Baltic States.[47]

For this and other reasons Western and Soviet military observers and political planners showed no respect for the Baltic Entente and its armed forces. They agreed that the Baltic armed forces, being divided and uncooperative, had no military value whatsoever and could not be considered as a power factor.[48] It would be idle to pretend that the Baltic States were a factor of first importance in European affairs; nevertheless, placed as they were between Russia, Poland, and Germany, if united, they could have played a respectable role in northeastern Europe. Their fate during the months that followed, then, would probably have been somewhat different.

During the critical days of September and October 1939 the Baltic Entente functioned so badly that there was no political or military co-operation between the Baltic States. In negotiating with the individual Baltic countries the Soviet Union succeeded in splitting the Baltic Entente.[49] Only after the Soviets had established military bases in the Baltic States did the Baltic leaders start to think seriously about military co-operation. But it was too late.[50]

When Molotov accused the Baltic States of a military conspiracy against the Soviet Union in June 1940, he knew that there was in fact no Baltic military alliance to speak of.[51]

The Baltic States had wasted twenty valuable years without establishing themselves as a respectable buffer zone, as was expected of them. The Baltic States were an important natural obstacle to the aggressive tendencies of the Soviet Union and Nazi Germany. Russia and Germany jointly managed to remove the Polish-Baltic barrier, and World War II was started in this area. Today, with that barrier gone, the Soviet armies are in central Europe, Germany is divided and amputated, all of Eastern Europe is under Soviet domination, Western Europe, crippled and shorn of power, is under the Soviet shadow, and the United States of America is paying the bill.

IV

World War II and the Baltic States

The Baltic Question in World Politics

BORIS MEISSNER

For centuries the Baltic countries have constituted the bridge or the barrier between East and West. In the struggle for the *Dominium maris baltici* their possession signified the key to predominance in Europe's northeast. The instability of the power relationships, along with the concomitant and related changeability of historical fate, has not only hindered the independent national development of the Baltic peoples but has also preserved their national character and steeled their will to self-determination. This will enabled them to obtain, through the right to national self-determination established under the terms of the 1920 peace treaties with Soviet Russia at the close of World War I, the state sovereignty so long denied them.[1] The consolidation of this sovereignty ensued, however, within the framework of an uneasy peace. It was created by the Western Allies at Versailles at Germany's expense and without the participation of Russia. The Baltic States had thereby become a component part of the *cordon sanitaire* that was to isolate Bolshevik Russia from the Western world. The necessary anchorage, however, whether in a regional security system or in a stronger association with Germany or Poland, was lacking. As a consequence of Lithuania's special situation, such an association was prevented on the one hand by the Klaipėda question and on the other by the Vilnius question.

There was no shortage of plans designed to guarantee the security of the Baltic States.[2] These were based in part on larger or smaller federate alliances, in part on the neutralization of the Baltic Sea, and in part on agreements between the Baltic States themselves.

The nonaggression pacts that the Baltic nations concluded from 1926 to 1932 with the Soviet Union and in 1939 with Nazi Germany did not substantially increase their security. The same is true of the 1933 conventions on the definition of aggression.[3] Since 1933–1934 the general power alignment in Europe's northeast had evolved in an extremely dangerous situation for the Baltic States. This became particularly clear in December

1936, when Party Secretary Andrei Zhdanov, one of Stalin's most influential associates, announced the Kremlin's intention of "expanding the small window toward Europe," with the help of the Red Army, if need be.[4]

On the other side, Nazi Germany's growing urge for expansion gave the Baltic nations considerable cause for concern, as did the increasingly unrealistic major-power politics of post-Pilsudski Poland expressed as a conception of a "Third Europe"[5] by Colonel Józef Beck, the director of Polish foreign policy.[5] Hans J. Morgenthau has pointed out that the disaster that engulfed Poland was caused in large measure by that nation's attempt at playing the role of a superpower without possessing the necessary prerequisites.[6] Michael Freund characterizes Poland's history in the years immediately preceding World War II as a "history of heroism and foolishness."[7] Neither in 1939 nor earlier was Poland equipped to oppose Germany in a settling of the corridor question. But she also rejected the possibility of a passage by the Red Army through Polish territory in the event of war and therefore made impossible an alliance between the Western powers and the Soviet Union—which alone could have frightened off Hitler.

The one-sided guarantee given to Poland by Great Britain on March 31, 1939, in a reversal of its traditional policy was strengthened even more by the rigid attitude of Colonel Beck. That same day Sir Alexander Cadogan told American Ambassador Joseph Kennedy that for the first time in history Great Britain had left to another power the decision whether to fight or not to fight outside its own borders.[8] Through the British guarantee the German-Polish war was not averted, but rather accelerated, and at the same time the possibility of a local confinement of the conflict was excluded.[9]

The preliminaries to World War II were characterized by parallel secret negotiations conducted by the Soviet Union, a direct application of the two-pronged course of policy announced by Stalin in his speech of March 10, 1939. On the one side were Great Britain and France; on the other side Nazi Germany was the partner in the negotiations.[10] The independence of the Baltic States was the price Stalin demanded for the support of the one side or the other. Hitler was unscrupulous enough to offer this price. The Western powers, in spite of the delays caused by Britain's resistance, were about to do the same, as is clearly evident from the minutes of the negotiations and from the memoirs of Sir William Strang. The French, according to the reports by Edouard Daladier and Georges Bonnet, were prepared from the start to take such a course.

The Soviets insisted on a connection between the political treaty and the military convention and pushed through a common guarantee of the Baltic States. They could doubtlessly have attained a formulation of "indirect aggression"—which they had had at heart since 1934—that would have given them free reign in the Baltic area Nevertheless, the realization of their imperialistic intents in the event of an assistance pact with the Western powers would have been considerably more difficult than on the basis of the nonaggression pact with Nazi Germany. This assistance pact never came about, not on account of British restraint but rather because of Poland's refusal to condone the right of Soviet troop passage as a condition of the military convention. "With the Germans we run the risk of losing our liberty. With the Russians we will lose our soul," was the reasoning reportedly offered by the Polish commander in chief Marshall Edward Rydz-Smigly in explaining the rejection.[11] To be sure, Polish fears, as later developments revealed, were not unfounded. Nevertheless, the situation required that Poland, in rejecting the German demands, assume certain risks. By not utilizing this opportunity the Polish leadership at the time made possible the collaboration between Hitler and Stalin to which not only Poland but also the completely innocent Baltic States were to fall victim.

The secret accord of the German-Soviet nonaggression pact of August 23, 1939, which afforded Hitler the possibility of attacking Poland with the later participation of Stalin, contained a delimitation of their mutual spheres of interest in the Baltic area and in Poland. Von Ribbentrop first intended the Daugava line as the boundary of the German and Soviet spheres in the Baltic region. Stalin demanded all of Latvia. He later explained to the Latvian foreign minister Munters that the partition of a nation would be in contradiction to the basic principles advocated by the Soviet Union. After World War II, as the case of Germany shows, he no longer had such reservations. Of course he was also not prepared to let all of Latvia fall within the German sphere of interest, once the Soviets had announced during the Moscow negotiations their particular interest in Finland, Estonia, and Latvia and to a lesser degree in Luthuania. Since the return of the Klaipéda region to Germany through the treaty of March 22, 1939, Lithuania had been considered to be under German influence. However, the allegation that Lithuania supposedly played no role in the negotiations with the Western powers is incorrect. The drafts of the political accords of July 23 and 24, 1939, offered by Strang and Bonnet, respectively, differ on the matter of the secret supplementary proceedings precisely in the fact that the French version also names Lithuania.[12]

The wire containing Hitler's agreement to the inclusion of all of Latvia within the Soviet sphere of interest followed so quickly that it made Stalin's head spin. His later conversation with Munters clearly shows that he was not completely certain of his case. The conclusion of the assistance pacts with the Baltic States[13] indicates that Stalin did not dare to proceed immediately with the occupation and absorption of the entire Baltic area. In connection with the German-Soviet boundary and friendship treaty of September 28, 1939, which was concluded after the Red Army's entry into the Soviet sphere of interest in Poland, Stalin achieved the inclusion of the remaining portion of the Baltic region into the Soviet sphere. For an essentially insignificant portion of Poland he obtained Lithuania. A special arrangement was made only for the district around Mariampolė (currently Kapsukas).[14] Hitler's rapid acquiescence seems in this case as well to have been not totally uncanny to Stalin, as the later wrangling over the return of the principal portion of the Vilnius district to Lithuania showed. Significantly, the universally known existence of the secret accords on the demarcation of the spheres of interest in East Central Europe has to date not been officially admitted by the Soviets.

The German advance in the West was used by the Soviet regime on June 15 and 16, 1940, to demand under idle pretexts and in the form of an ultimatum the total occupation of the Baltic States by the Red Army and the formation of regimes friendly toward the Soviet Union. Upon the acceptance of the ultimatums the Soviet government declared itself prepared to preserve the national independence of the three republics within the framework of the applicable treaty provisions. Under these fundamental preconditions the Soviet ultimatums were accepted by the governments of Lithuania, Latvia, and Estonia, especially since military resistance to the Soviet demands would have had no chance of success.

The Soviet regime did not honor these commitments. After the occupation of the area the Kremlin quickly ended the intermediary stage of "people's democracy." Following sham elections held on July 14 and 15, 1940, in violation of the existing constitutions and election laws, a dictatorial Communist regime was installed and an accelerated sovietization was set in motion.[15] The Baltic annexation offers an excellent case study both of the methods of Communist takeover and of individual measures of sovietization.

The transformation of the free Baltic States into Soviet Socialist Republics was undertaken in Tallinn by Party Secretary Zhdanov, one of Stalin's closest associates, with the assistance of Andrei Vyshinski, Molotov's assistant, in Riga and of Vladimir G. Dekanozov, one of Lavrenti Beria's trusted aides, in Kaunas. This combination indicates that among the members of the Politburo Zhdanov, Molotov, and Beria, along with Stalin, were considered to be the chief advocates of an expansionist Soviet policy toward the Baltic area and also of closer collaboration with Nazi Germany. In Estonia the election propaganda was initially conducted by the Communist electoral bloc under the slogan of the retention of national independence for the three Baltic republics. The new slogan of annexation to the Soviet Union was first announced by Zhdanov on July 17 following his return from Moscow. On July 18 Communist demonstrations were held in Tallinn and other Estonian cities demanding the transformation of Estonia into a Soviet republic and its incorporation into the Soviet Union. On July 21 the Communist puppet parliament convened for its first session. It accepted a declaration concerning executive power in Estonia by which the free state of Estonia was proclaimed a Soviet Socialist Republic. On July 22, in Zhdanov's presence and in a parliament building surrounded by troops of the Red Army, a debate was held on the "proposal" by Johannes Vares' people's democratic government to incorporate the Estonian Soviet Socialist Republic as a member state of the Soviet Union. In conjunction with this debate a declaration concerning Estonia's entry into the Soviet Union was accepted.

Identical resolutions preceded by similar sham elections were drawn up on July 21 and 22, 1940, by the new "people's parliaments" of Latvia and Lithuania. Before the convening of the new Latvian *Saeima* (Diet) August Kirchensteins' government amended the 1936 law under which Ulmanis had become president of Latvia. Kirchensteins, in violation of the provisions of the 1922 constitution, assumed the powers of the president. Ulmanis was deported to the Soviet Union. The same fate befell the Estonian president Päts, who had contributed so significantly to the maintenance of a democratic government in Estonia. The Lithuanian president Smetona went into voluntary exile following the Soviet occupation.

The absorption of the three Baltic republics into the Soviet Union was already completed at the beginning of August 1940. The three "applications for admission" submitted to the Supreme Soviet of the Soviet Union were ratified with the customary ritual. Molotov, in a speech on August 1, 1940, which constitutes a masterful falsification of history, declared that in the annexation of the Baltic States the Soviet Union sought to obtain access to the Baltic Sea and to its ice-free ports. These, he said, were of primary significance to the Soviet Union. Stalin, significantly, used the same argument at the Tehran summit conference in 1943 in order to obtain the transfer of Königsberg and Klaipėda to the

Soviet Union. According to the Soviet minutes of the conference Stalin explained: "The Russians have no ice-free ports on the Baltic Sea. Therefore the Russians need the ice-free ports of Königsberg and Memel and the corresponding portion of the territory of East Prussia."[16] Both statements were untrue. In Liepāja and Ventspils the Soviets had already acquired ice-free ports. Moreover, Slavs had never settled in the northern part of East Prussia, as he claimed. The Soviet government was interested in much more than these limited aims. At the negotiations with Hitler in Berlin in 1940 Molotov, on Stalin's orders, demanded not only the incorporation of Finland—which had lost considerable territory before stemming the Soviet onslaught—into the Soviets' direct sphere of influence, but also the right to a voice in the control of the accesses to the Baltic Sea (Store Baelt, Lille Baelt, Sund, Kattegat, Skaggerak).[17]

The program of Soviet expansion developed by Molotov, which also focused on the Turkish straits and on the Balkans, strengthened Hitler in his fateful decision to attack the Soviet Union. Thereby the *cordon sanitaire* so carefully erected in East Central Europe by the Western powers finally collapsed, and the door was opened to the advance of the Soviet forces westward. In Tehran Stalin again took up this question and announced Soviet interest in the control of the Kiel canal. After Yalta the Soviets expressed interest in the occupation of the island of Fehmarn, over which the shortest connecting route from Denmark to Sweden now runs. Only with considerable effort did the Allies succeed in persuading the Soviets to evacuate the Danish island of Bornholm in the Baltic Sea. It was due solely to Churchill's intercession that General Bernard Law Montgomery received the necessary reinforcements to reach Lübeck ahead of the Red Army and thereby prohibit a Soviet advance to Schleswig-Holstein.

The occupation of central regions of Germany (the present-day German Democratic Republic) and the dependency of Poland—enlarged through the addition of Germany's eastern regions, including Danzig (Gdansk), made it possible for the Kremlin to turn the Baltic Sea into a primarily Soviet *mare clausum*. The Soviets did not succeed, however, in breaking through to the open sea on this important flank.

In certain respects the expansionist policy pursued by Stalin—to which the Baltic States were the first to fall victim—seems a continuation of Tsarist Russia's traditional foreign policy, which was characterized particularly by a push toward the sea and by pan-Slavic ambitions in East Central and Southeastern Europe.[18] The concealment of old Russian expansionist aims in the disguise of ideological formulas became abundantly clear in talks between the Baltic statesmen and the Soviet leaders. Vincas Krėvė-Mickevičius, the prime minister and foreign minister of the Lithuanian transition "people's" government following that country's occupation by the Red Army in June 1940, was told by his Soviet counterpart Molotov: "If the Russian Tsars since Ivan the Terrible were already intent in reaching the Baltic Sea, it was not on account of their personal desires, but rather because the course of development of the Russian state and the Russian nation demanded it."[19] Stalin made similar comments to the Estonian foreign minister Selter and the Latvian foreign minister Munters at the time of the conclusion of the assistance pact in the autumn of 1939. He expressly pointed out that Peter the Great's efforts at gaining for Russia an outlet to the sea had not been motivated by mere personal aspirations for power.[20]

But even in the Baltic case, where the element of Bolshevik Russia's imperial power politics is so clearly in evidence, the world-revolutionary element should not be overlooked. In the Baltic States the very process of sovietization, which was repeated in Central Europe over a longer period of time according to the "salami strategy," was carried out in a compressed time period. The difference lay solely in the fact that the "people's democratic countries" did not completely forfeit sovereignty and therefore were not subjected to Russification in such great measure. The Baltic nations, as "Soviet Republics," were even granted limited autonomy much like the three Baltic provinces had possessed under the Tsars up until the time of the Russification during the reign of Tsar Alexander III and in part beyond that time.

The Soviet Union's conduct toward the Baltic States, which was in violation of international law, met all the conditions both of "direct aggression," which she herself had defined in the conventions of 1933, and of "indirect aggression," the definition of which she had considered so important at the secret negotiations with the Western powers. The incorporation of the Baltic States into the Soviet Union, which ensued pursuant to the Soviet laws of August, 3, 5, and 6, 1940, constituted not a voluntary unification on a federative basis but a forced appropriation of the sovereign territory of a foreign state, that is, an annexation forbidden by modern international law. The legal arguments put forth from the Soviet side in justification of this illegal acquisition of territory are easily refuted.[21]

The public institutions of Soviet rule were based on the bayonets of the Soviet occupation forces and not on the will of the Baltic peoples. These institutions therefore could not express the right of self-determination of the respective nations. The Soviet Union contracted with itself, as it were, and through the act of annexation clearly violated not only the sovereignty of the Baltic States but also the right to self-determination of the Baltic peoples. Even the invocation of the right of self-preservation in case of necessity—which is found under the heading "Falsifiers of History" in the Soviet reply to America's publication of documents on the relations between Nazi Germany and the Soviet Union from 1939 to 1941—was unfounded. The security of the Soviet Union was largely guaranteed by the articles set forth in the assistance pacts. No direct threat existed in the summer of 1940. Even if one conceded this Soviet justification, the Soviet Union would have been obligated to restore the original conditions and therefore the independence of the Baltic States following the victorious conclusion of the war. That aside, the Kremlin, in invoking the right of self-preservation, would never have been justified in carrying out, in violation of the Hague Regulations of Warfare on Land, such a thoroughly revolutionary structural change of the occupied countries according to the Soviet model.

To this day the international community has to a substantial degree not accepted the Soviets' conduct on the basis of its illegal nature in regard to international law.[22] The United States, in a statement by Under-Secretary of State Sumner Welles on July 23, 1940, refused to recognize the unlawful annexation of the three Baltic States. The British government, in a speech by Winston Churchill in the House of Commons on September 5, 1940, adopted the same position. On October 15, 1940, it was underscored by President Franklin Roosevelt at a reception for the delegation of the Lithuanian American Council. After Hitler attacked the Soviet Union, the formation of the Grand Alliance led Roosevelt and Churchill to vacillate for a time over whether they should yield to Soviet pressure on the question of recognizing the annexation of the Baltic States. In this case, Roosevelt considered a resettlement of all Estonians, Latvians, Lithuanians, and Finns who opposed the annexation by the Soviet Union. It was due to the efforts of the longtime American secretary of state Cordell Hull that this recognition was never granted during the course of the war. A similar proposal by Stalin at the Yalta conference was also rejected.

There has been no change in this fundamental attitude since the war, as evidenced both in the numerous statements by the United States government and the House of Representatives on the occasion of the Baltic States Independence Day festivities and in the conduct of the British government. Secretary of State Dean Rusk, in a letter commemorating the forty-fifth anniversary of the Estonian declaration of independence, stated: "Standing on the principle that the right of a people to national self-determination cannot be suppressed, the United States continues to refuse recognition of forced incorporation of Estonia in the Soviet Union."[23] In the foyer of the State Department hang the flags of those nations with which the United States maintains diplomatic relations. Among them still are the flags of the three Baltic States. The United States has accorded neither *de jure* nor *de facto* recognition to the Soviet annexation of the Baltic countries. In the case of Great Britain there is a *de facto* but not a *de jure* recognition. This means that from the standpoint of the Anglo-Saxon powers the Baltic States continue to enjoy recognition in a legal sense.

As a result of the German-Soviet war, an exchange of the already-completed ratification documents of the German-Soviet border treaty of January 10, 1941, never took place. *De jure* recognition of the Soviet annexation has therefore not been granted by Nazi Germany. From the standpoint of the Federal Republic of Germany, the Baltic States have not forfeited their sovereign international rights.[24] The competent German federal authorities have consequently continued to recognize Estonian, Latvian, and Lithuanian citizenship on the basis of passports issued by the official representatives of the Baltic States. The German position on the Baltic question has not changed through the conclusion of the Moscow Treaty of August 12, 1970. In a statement of September 14, 1955, which was unanimously approved by the *Bundestag*, the Federal Republic's government expressly stipulated that the establishment of diplomatic relations between the two powers did not constitute a recognition of existing territorial possessions of both parties.[25] In accordance with the renunciation of force agreement the Moscow Treaty speaks only of the parties' mutual responsibility "to respect the territorial integrity of all European states within their present boundaries." From this formulation there emerges no *de jure* recognition of the Soviet annexation of the Baltic States, especially since the question of the Soviet Union's western boundary is excluded from the treaty. The German Foreign Office, in response to a petition from the Baltic side, has therefore stipulated in a communique of August 27, 1970,[26] "that the Federal Republic has not altered its commonly known position on the question of the Baltic States." In this connection it is essential to point out that the *Exequatur* of West Germany's newly established Consulate General in Leningrad also extends to the cities of Tallinn and Riga but not to the two union republics.

The Soviet Union's efforts to attain multilateral *de jure* recognition of its territorial possessions have also met with no success to date. The course of the preliminary discussions on a Conference for Security and Cooperation in Europe (CSCE) in Helsinki showed that the Western nations were prepared only to reach an agreement on a list of principles and not to conclude a Pan-European renunciation-of-force treaty that would first and foremost have the character of a boundary agreement. The Soviet Union did of course succeed in gaining the inclusion of the "inviolability of borders" as a separate article in the "Declaration of Principles" adopted by the Helsinki Conference on August 1, 1975. On the other hand, she was forced to consent to Western urgings for a clarification on the admissibility of peaceful and mutually agreed-upon changes in boundaries.[27] Also of particular significance for the Baltic situation is the acceptance of the right of national self-determination as a separate article in the "Declaration of Principles." It clearly expresses a universal principle that is equally valid in Europe and in the developing areas of the world.

The Baltic case is instructive in more than one way. It helps to explain the prehistory of World War II. It also reveals that guarantees and treaty assurances against the threat of totalitarian powers make sense for small nations—and in the atomic age this applies to larger powers as well—only when they are made in conjunction with a clearly recognizable deterrent. The events of 1939–1940 have again proved correct the words spoken in 1870 by a high Tsarist official and former governor general of the Baltic provinces to a representative of the Livonian knighthood: "You can... preserve the historical role of your provinces: to be the battlefield of high politics."[28] These words are hardly a solace for the three Baltic nations which, through the tragic developments of recent years, have suffered the loss of their national sovereignty and have again been forced to live under foreign domination.

The restoration of national independence to the Baltic states appears unlikely at present, for the existing alignment of powers and the unsatiated character of the Soviet Union seem to militate against such a possibility. Yet power alignments are ephemeral, and the intensity of political ideologies customarily dissipates with the passage of time. A situation is conceivable in which a solution of the Baltic question in accordance with international law—or in any case the granting of greater independence to the Baltic republics—could be in the best interest of a Russia intent upon inner renewal.

The Catholic Church and the Soviet Government in the Baltic States, 1940–1941

DENNIS J. DUNN

Having occupied the Baltic States, the Soviet Union in 1940 instituted antireligious measures similar to those adopted the previous year in Soviet-occupied Poland. Simply stated, the Soviets were hostile toward the Baltic Catholic churches. However, the Kremlin's specific policies were dictated by the internal priority of sovietizing the new regions and by the threats to its position that resulted from the twists and turns of foreign affairs.

Compared to the violent forays of the 1920s and 1930s in the Soviet Union, the Soviet government's anti-Catholic behavior in the Baltic States, as it had been in Eastern Poland, was mild. Almost without exception the Soviets restricted their antireligious proclivities in the occupied regions to nonviolent administrative tactics.

Such leniency probably had three causes. First, affairs of the Church were of relatively low priority. The Soviet government was preoccupied with integrating the newly occupied territories into the Soviet system as quickly as possible. The procedure was not dissimilar to that in the Soviet Union during the first years of Soviet power when churches were left alone while the Communists consolidated their political position. Second, Moscow at first tolerated the Catholic Church to avoid antagonizing Western public opinion even more than it already had. Finally, and most importantly, during the first year of occupation the Kremlin treated the Baltic Catholic Church cautiously for fear that an outright persecution in the newly absorbed but not yet digested territories would create sympathies for Hitler. The Soviet leaders knew that Hitler was an incorrigible anti-Communist, who controlled an awesome military machine. Though the war had started in September 1939, it was not until April 1940 that the Germans and the Western states became directly engaged. The Reich then annihilated France and had forced England off the Continent by the middle of June. At no time, except for a few months in the spring of 1940, did the powdery Western war, which Moscow had banked upon when it signed the Nazi-Soviet pact, seem to be on the verge of burgeoning. Thus it was of the utmost importance that the Soviet government remove or forestall any complications in Russian-German relations, for without the exigency of a Western front Hitler might tear up the Molotov-Ribbentrop agreement and move against the Soviet Union.

Moscow no doubt felt that a strenuous persecution of the Catholic Church in Eastern Europe would place the Kremlin at a disadvantage vis-à-vis Hitler. Popular resistance to open assaults on religion in the newly occupied territories would complicate and possibly weaken Soviet control. This, in turn, might tempt the Germans to invade Soviet territory. At the very least, it would lower Hitler's opinion of Soviet strength, causing him to disregard Soviet interests. To present Hitler with such possibilities was politically asinine, and the Soviets were not about to commit such an error. An all-out persecution in Eastern Europe, in addition, might rekindle Hitler's militant but at the time latent anti-Communism. Antireligious attacks were a well known Communist policy. If Soviet authorities launched an anti-Catholic pogrom in Eastern Europe, Hitler might lose his illusion, which Ribbentrop had assiduously fashioned, of Stalin as a non-Communistic Russian nationalist.

Furthermore, the vast majority of the people in Soviet-annexed Eastern Europe were Catholic—either Latins or Uniates—and the Kremlin certainly was aware of the fact that Hitler had diplomatic relations with the Vatican. This must have seemed perplexing. Why would the most powerful country in Europe maintain formal ties with a man who had "no divisions"?[1] The Soviets could not but conclude that for Hitler Catholicism was significant, at least as a tool of expediency. An attack on that Church might upset Hitler, since he had his own Catholic population of Germany to think about.

The Catholic Church was strongest in Lithuania; about 90% of Lithuania's three million inhabitants were Catholics. At the time of Soviet occupation in June 1940 Lithuania had three archbishops, eight bishops, six dioceses, and one prelature served by more than 2000 priests and religious. In 1927 the Vatican had negotiated a favorable concordat with the Lithuanian government, which provided for obligatory religious instruction in all primary and secondary schools and for the state's recognition of canonical law.[2] In Latvia the Church had fewer members—of the two million Latvians who lived in the second largest Baltic state only 25% called themselves Catholic. Nonetheless the Papacy had in 1922 concluded a suitable accord with Latvia, by which the Church received 7500 acres of land and a yearly stipend from the government for the Church's upkeep. The Catholic Church enjoyed complete freedom, as did the Orthodox and dominant Lutheran churches.[3] In Estonia the Catholic Church was minute and rather unimportant. Out of a total population of one million in 1938 only about 2000, or 2%, were Catholic. Since 1926 a German Jesuit, Monsignor Edward Profittlich, residing in Tallinn, had acted as the Apostolic Administrator for all of Estonia. He was assisted by eleven secular priests and some twenty nuns and religious priests who were mainly German missionaries.[4]

The lack of strong religious persecution under the first Soviet occupation is attested to by bishops and Nuncios who were in or near the occupied Baltic States.[5] This is corroborated by unofficial accounts issued by both Soviet and Papal news media, the latter apparently based partly on official reports from local dioceses and partly on information from unidentified sources.

Throughout the Baltic States—as they had in the regions annexed in 1939—the Soviets immediately upon occupation implemented a number of broad overall policies. All churches and ecclesiastical properties were nationalized and assessed taxes. All schools were taken over by the state, and religion was eliminated from the curricula. All religious publications were proscribed. Almost all monasteries and seminaries were confiscated and usually used to quarter the Red Army. The monks and religious were dispersed and forced to find new housing. Atheistic propaganda was organized and supported by governmental authorities. Communication with the Vatican was disrupted and made exceedingly difficult. Arrests of clergymen began, and pressure was used to enroll some of them as informers for the secret police. And, finally, arrests and deportation of lay religious activists were initiated.

In addition, each Baltic country and, for that matter, practically each diocese had its own distinct experiences. Given below is a chronological summary of the reports of individual bishops or Nuncios to the Vatican during and immediately after the first Soviet occupation of the Baltic States. They are interspersed with brief descriptions of Papal-Soviet relations during 1940 and 1941. Some of this material, especially that dealing with the Soviet Union, is of necessity conjectural.

The first official report from the Baltic States came from Monsignor Louis Centoz, the Nuncio at Kaunas. His letter did not mention religious persecution, but the Vatican, fearing the worst, on June 25 extended extraordinary powers to the bishops of the Baltic States. On July 3 Centoz informed Cardinal Luigi Maglione, the papal secretary of state, that the new Lithuanian government, appointed in June under Soviet auspices, had denounced the concordat with the Church. On the same day, in another letter to Maglione, Nuncio Centoz wrote that the bishops of Lithuania had gathered recently in Kaunas under the leadership of Archbishop Joseph Skvireckas, the Metropolitan of Kaunas, to review the religious situation in Lithuania.[6] Although the Nuncio did not elaborate upon the findings of this assembly, the fact that it took place was testimony to the tempered approach of the Soviets toward the Church. On July 5 Radio Moscow indirectly confirmed that the Lithuanian-Catholic concordat had been put asunder by reporting that the new Lithuanian government had stopped paying "the vast sums" of money received by the clergy and the churches under Smetona.[7]

On July 5 and 9, in a move to strengthen its episcopal structure in Lithuania, the Vatican informed Nuncio Centoz that Bishop Mečislovas Reinys had been appointed auxiliary of Vilnius.[8] On July 16 Nuncio Centoz asked Monsignor Cesare Orsenigo, the Nuncio in Berlin, to inform the Pope that the Soviets had arrested and expelled a few priests from Lithuania.[9] These priests were not identified, nor was reason given for their arrest and exile. In view of the Soviets' assuasive antireligious policy, the victims were likely to have been either Poles, selected for harassment to impress the Lithuanians with the cultural liberator role of the Soviets, or Lithuanians actively opposing Soviet-forced incorporation.[10]

On July 29 the Vatican Radio announced that the Soviets had implemented in the Baltic States their usual antireligious policies: church land and property had been nationalized, departments of theology and philosophy at the universities had been closed, and "exorbitant taxes" had been imposed on the clergy.[11] On August 6 Nuncio Centoz reported that the Soviets had sequestered the seminaries of Vilkaviškis, Vilnius, and Telšiai for quartering Russian troops.[12] On August 13 the Vatican Radio noted, among other things, that throughout the Baltic States antireligious propaganda was widespread.[13]

On August 14 Nuncio Centoz, again in a letter to Cardinal Maglione, mentioned that in Lithuania the dwelling space per person allowed to clerics was 9 square meters.[14] On August 13 Nuncios Centoz and Antonio Arata, the Papal representative to Latvia and Estonia who resided in Riga, informed Cardinal Maglione of the closing of their respective embassies and their expulsion.[15] Though on August 14 Maglione advised the Nuncios to stay at their posts as long as possible,[16] on August 19 and 24 the Latvian-Estonian and Lithuanian Nuncios, respectively, were forced to leave.[17]

On August 31 Monsignor Vincent Brizgys, auxiliary bishop of Kaunas, wrote to Nuncio Centoz, now in Rome, that a new academic year was to begin at the Seminary of Kaunas on September 16 and that the bishops of Lithuania had held another pastoral conference in Kaunas to discuss the administration of the Kaunas Seminary and general pastoral conditions. He concluded his letter by asserting that thus far the Communists had been restrained in their conduct toward the Church.[18]

On September 17 the Vatican Radio reviewed the religious situation in the Baltic States. According to the broadcast, the Soviets, though they had appropriated religious colleges, had not yet closed churches or excessively interfered with clerical duties.[19] On October 2 Nuncio Orsenigo reconfirmed for the Vatican that the seminary in the diocese of Vilnius had been sequestered. Also in early October Bishop Brizgys informed Nuncio Orsenigo that the Kaunas Seminary was functioning with 180 students under his rectorship and the vice-rectorship of Monsignor Francis Ramanauskas.[20]

On October 25, for the first time since the Soviet occupation of the Baltic States, the Vatican received an official report from Estonia—from Monsignor Edward Profittlich, the apostolic administrator. The monsignor informed the Papacy that the Soviets were about to require all foreigners to leave the country, including him and the bulk of the Catholic clergy, and inquired whether the Vatican would object if he changed from a German national to a Russian national. He was told to feel free to choose any nationality that suited him. On October 31 the Estonian representative reported that all Germans had been told to return to Germany, or else to apply for Soviet citizenship under threat of being deported to Siberia.[21]

On December 12 the Vatican Radio issued fresh information on the status of the Church in Latvia. According to the radio, no mass arrests or executions of priests had occurred, although ecclesiastical property had been nationalized and some clerical domiciles had been confiscated for the use of occupying troops. The broadcast asserted that all clerics had been excluded from old-age relief, that religious instruction had been banned in all schools, and that private schools had been closed.[22]

The Vatican reacted to Soviet persecution in Eastern Europe in 1940, by and large, as it had in similar circumstances in 1939. It persisted in downplaying the antireligious nature of Communism and the threat that such an atheistic philosophy posed for humanity and Western civilization. It also continued to reprove Germany, publicly and privately, for its alliance with the Soviet Union.[23] And it worked diligently with the United States to keep Italy out of the war, simultaneously pressuring the

United States to obtain information on Soviet anti-Catholic measures in Eastern Europe. The first was intended to protect France and prevent an invigoration of the German-Russian alliance. The latter, apart from reflecting the Vatican's legitimate thirst for knowledge, were intended to remind Americans that the Soviets were Communists who ravished God's temples and thus cool any actual or potential American penchant for an alliance with the Soviet Union.[24]

The Papacy, in addition, sustained its anathemas against Soviet aggression. In early 1940, with the Soviets bogged down in Finland, the Vatican Radio condemned the attack on Finland and pointed to the Soviet Union's inability to conquer the Finns as evidence of that country's weakness.[25] It ascribed Soviet debility to "the inborn wickedness of Bolshevik Communism." Though this was in line with the Vatican's denunciatory policies, the emphasis placed on the Soviet Union's weakness was undoubtedly a red herring to be dangled before Hitler to convince him that the Red Army was, to borrow from Mao Tse-Tung, a "paper tiger."[26] In the middle of the year, when the Soviets annexed the Baltic States, Bessarabia, and northern Bukovina, the Papacy again condemned what it termed Communist aggression and, by way of a rebuke to Hitler, added that "whoever likes Stalin has not the right to call himself a paradigm of civilization."[27] By that time the Vatican's censures of Communism and Soviet incursions served not only to upbraid Germany, but also to obviate the possibility, made more real after the defeat of France and the deterioration in German-Russian relations, that the English might seek out the Soviets as potential allies.

The Papacy also persevered in its drive for peace. The Vatican's major effort in this direction came after the surrender of France, when Cardinal Maglione sent telegrams to the Germans, Italians, and English, inviting them to negotiate a settlement.[28] The Germans were in favor of peace and, in fact, made a proposal of their own. The British, as could be expected, replied that "they are determined not to allow Europe and Britain themselves to fall under Nazi domination, and they are ready to fight against this to the end."[29] Nevertheless, the Papacy continued to agitate for peace for the remainder of 1940.[30] Had peace been secured on the Continent, the Soviet Union would have been in desperate straits—there could have been no alliance with England in case of a German attack.

By the end of 1940 the Vatican's policies evidently had begun to arouse the Kremlin.[31] By that time Soviet fear of Germany had mushroomed. The Nazis had already soundly defeated France and were bombing England into rubble. Berlin was becoming more and more abrupt and insulting toward the Soviets. In November the Soviet Union offered to surrender some Bulgarian territory to the Germans—who never replied![32] Given such crescendo defiance on the part of the Nazis, the Soviet government could not help but view with increasing apprehension the Vatican's anti-Communist policies, which, even if not seen by the Soviets as having contributed to the decline in Nazi-Soviet ties, had certainly not enhanced them.

By early 1941 the Soviets had evidently decided to curry the Vatican's favor in the hope of at least diluting the Church's vehement anti-Communism. The goal may have been to seek a redress of balance in the worsening Russian-German relations, but Moscow was also embarking on a zigzag course in its religious policy. Its courting of the Vatican, handled somewhat awkwardly and obtusely, was complicated by four factors.

First, since the Kremlin deemed religion *per se* to be politically useful, Russian Orthodoxy loomed as the Soviet Union's first and necessary ally. This further worsened Soviet relations with the Papacy because of Orthodoxy's anti-Catholic (especially anti-Uniate) proclivities. In effect, by withdrawing *a fortiori* from Catholicism Stalin's government was moving closer to Orthodoxy. This placed increased governmental pressure on the Uniates as well as on Leopold Braun, the Vatican's apostolic administrator in Moscow (who since 1934 had also served as chaplain to the American Embassy). Second, Soviet leaders had to obscure the anomaly of the Marxist-Leninist state aligning itself with religion to avert being charged by the Trotskyites of the world with debasing Marxist dogma. In other words, the Kremlin felt compelled to present an anti-religious facade, if not against Orthodoxy, at least against some type of religion. Since the government was already inclined, due to its closing embrace with Orthodoxy, toward an anti-Catholic position, it was convenient to go on using the Catholic Church as a target for invective. Third, as the German threat increased, the Soviets sought to build up their western defenses, both by concentrating troops there and by intensifying the deportation of persons considered to be untrustworthy. This policy led Moscow to the billeting of troops in Church domiciles and dwellings that had not yet been confiscated. It also led to the deportation, in June 1941, of large numbers of Catholics, since they were deemed to be more unreliable, for atavistic reasons, than Orthodox, borderland peoples.[33] Fourth, as emphasized earlier, the Kremlin, aiming at sovietization, wished to control the Church and break the back of Baltic nationalism (of any type). The Church, as a pillar of national identity for many Balts and an apologist for a world view irreconcilable with Soviet ideology, stood in the way of a rapid, successful integration of the Baltic republics. Its vigorous members and leaders were therefore marked for deportation, abuse, and discrimination.

Thus the Communists, in their desire to ingratiate themselves with the Vatican, faced a dilemma. To deflect even slightly the German juggernaut and to win sympathies in the democratic West, they tried to resolve the dilemma, first, by having Catholic clerics in Lithuania inform the Vatican that the religious situation in the Russian-controlled parts of Eastern Europe was good and that the Church should curb its inaccurate pronouncements on Soviet persecution.[34] Second, the Kremlin contacted the Vatican directly by sending, on January 11, 1941, Vladimir G. Dekanozov, its new ambassador to the Reich, to Nuncio Orsenigo to impress upon the Church official that the Soviets were not attacking the Catholic Church in Russia and the Baltic States and that the Church's position in those countries remained the same as it had been before the war.[35]

The Pope received the first episcopal report on conditions in the Baltic States on March 21, 1941, from Bishop Vincent Brizgys, the auxiliary of Kaunas. The Soviets, he wrote, continued to impede religious practice, but the faith was growing and even Soviet military personnel were visiting churches and practicing religion. On May 15, 1941, Father Leopold von Ebersberg, O.F.M. Capp., the head of the Capuchins in Estonia and Latvia, who had been forced to leave the Baltic States in March 1941 for Rome, informed Pius XII that the hierarchy and clergy remained faithful to the Church.[36]

By the end of June 1941 the Baltic States were firmly in the hands of the Germans, but correspondence with the Vatican continued for a while to summarize the religious conditions during the Soviet occupation. On September 18 Cardinal Maglione received bad news from Nuncio Orsenigo in Berlin. The Nuncio reported that on June 28, 1941, the Soviets had deported Edward Profittlich, the apostolic administrator in Estonia, across the Urals.[37]

On September 20, 1941, Bishop Springovičs of Riga wrote Pius XII that, although the Church was taxed, the faithful arrested and deported, particularly in June, and the clergy buffeted, Christian life in Latvia had not diminished under the Bolsheviks. On October 10, 1941, Joseph Skvireckas, archbishop and metropolitan of Kaunas, communicated to Pius XII that the Church in Lithuania had suffered greatly under the Communist yoke, but that the clergy and faithful had remained committed to Catholicism. On February 14, 1942, Archbishop Jałbrzykowski, in a letter to Cardinal Maglione, claimed that Church life in Vilnius had remained strong during the Soviet occupation. On August 8, 1942, Bishop Springovičs capsulized, for Cardinal Maglione, the position of the Church in Estonia. According to the bishop, there were approximately 2340 Catholics in Estonia in 1942, which was close to the prewar number; of the fourteen clergy in Estonia before the war, however, only four remained, most of the others having been expelled. A final letter, dealing with the Bolshevik tenure, was received at the Vatican in October 1942 from the Lithuanian bishops. They informed the Pope that, though hampered in their work, they had in fact become the people's leaders and active defenders of religion.[38]

As these reports indicate, the Communists, though harassing the Catholic Church, did not magnify their incubus in the Baltic States until June 1941. In fact, as mentioned earlier, to convince the Papacy that they were not persecuting the Catholic Church they obliquely even courted the Vatican. Undoubtedly, the Soviet Union's desire to improve its image in the eyes of the Papacy was reinforced by a number of developments in early 1941. First, the Japanese foreign minister, Yosuke Matsuoka, whom the Soviets were desperately attempting to convince to sign a nonaggression pact, visited Pius XII in March.[39] That event must have brought it home to the Kremlin that the Pope, even if he did not have an army, had some powerful friends. Second, Germany was becoming even more belligerent. In March the Nazis initiated flights over the Soviet Union and in April, with devastating power, conquered Yugoslavia and Greece.

To their misfortune, Soviet efforts to placate the Vatican were thwarted by some complicating factors: their need to present an atheistic front, their increasing anti-Uniate position (or pro-Orthodox proclivity), their desire to bolster their defenses, and their totalitarian aspirations. These components, singularly or in combination, led Moscow, first, to name, in March 1941, an Orthodox bishop, Panteleimon Rudyk, for the Uniate diocese of Lviv, whose obvious purpose was to prepare the Uniates for "reunion" with the Russian Orthodox Church.[40] Second, the Soviets were induced to instigate (under the NKVD) a terror campaign of arrests, torture, executions, and deportations, which grew in proportion to the proximity of the German invasion.[41] Third, the Russians were moved to confiscate more Baltic church buildings, including the Kaunas Seminary, for quartering army troops.[42] Finally, the Russians felt compelled to increase Leopold Braun's tribulations in Moscow.[43]

The Vatican did not respond favorably to Moscow's overtures. Even apart from the contradictory measures that accompanied them, there was still the Vatican's view of Communism as a dire threat to Catholicism, Western civilization, and humanity. Throughout the spring of 1941 the Vatican persisted in the policies it had pursued against Stalinism in 1939 and 1940.[44] Accordingly, the Papacy was no doubt exhilarated by the growing number of reports from Nuncios presaging a Nazi-Soviet clash. On February 7 Nuncio Angelo Roncalli, the future Pope John XXIII and the current legate to Turkey, informed Cardinal Maglione that the Germans were concentrating troops in Romania.[45] A little over a month later Nuncio Filippo Bernadini in Bern, Switzerland, reported widespread rumors of a war between Germany and the Soviet Union. On June 13 Nuncio Andrea Cassulo in Bucharest declared in a letter to Maglione that a break in Nazi-Soviet relations was very near. And on June 19 Nuncio Bernadini wrote the Vatican that hearsay had it that war was imminent between the Communists and the fascists.[46] The Kremlin, which was also privy to such rumors and information, was certainly, in contrast to the Papacy, depressed and unnerved.

On June 22 the Nazis raged into Eastern Europe. Within a few days the Soviet siege of the Catholic Church in the Baltic States was lifted, thus ending the Baltic Catholic Church's first contact with the Soviet government.

Morality or Expediency? The Baltic Question in British-Soviet Relations, 1941–1942

DAVID KIRBY

When Anthony Eden returned to the Foreign Office at the end of 1940, British-Soviet relations were at a particularly low ebb. In spite of the frequent and often exasperated pleas of Sir Stafford Cripps, appointed ambassador to the Soviet Union in May 1940, for some sort of British initiative toward Moscow, little had been achieved. In Cripps' view, the British government should have been prepared to make concessions over matters arising out of the incorporation of the three Baltic States into the Soviet Union. He felt that the Russians were determined to make the Baltic question a test of British willingness to cooperate. Once this obstacle had been overcome, the way would be open to more durable and profitable relations.

Cripps' view was not shared, however, by the clerks of the Northern Department of the Foreign Office, who believed that Cripps was obsessed by the Baltic States and wrong in his conviction that concessions on such matters as frozen Baltic assets and requisitioned Baltic shipping, not to mention recognition of *de facto* Soviet sovereignty in the area, would lead to an improvement in British-Soviet relations. Cripps' attempts to initiate discussions on the Baltic question had run into the sand: British policy remained one of "wait and see." If the Russians were prepared to make counterconcessions, then the British were prepared to negotiate a settlement of the Baltic question. But since such concessions seemed unlikely, it would be unwise to risk the wrath of American opinion and to jeopardize the postwar status of Poland by giving way to Soviet demands for recognition of their claims in the Baltic States.[1] Eden chose at first to adapt to the Foreign Office's "wait and see" line, but the German attack on the Soviet Union and the forging of a British-Soviet alliance in July 1941 soon made this policy untenable.

The July 12 agreement signed in Moscow was confined to pledges of mutual assistance and nonconclusion of a separate peace with Germany. In his original draft reply to Stalin, however, Churchill had included a paragraph that embodied the principle he had enunciated before the House of Commons on September 5, 1940. He stated that at the final peace settlement, in which the United States would certainly play a leading part, "our line would be that territorial frontiers will have to be settled in accordance with the wishes of the people who live there and on general ethnographic lines, and ... that these units, when established, must be free to choose their own form of government and system of life, so long as they do not interfere with the similar rights of neighbouring peoples."[2] This paragraph was omitted by the War Cabinet on the grounds that it might complicate negotiations between the Polish émigré government and the Russians.[3] The British government thereby sacrificed the opportunity of clearly stating to the Soviet Union a principle that was later embodied in the Atlantic Charter. The Atlantic Charter was a British-American affair, which the Soviet Union, although declaring its support in September 1941, regarded with a good deal of suspicion. There is no guarantee that Churchill's paragraph on territorial frontiers would have been accepted by Stalin or would have altered Soviet policy, but it would at least have presented the Russians with a principled statement of British war aims.

The limited agreement of July 12 soon proved inadequate, and the British government found itself having to deal with the demands of its ally. Throughout the autumn of 1941 Stalin demanded that the British government declare war on Finland, Romania, and Hungary, send more aid to Russia, and clarify its war aims. At the end of the Moscow conference in September Stalin told Beaverbrook that the Soviet Union greatly desired a treaty that would broaden and extend the July agreement to cover the postwar period. On November 21 Churchill informed Stalin that Eden would come to Moscow for discussions, which would include postwar aims. On November 29 Eden submitted a memorandum on policy to the War Cabinet in which he proposed that the principles of the Atlantic Charter should be taken as the basis for a peace settlement and postwar reconstruction. The British government should also associate itself with Stalin's statement of Soviet war aims, issued on November 6, which denied any intention of seizing foreign territory or subjugating foreign peoples.[4]

The guidelines of the Eden mission were carefully drawn up so as to avoid repercussions from Washington. The State Department was acutely sensitive on matters relating to the Soviet Union, especially the question of the Baltic States. Both Cordell Hull and Sumner Welles dispatched messages to Eden before his departure, urging him not to agree to Soviet incorporation of the Baltic States. Hull warned him against concluding secret agreements or any kind of agreement that contained specific terms for a postwar settlement.[5] The British government found itself in a difficult situation. On the one hand, it was allied to a reprehensible and amoral power, which demanded decisions on matters affecting the conduct of the war and the making of the peace; on the other, it was morally but not militarily tied to the neutral United States, which urged procrastination in all dealings with the Soviet Union. The dilemma, for the time being centered in the Baltic question, was well summed up in a Foreign Office analysis of the principles of the Atlantic Charter:

> If, for instance, the USSR decided after the war to absorb the Baltic States, we might be compelled to recognise the facts and for the sake of peace in Europe, and our own wider interests, to maintain friendly relations with Russia. The United States would also tolerate the facts, but might refuse to give them formal recognition on moral grounds whilst accusing us of a selfish surrender of principle.[6]

Caught between the demands of an amoral ally and the warnings of a moral friend, Eden was bound to have problems, as he himself ruefully noted on his return from Moscow.[7]

From the very first meeting of the two sides in Moscow on December 16, 1941, it was obvious that Eden's hopes of confining discussion of frontiers to the general terms outlined in the Atlantic Charter were not to be realized.[8] According to Soviet ambassador Ivan Maiskii, who was present at the discussions, Eden seemed disposed to accept the Soviet draft on postwar organization, which provided for recognition of the Soviet Union's June 1941 frontiers, but refused to commit his government to Stalin's secret protocol, which came as a "complete surprise" to Maiskii. This demanded the immediate recognition by Britain of the 1941 frontier, and it was to prove the major theme of the discussions.[9]

The frontier question was immediately raised by Stalin at the second round of talks on December 17. When Eden tried to stall by referring to the Atlantic Charter and the necessity of consulting his government, Stalin retorted that the question of the Baltic States was "absolutely axiomatic" and ought not to require any governmental decision. He bluntly asked if Eden's government would support the entry of the three states into the Soviet Union at the end of the war. Eden replied that his government was bound by its promise to the United States not to commit itself to any decision on frontiers before the end of the war without prior consultation with the United States government. He was, however, prepared to seek such a decision from his government and to consult Washington on his return to London. Eden also admitted that the Soviet Union was recognized as possessing *de facto* sovereignty of the Baltic States, a point that the Foreign Office had been anxious not to concede in public, but one that Stalin contemptuously brushed aside. In his view, the western frontiers of the Soviet Union had been the major cause of the war with Germany, and if Britain was not prepared to support her ally in regaining these western frontiers, there was no point in concluding any agreements. The discussion was finally postponed until the following day, with the British delegation left in no doubts that the Russians would sign no treaties without British recognition of the 1941 frontiers.[10]

The following day Eden sought to develop what was to become a major tenet of his policy, the settlement of the frontier question by tripartite negotiation. Stalin was unwilling to accept the introduction of the United States into what he saw as a straightforward British-Soviet agreement. Stalin had amended Article 4 of the British draft agreement on postwar reconstruction. In addition to reconstruction on the basis of nonaggrandizement and noninterference in the affairs of other peoples, the amended article also made provision for the interests and security of both parties, and for the Soviet desire "for the restoration of its frontiers violated by the Hitlerite aggression." This Eden could not accept. At the final round of talks on December 20 both parties agreed to postpone signature of any agreement, and Eden promised to report Stalin's views to his government.[11] The War Cabinet had in fact been informed of the substance of Stalin's demands on December 18 and at its meeting the next day had decided that the terms proposed were unacceptable, although refusal at this stage to recognize Soviet territorial claims did not mean that Britain would oppose them at a future peace settlement.[12] The prime minister, who was in the United States at the time, also rejected the terms as incompatible with the principles of the Atlantic Charter.[13]

Eden returned from Moscow convinced that Stalin viewed the frontier question as "an acid test of our sincerity," as he informed the prime minister by telegram on January 5. In his telegram he argued the case for "immediate recognition" of the Soviet demands, basing his argument on the necessity of close collaboration with Moscow, on the fact that nothing the British or Americans could say or do would affect the situation at the end of the war with regard to the Baltic States, and on the Russian need for security, since "it is in our interest too that they should be in a strong position in the Baltic."[14] Churchill's reply was sharp to the point of rudeness. He expressed his surprise at Eden's telegram. The 1941 frontiers had been acquired by "acts of aggression in collusion with Hitler," and British acquiescence to this "would be contrary to all the principles for which we are fighting and would dishonour our Cause." He repeated that the question of frontiers could be resolved only at the peace conference, a policy fully supported by Roosevelt, and he refused to be an advocate for any British cabinet bent on departing from that line.[15]

Although Eden is reticent on this matter in his memoirs, it is clear that he returned from Moscow convinced of the necessity of forging closer ties with the Soviet Union, and prepared to depart from the principles of the Atlantic Charter in order to do this.[16] It must be remembered that in the winter of 1941–1942 the war was going extremely badly for Britain and the United States. The latter was as yet an untried ally, and although British statesmen believed the United States would play an important part in postwar reconstruction, there was no guarantee in 1942 that America would not once more slide into isolationism after the peace conference. Soviet Russia, on the other hand, was managing to hold her own against the Germans, and was clearly destined to play a major role in Europe after the war. It was therefore essential that the British government come to terms with this hard fact, as Eden's memorandum to the War Cabinet of January 28, 1942, underlined.

The memorandum dealt with two aspects of British-Soviet relations: the western frontiers of the Soviet Union and postwar British-Soviet cooperation. The memorandum found the Soviet frontier demands superficially reasonable, although admitting that there was no knowing if they were final. Britain's strategic interests might well be served by a strong Russian presence in the Baltic as a check to Germany, although any concessions here would have to be matched by a *quid pro quo* such as a Soviet acknowledgment of Britain's right to establish bases on mainland Europe (a bait already offered by Stalin during the Moscow talks) and Soviet approval of the principle of federation in southeastern Europe. The major obstacle to British agreement to Soviet demands was the Atlantic Charter and the "exaggeratedly moral" policy of the United States. Should Britain be forced to choose, however, Eden had no doubt that "we should . . . decide that Anglo-American cooperation is more indispensable, and the more natural because it rests on broader and older foundations than Anglo-Russian cooperation." The only way around this dilemma was to seek tripartite solutions to problems as they arose.[17]

At the War Cabinet meeting of February 6 Eden suggested three lines of approach to the frontier problem. Stalin's demands could be accepted, subject to American acquiescence; the Soviet Union could be granted the right to have bases in the Baltic States, a suggestion that Eden himself seemed to favor; or the Soviet Union could have overriding control of the defense and foreign affairs of the three countries, a suggestion put forward by Lord Halifax but not much favored by his successor at the Foreign Office. The cabinet decided to approach the United States government for its consent to a British recognition of the 1941 frontiers. Should this prove difficult, American support for the establishment of bases or some sort of Soviet control of the defense and foreign policy of the Baltic States would be sought. The only dissident voice was that of the Lord Privy Seal, who echoed Churchill in warning that the proposed course of action "might, indeed, stultify the causes for which we are fighting."[18]

In Washington the State Department was already preparing the President for a British approach on the frontier question. Cordell Hull, in a lengthy memorandum to Roosevelt on February 4, expressed the view of the State Department that any bargaining over frontiers by the British government would be unfortunate, since at best this would create little more than a temporary improvement in British-Soviet relations. Stalin was seeking to break down the British-American principle of not recognizing wartime territorial changes before the peace conference. His frontier demands were in clear defiance of the principles of the Atlantic Charter, and Eden's attempt to suggest that the plebiscites of July 1940 in the Baltic States in some way did meet the Charter's demand that the wishes of the inhabitants be taken into account was tartly dismissed by the secretary of state. Such casuistry would only serve to undermine the whole structure of the Atlantic Charter. In Hull's view, Soviet security needs could best be met by a strong postwar organization; the absorption of the independent Baltic States was certainly not necessary to the interests of Soviet security.[19]

Thus forearmed, President Roosevelt met Lord Halifax on February 17. The conversation was confined to generalities, although Roosevelt apparently put forward a compromise suggestion with regard to the Baltic States similar to that advocated by the British minister to Washington himself, that is, some degree of Soviet control of defense and foreign affairs. Halifax "got deeper" with Sumner Welles the following day. Having presented the undersecretary of state with the alternative lines of approach approved by the War Cabinet, and the British rationale for closer British-Soviet cooperation, the ambassador requested Welles' own views on these questions. Welles' reply was uncompromising. He took his stand on principle, without which he professed to see no hope for a peaceful world in the future. In Welles' own report of the conversation, Halifax epitomized "the worst phase of the spirit of Munich." Halifax for his part came to regard Welles as the moving spirit of American opposition to British-Soviet rapprochement involving even the slightest concession on the frontier question.[20] When the two men met again two days later, Welles had seen and briefed the President, who, after careful study of the documents, chose to describe the British proposals as "provincial." When Halifax had recovered from this blow, Welles went on to say that Roosevelt felt that the question of Soviet frontiers could not be discussed or settled until the end of the war, and that he would take up the matter directly with Stalin.[21]

The threat of direct personal intervention by the President of the United States greatly upset the British government. Churchill, while seeing some merit in Roosevelt's proposed action, feared that British-Soviet relations might be endangered if the United States were allowed to take the lead in negotiations. Eden suggested that pressure be brought to bear on the President through the agency of the United States ambassador to London, who was due to return to Washington for consultations, and an *aide-mémoire* for transmission to the President was approved by the War Cabinet.[22] Eden and the Soviet ambassador Maiskii impressed upon Ambassador John Gilbert Winant before his departure their belief that American interference in British-Soviet discussions at this stage would only serve to delay matters and might well cause a further deterioration in British-Soviet relations. Eden sought to make a virtue of necessity and hinted at the advisability of tripartite negotiations.[23] Prime Minister Churchill, "under the pressure of events," was now prepared to give way to Soviet demands, and at Eden's suggestion on March 7 sent a personal telegram to Roosevelt, in which he pointed out that

> the increasing gravity of the war has led me to feel that the principles of the Atlantic Charter ought not to be construed so as to deny Russia the frontiers she occupied when Germany attacked her. This was the basis on which Russia acceded to the Charter, and I expect that a severe process of liquidating hostile elements in the Baltic States, etc., was employed by the Russians when they took these regions at the beginning of the war. I hope therefore that you will be able to give us a free hand to sign the treaty which Stalin desires as soon as possible.[24]

This brusque and somewhat crude appeal did little to alter the views of the President. He contemplated telling Stalin that although the United

States recognized his need for security, it was impossible for the American government to agree to any commitments at the present time, since this "would lead to dangerous explosive opinion" in the United States. With regard to the Baltic States, Roosevelt admitted that, were the area to be reoccupied by a victorious Red Army, neither Britain nor the United States could or would do anything about this. Why, then, should Stalin worry? In other words, Roosevelt was quite happy to bow to the inevitable, but did not wish to compromise by prior agreement the principles for which his government was fighting.[25] Roosevelt was under considerable pressure from his own State Department to stand firm on the principles of the Atlantic Charter. Welles, in charge of the Department during Hull's illness, even opposed the idea of admitting that Stalin would be able to hold on to the Baltic States after the war by virtue of military occupation.[26]

Roosevelt had discussions with Winant on March 10, two days before meeting Litvinov, the Soviet ambassador, who was to act as intermediary between the White House and the Kremlin. It would appear that Winant was unable to dissuade the President from interfering in British-Soviet negotiations. In his conversation with Litvinov, Roosevelt complained that Stalin had not troubled himself to consult the United States government on a matter of vital interest to that government. He impressed upon the ambassador the unwillingness of his government to be a party to any treaty on frontiers until the war was won, when the United States would be willing to give full support to Soviet efforts to achieve "legitimate" security. Eden's reaction to the news of the Roosevelt-Litvinov conversation was to describe it as "a dismal tale of clumsy diplomacy." The President had shown no consideration of British views, and had increased Britain's difficulties. All that was left now was to await Stalin's reaction.[27]

The reaction of the Soviet government was milder than had been feared. On March 23 Maiskii informed Eden that his government regarded Roosevelt's observations as intended to indicate the American point of view to the Soviet Union. No reply had been sent, since it was not with the United States government that Moscow wished to make an agreement.[28] Eden now decided to press ahead and enter into negotiations with the Soviet Union, a decision that his permanent undersecretary felt bound to resist.[29] A draft dispatch to the British ambassador in Moscow was prepared in the Northern Department, probably at Cadogan's instigation, which sought to postpone negotiation of Stalin's demands in view of the adverse effect this would have on Anglo-American relations. Cadogan felt that this dispatch might be used as a *ballon d'essai*, but Eden did not take up his suggestion that it be circulated to the War Cabinet. The cabinet meeting of March 26 did in fact endorse Eden's proposed initiation of talks with Russia, with the proviso that Washington be informed first of His Majesty's government's intention of going ahead with negotiations on the basis of settlement of the 1941 frontier claims.[30] Lord Halifax was instructed to inform the President that in view of the urgency of making some sort of more positive agreement with the Soviet Union, the British government now proposed to negotiate a treaty on the basis of Stalin's frontier claims, with the exception of the Russian-Polish frontier. It was hoped that the President would at least understand the British position, even if the pressure of public opinion made it difficult for him to express approval.[31]

Halifax met with Welles on March 30 and again on April 1. The President, Welles reported, saw no useful purpose in seeing the ambassador again. He would try to remain silent when the issue became public knowledge, but this would have to be construed as a sign of his disapproval. Roosevelt did make one suggestion, however: it would soothe opinion in the United States if the final treaty were to contain a stipulation obliging the Soviet Union to permit anyone wishing to do so to emigrate with their property from the Baltic States.[32]

The State Department kept up its relentless and forceful opposition to any concessions over the Baltic States. Assistant Secretary of State Adolf A. Berle expressed grave reservations on the President's suggestion on free emigration. He feared that the situation was developing into a "Baltic Munich," in which the United States would find herself both morally and practically compromised. Welles agreed fully with Berle's sentiments. The proposed treaty was in clear violation of the terms of the Charter, and "indefensible from every moral standpoint, and equally indefensible from the standpoint of the future peace and stability of Europe." The attitude of the British government was not only morally wrong but "extraordinarily stupid" and would only lead to further demands from the Soviet Union.[33]

The Foreign Office received further indications of American hostility as preparations for negotiations were made. Polish pressure groups in particular were active, threatening "a hell of a row" in the United States should the treaty be signed.[34] Informal soundings revealed that the governments of Canada, New Zealand, and South Africa disliked the proposed treaty and did not wish to be associated with it.[35] Within the Foreign Office itself, Cadogan maintained a determined, if loyal opposition to his chief, whom he characterized in his diary as galloping gaily over ground that would give way under him one day. Cadogan, who was firmly attached to the principles of the Atlantic Charter, believed that it was better not to "crawl to the Russians over the dead bodies of *all* our principles."[36] Eden, on the other hand, was apparently quite prepared to throw to the winds all principles that he had not drafted in order to crown his Moscow trip with glory.[37]

Cadogan's private comments on his chief may be unkind, but they hint at a degree of vanity and self-centered blindness that were to prove Eden's final undoing. It must be said that Eden was no devoted champion of small nations, but neither was Cadogan, nor indeed any man of rank at the Foreign Office. The sentiment expressed by the Foreign Office's Russian expert Dew in a memorandum on the Baltic States in December 1941 ("I do not feel that the independence of the Baltic States is a European necessity") was undoubtedly shared by others.[38] Sentimental considerations were highly unlikely to move Eden. And the ethical considerations of Britain's pledges on the nonrecognition of frontier changes during the war may well have irked Eden, who had had no part in making these pledges and yet was now faced with the responsibility of meeting demands that flew in the face of these moral pronouncements. British public opinion cared little for the fate of the Baltic States, but it was impressed by the Red Army's fight against Germany, and would welcome closer relations with the Soviet Union. For the British, however, the war was going badly. The possibility of opening a second front was practically nil, which made it all the more important to offer Stalin an acceptable substitute. Stalin's Order of the Day on February 23, which had seemed to hint that the Soviet Union might drop out of the war once she had regained her lost territories from the Germans, was an additional incentive toward negotiations on the basis of recognition of the 1941 frontiers of the Soviet Union.

The draft political treaty was prepared in the Northern Department during the first week of April. It incorporated four points that the British government regarded as essential. British-Russian collaboration must be within the framework of the United Nations; there must be a joint statement safeguarding the question of the future Russian-Polish frontier; the general principle of nonaggrandizement and noninterference in the affairs of other nations must be clearly recognized; and there must be mention of the idea of federation in southeastern Europe. The draft also contained a stipulation permitting subjects of a new sovereign power to emigrate freely.[39] Eden also asked Maiskii at the end of preliminary discussions on the draft treaty if the Soviet government might be willing to make some kind of declaration at the time of signing the treaty indicating that the former Baltic States would enjoy some measure of autonomy as guaranteed by the 1936 Soviet constitution.[40]

The Soviet counterproposals were presented to Eden by Maiskii on May 1. They failed to meet the British terms in a number of important respects. There was no mention of the United Nations declaration, nor of the planned federation of states in southeastern Europe. The question of the Russian-Polish frontier was regarded by Moscow as being outside the competence of any British-Soviet agreement. Similarly, the Soviet government refused to countenance any clause on the right of emigration, and Maiskii made it clear that his government was not willing to make any statement in respect to autonomy for the Baltic States. Eden was openly disappointed.[41] A further meeting with Maiskii failed to break the deadlock. Cadogan noted in his diary on May 4 that Eden was beginning to realize that there was no point in haggling with the Russians. At a meeting at the Foreign Office the following day the permanent under-secretary urged the drafting of an alternative political treaty for "mutual guarantees or something." It was agreed that the Northern Department should attempt a draft along these lines, but in the meantime Eden presented a revised version of the original draft political treaty to the War Cabinet meeting of May 7. This redraft omitted the article on the right of emigration and went some way toward more open support of Soviet frontier demands. According to Cadogan, the redraft met with stiff opposition. The cabinet as a whole, with the exception of Cripps, who was late, was against Eden giving way to the Russians. Further discussion of the proposed treaties was postponed, however, and the cabinet did not return to the matter until May 25.[42]

In the meantime, the Northern Department had come up with a new draft treaty, which offered the Russians a postwar alliance against German aggression, but omitted all reference to frontiers. Eden welcomed the new draft as being in keeping with British policy in general. If the Russians were less obsessed with the Baltic States, the foreign secretary thought, it would do admirably. The new draft was circulated to the War Cabinet on May 18.[43] Eden was tempted to try it out on Maiskii, but was advised against this by Cadogan, and when negotiations began with Molotov on May 21 only the original drafts were on the agenda.

At the first meeting of the two sides at No. 10 Downing Street, Molotov invited Churchill to explain why the Soviet draft political treaty was unacceptable. Churchill replied that it could be interpreted as being contrary to the principles of the Atlantic Charter, and it was clearly unacceptable to the President of the United States, as indeed was the British draft version. However, Britain was prepared to sign the latest British draft in order to secure Soviet friendship. Molotov maintained that the Soviet version outlined the minimum acceptable conditions for his government and public, and he left the British in no doubt that "minimum conditions" meant the frontiers of June 22, 1941.

In the afternoon session Eden explicitly stated that his government was prepared to accede to Soviet demands with regard to the Baltic States, and was ready to agree to the Soviet draft treaty on this point. The real point at issue was no longer the Baltic States, but the Russian-Polish frontier, and the negotiations began to grind to a halt over this question. On the evening of May 22 Churchill and Eden suggested to Molotov that the alternative draft treaty might be introduced into the discussions. A copy of this treaty was handed to the Russian delegation the following day. According to Maiskii, the Russian reaction was "sharply negative," since the alternative proposals completely ignored the frontier question. A cable conveying this feeling accompanied the alternative draft proposals to Moscow. The two sides continued to go through the original drafts, with Eden making great play of the article on the right of emigration (omitted in his revised draft of May 7). Molotov even produced a Soviet revision of this article, which would recognize the desirability of making appropriate provision in the peace settlement to ensure as far as possible the right of free emigration to inhabitants of territories under a sovereignty different from that of January 1938, provided these inhabitants *belonged to national minorities*. Thus, said Molotov, the Soviet Union would have no objection to Poles leaving Lithuania. Pressed by Eden, he admitted that no Lithuanian would be allowed to leave.[44]

While these rather pointless diplomatic exchanges were going on, a great deal of "twisting of tails," in Cadogan's words, had been occurring behind the scenes. The American ambassador conveyed to Stalin his government's strong feelings about any conclusion of frontier treaties and dangled the bait of a second front. Churchill and Eden both pressed Molotov to give urgent consideration to the new draft treaty. Molotov appeared to be convinced that there would be serious repercussions in the United States if the frontier treaty was signed. It appears that the Kremlin was similarly convinced, for on May 25 Molotov signified his willingness to discuss the new British draft. The treaty was in fact signed the following day.[45]

The conclusion of the twenty-year treaty was seen at the time as a personal triumph for Eden. In retrospect, however, it appears as a rather doubtful expedient designed primarily to avoid the moral obloquy that a British recognition of the Soviet Union's 1941 frontiers would have created. Even Wheeler-Bennett and Nicholls, who warmly praise Eden's statesmanship during this period, admit that the treaty did not achieve what was hoped of it.[46] Furthermore, it is clear that the British government was prepared to accede to Soviet demands in regard to the Baltic States, as it was later prepared to give way on the Polish frontier. It was only Soviet intransigence on this latter issue in May 1942 that prevented the conclusion of formal British recognition of Soviet claims to the Baltic States.

Why did the Soviet government switch course so abruptly at the end of May 1942? Admiral William H. Standley, United States ambassador to Moscow, believed that the reason for the sudden change of tactic was the promise of something equally valuable—the second front.[47] When Molotov visited Washington after the London negotiations, he was offered a second front by Roosevelt in return for postponing the Soviet demand for recognition of the 1941 frontiers. The failure of the Allies to provide a second front, which caused a deep rift with Moscow, and the launching of the Red Army drive westward in 1943 proved to be decisive factors. The Soviet government was no longer so anxious to obtain recognition of frontiers the Red Army was now about to man. Roosevelt's rather cynical prediction was coming true. When he met Eden in Washington in March 1943, he expressed the hope that Moscow would make the absorption of the Baltic States more palatable to American opinion by holding plebiscites, but he could see no way of preventing the Soviet Union from implementing its declared intention of regaining the lost territory of the Baltic States.[48] Roosevelt attempted to put this point over to Stalin at the Tehran conference, but met with little success.[49] The President acknowledged the reality of the situation, but was dogged by the incubus of a heightened morality in foreign policy and American public opinion.

The British government was more fortunate in this respect. It had no Cordell Hull or Adolf Berle at the Foreign Office, and British public opinion was by and large apathetic to the fate of small East European nations. There was no organized, strong pro-Baltic lobby in the country or in parliament. The representatives of the three Baltic States were received politely but unofficially by the Foreign Office and made no impact there. The prime minister, who in December 1941 firmly defended the principle of nonrecognition of territorial changes during the course of the war, soon accommodated himself to the necessity of making concessions to the Soviet Union. In January 1944 he dispatched a personal minute to Eden, in which, having reminded the foreign secretary of his earlier opposition to British recognition of the absorption of the Baltic States by the Soviet Union, he asked himself how matters now stood:

Undoubtedly, my own feelings have changed in the two years that have passed since the topic was first raised during your visit to Moscow. The tremendous victories of the Russian armies, the deep-seated changes which have taken place in the character of the Russian state and government, the new confidence which has grown in our hearts towards Stalin—these have all had their effect.[50]

Two months earlier he had written to Eden, reaffirming the principles of the Atlantic Charter, but noting significantly that Soviet accession thereto was based on the frontiers of Russia on June 22, 1941. Churchill also took note of the "historic frontiers" of Russia; in his January memorandum to Eden he spoke approvingly of Soviet claims falling far short of the 1914 frontiers.[51]

There can be little doubt that Eden and Churchill were prepared in 1942 to forgo their principles and acknowledge the Soviet absorption of the Baltic States—as the protocols of the May meetings indicate[52]—but they were saved by Soviet greediness. Stalin, unlike Hitler, sought to obtain too much at one go. The frontier question was shifted to one side and replaced by the twenty-year treaty and the offer of a second front. The second front did not materialize in 1942. Russian forces moved westward in 1943 to secure by main force that which their allies had been unwilling to grant them a year before. The conclusion of the twenty-year treaty saved Britain the embarrassment of publicly reneging on her pledge not to recognize territorial changes during the course of the war, but it did little to create an atmosphere of mutual trust and confidence between Moscow and the West. The "Baltic Munich" so feared by Berle did not occur. The British and American governments managed to avoid recognition of the Soviet incorporation of the three states, and since there has been no general European peace settlement, they are still burdened with their moral obligations. The Soviet Union in the meantime has reoccupied the Baltic States, which have functioned as Soviet republics for over thirty years. Moral postures in the harsh world of power politics may acquire a certain nobility in their very futility. But, as this chapter has attempted to show, when tainted by a history of compromise and failed bargains, they tend to appear somewhat shabby.

Soviet Historiography on World War II and the Baltic States, 1944–1974

ROMUALD J. MISIUNAS

That Soviet historiography fluctuates with Soviet politics has been fairly well established. As the most politicized of the arts and sciences, history in Soviet society has an instrumental function. It seeks not truth *per se*, but serves as a tool for the legitimization of Soviet institutions as well as for the support of official mythology and hagiography. Soviet historiography on World War II has provided a cornucopia of source material for investigating the relationship between scholarship and politics.[1] However, relatively little attention has been paid to the subtopics provided by the study of local histories of the war.

This chapter surveys available Soviet historiography on the Baltic region during the war published through 1975, whether emanating from all-Union institutions or produced locally in the Baltic republics. Because of linguistic difficulties, only works published in Russian and Lithuanian are discussed. Latvian works published in Russian seem to provide a good picture of the historiographical trends in Riga. It has, however, proved more difficult to find Estonian historiography on the war in Russian. The discussion here, therefore, will probably not adequately cover the topic as it applies to Estonia.

The Stalin Years

It is relatively simple to divide Soviet historiography on World War II into two periods separated by the watershed of the Twentieth Party Congress. The war had been a source of embarrassment to the regime in too many ways for an open discussion of it to be allowed. In Stalin's day his collected wartime speeches[2] and the article in the second edition of the *Bol'shaia sovetskaia entsiklopediia*[3] constituted the main body of

Soviet historiography on the war. A 1947 report on the work of the Sector on Contemporary History of the Historical Institute of the Academy of Sciences of the USSR mentioned that the first volume of wartime history had been sent to press; what became of it is unknown.[4] A few document collections and secondary works did appear. Notable among them is a two-volume edition of captured German documents[5] released as a cold war countersalvo after the U.S. Department of State published *Nazi-Soviet Relations, 1939–1941* in 1948. These documents were intended to further the image of the Western powers as crypto-allies of Hitler whose prewar policy had been to embroil the Soviet Union in a war with Germany.

The ugly reality of what the war years and the occupation had done to the population could sometimes be seen mirrored more distinctly in the works of established litterateurs than in the works of historians.[6] And even here a reaction set in against such lapses as Aleksandr Fadeev's failure in his *Molodaia Gvardiia* to show an evacuation carried out in an orderly fashion under constant party supervision.[7]

A lame explanation for the paucity of Soviet works on the war was attempted by one researcher in the early 1960s, who viewed the rather small literature about the war that appeared during the first ten postwar years as important, but fraught with mistakes and tendentious in nature, particularly in exaggerating Stalin's role in the Central Committee. He euphemistically attributed the lack of quality to intensive work in classifying and cataloging archival materials, which surpassed in quantity the research done on them.[8]

If bleak on the all-Union level until 1955, historiography on World War II was even bleaker in the republics. The 1969 bibliography of Soviet Lithuanian historiography,[9] which lists the books, scholarly and popular articles, and pamphlets published in the various languages of the Soviet Union, contains only 5456 entries on the entire span of Lithuanian history. Of the approximately 450 entries covering the war years, only 103 were published between 1944 and 1955. Of these, 50 appeared in 1944 and 24 in 1945, with only 29 issued during the following ten years. Not a single work appeared in 1950.[10] Most of the 103 entries are newspaper articles. Of the few works published each year between 1946 and 1955 most are concerned with such safe topics as fascist German atrocities.

A 1964 article surveying Latvian historiography on the war also mentions relatively few works of any kind dating from the Stalin years.[11] Another scholar in the same collection deplores the historiographical activity of the "bourgeois" émigrés and laments the ill effects of the personality cult on Soviet Latvian historiography, but considers that a good foundation was laid by Aleksandrs Drīzulis in the early 1950s.[12] A 1970 survey of Soviet Latvian historiography[13] mentions no works dealing with the war years published before 1955 apart from those of Drīzulis.

Among the few Soviet Lithuanian works on wartime historiography during the Stalin era the 1949 booklet by Juozas Žiugžda, entitled (in translation) *The Aid of the Soviet Union to the Lithuanian Nation in Its Defense of Liberty and Independence in 1939 and 1940*,[14] stands out in light of the circumstances that produced it. In 1948 the Soviet Information Bureau responded to the publication of *Nazi-Soviet Relations* in the United States in the form of a pamphlet entitled *Falsifiers of History*.[15]

Up to that time a rather simple and straightforward explanation of the events culminating in the incorporation of the Baltic States into the Soviet Union had been in effect. According to it, the internal revolutionary situation, aggravated by the European war, led to the overthrow of the "fascist bourgeois" regimes. Only the fact that the Soviet ultimatums to the three Baltic States in regard to their inadequate fulfillment of the mutual-assistance pacts, which preceded the introduction of unlimited Soviet troops into these countries in mid-June of 1940, coincided in time, had prevented foreign imperialists from aiding the indigenous bourgeoisie in crushing the popular revolutions. The Soviet role in relation to the revolutions thus had been basically passive.

The Soviet Information Bureau pamphlet, in castigating Western plans either to deflect German aggression eastward or to strike themselves at the Soviet Union, placed the Soviet presence in the Baltic States mainly in the context of eventual defense needs against Nazi Germany. An analogy was made with Great Britain stationing troops in Egypt and the United States landing its forces at Casablanca in the face of Egyptian and Vichy protest and military resistance, respectively. It was claimed that by establishing its first line of defense west of the 1939 Soviet frontier, the Kremlin had shortened the war by at least two years.[16] Significantly, the pamphlet said nothing about the "spontaneous" Baltic revolutions.

It became Žiugžda's task, then, to reconcile the Soviet Information Bureau line of *raison d'état* on the part of the Soviet Union with the prevalent explanation of the Baltic revolutions. He did this by stressing two points. First, it had been the policy of *all* bourgeois parties to erode Lithuanian sovereignty by slowly turning the country into a satellite of Nazi Germany. Second, the class struggle in Lithuania, extant through-out the interwar period of independence, had reached a particularly intense level in 1939–1940, creating a revolutionary situation. Popular pressure had forced the Smetona regime to accept the mutual-assistance pacts offered by Moscow. The working masses of Lithuania had been inspired by the Soviet Union; the Lithuanian nation must therefore thank the Soviet Union, the Communist party, and Stalin for the revolution of June 1940.[17]

The main peculiarity of Žiugžda's account is his undocumented charge that the Germans had plotted to take over Lithuania on June 15–16, 1940, with Smetona's aid, and that the plot was foiled in the nick of time by the introduction of additional Red Army units into the country. To my knowledge, this charge has never been repeated in subsequent Soviet historiography. According to Žiugžda, the pro-German *coup d'état* was masked by the sports festival of the German *Kulturverband* in Lithuania, which began on June 15. Reich agents had been sent into Lithuania disguised as sportsmen, though the only sport in which they were planning to compete was putsch-making. The emphasis in Lithuania's official press on Smetona's planned visit to Vilnius on June 23, in preparation for which various fascist organizations were assembling their active memberships, was merely a ruse for the collection of antipopular forces in one place. The scenario supposedly called for the provocation of clashes with Red Army units based in the country and an appeal to Germany for help in restoring order once the fighting had commenced. The only evidence that Žiugžda presents for all of this is a quotation from the June 22, 1941, speech by Hitler, read by his Propaganda Minister Josef Goebbels, to the effect that at some unspecified time the Lithuanian government had requested military aid from Germany.

The Soviet ultimatum and the appearance of additional Red Army units in Lithuania, Žiugžda explains, demoralized the bourgeoisie, upset the German plans, and inspired the masses to proceed with their revolutionary business. Appropriate credit is given to the Soviet Union and the Red Army, which acted in accordance with the best interests of the anti-Nazi front implicitly and with those of the Lithuanian people explicitly. Thus the reasons for the June intervention given in the Soviet Information Bureau pamphlet are seemingly reconciled with the alleged native desire for a social revolution:

> Thus the sincere friendly aid of the USSR allowed the working people of Lithuania, marshalling their resources, led by the Communist Party of Lithuania, to destroy fascism, to overthrow the government of capitalists,

landlords and kulaks, to place power in the hands of workers and peasants and to save the liberty and independence of Lithuania.

But in spite of Žiugžda's attempt to reconcile the two Soviet versions of the events of June 1940, a note of ambiguity remains regarding who played the decisive role—whether the Soviet Union or the Lithuanian masses.

Another fact potentially relevant to the 1949 Soviet explanations of the 1940 events in the Baltic has recently come to the fore. Vladimir Dedijer, a Yugoslav historian, mentions a letter from Stalin, received in Belgrade on May 4, 1948, which expressed the belief that only the physical presence of the Red Army makes revolution possible:

> The fact that, for the moment, the French and Italian Communist Parties have less success than the Yugoslav Communist Party cannot be attributed to any particular qualities of the Yugoslav Communist Party but by and large to the fact that . . . the Soviet Army came to the aid of the Yugoslav people, routed the German occupying forces, liberated Belgrade, and created the conditions necessary for the Communist Party to take power. Unfortunately, the Soviet Army did not and could not extend such assistance to the French and Italian Communist Parties.[18]

Having never been published in the Soviet Union, this statement cannot have entered the canon of official pronouncements used by Soviet historians. Nevertheless, one cannot exclude the possibility of Žiugžda's knowledge of the existence of such opinions in Moscow. In the light of this statement, the preponderance of responsibility for the success of the 1940 Baltic "revolutions" would, by implication, shift from any native efforts during a revolutionary situation to the brotherly aid received from the east.

Such an evaluation comes through much more clearly in the 1955 study by Mykolas Požarskas. In this publication big-brother worship permeates the presentation to a far greater degree than in Žiugžda's work. Požarskas explains that Soviet power resulted first of all from the "historical friendship" between the Lithuanians and "the great Russian nation."[19] While presenting his arguments along the same lines as Žiugžda, he omits the claim of the planned German invasion on June 15, 1940. Požarskas merely insists that Smetona sought ways to sabotage the defense pact with the Soviet Union and to effect a German occupation.

The Thaw

The Twentieth Party Congress gave more attention to questions of historiography than had any other before it. Anastas Mikoyan, among others, remarked in a detailed and biting critique of Soviet historiography that "scholarly work in the history of the Party and of Soviet society is perhaps the most backward sector of ideological work."[20] The result has been a sharp increase in historical writing since 1956.[21] Apart from a temporary slack in works of military history during the period of Khrushchev's conflict with Zhukov, Soviet historiography on World War II has continued to increase steadily since that year. Quality, too, has been affected. The regime has become more comfortable with history[22] and has allowed more sophisticated explanations, thus necessitating at least some coverage of topics that had been taboo until then. The fall of Khrushchev has not changed this trend.

General Trends

A study of the Baltic region at war has not experienced quite so great a surge as has all-Soviet historiography. This may be due partly to the sensitivity of the topic and partly to a lack of available information, which local Baltic archival researchers had yet to provide for their colleagues in Moscow. Many of the all-Union works on World War II that appeared in the post-1956 period omit the Baltic region altogether. The sensitivity of the subject is well demonstrated by a 1959 teachers' handbook, which discusses the British-French-Soviet negotiations in the summer of 1939, the Winter War, and the annexation of Bessarabia, but leaves out the events in the Baltic area.[23] The works that do mention Baltic events go little beyond the official rationale of the early 1940s. Grigorii A. Deborin, the eminent military historian who later gained notoriety in spearheading the attack on Aleksandr M. Nekrich, ignored Soviet negotiations with the West in the summer of 1939, but touched on the Nazi-Soviet Pact.[24] His account of the events in the summer of 1940 is a short rehash of the official Soviet line of 1940.

The lodestar of Soviet interpretation of the war is the six-volume definitive history begun in the late 1950s by a special commission established for that purpose within the Central Committee's Institute of Marxism-Leninism.[25] Volume 1 appeared in 1960, and the project was completed in 1965 with the publication of Volume 6. As the main repository of Soviet knowledge and information on the topic, the work is overly oriented toward military history. Of the nonmilitary material, only Volume 1 intermittently touches on the Baltic area. Only 8 pages in the 530-page volume (covering the period before June 22, 1941) consider the Baltic "revolutions" of 1940 and their background. An additional section of 13 pages is devoted to the British-French-Soviet negotiations of 1939, and 3 more to the Nazi-Soviet pact. The standard Soviet argument of a sinister English plot to deflect German aggression eastward is elaborated with some reference to Baltic archival material, though sometimes in a rather oblique way. For instance, the statement of May 25, 1939, by the Estonian foreign minister Karl Selter to the Estonian Parliamentary Commission that Great Britain had no objections to the Estonian-German Non-Aggression Pact is used to demonstrate English interest in a Soviet-German war.

The section discussing Baltic events from September 1939 to August 1940 is surprisingly uneven in its presentation of fact. The morality-drama type of explanation is again utilized. First comes the "proof" that the "reactionary" Baltic governments were neither interested in nor capable of resisting Nazi Germany, hence were pursuing what is by definition an antipopular policy vis-à-vis their citizens. Then follows a demonstration of the size of the revolutionary sentiment in the Baltic lands from the fall of 1939 on, which is explained as stemming both from a feeling of love for the Red Army then stationed in the three states for the security it provided and from the deteriorating economic conditions that accompanied the beginning of the war in Europe. This section is considerably documented. The anti-Soviet activity of the bourgeois governments, according to this source, continued to the point where the Soviet government was forced to take steps to ensure the fulfillment of the mutual-assistance pacts and unilaterally lent some assistance through the introduction of additional troops in June 1940. This led the popular masses, now strengthened, to proceed confidently to topple the "bourgeois-fascist" regimes. Documentation becomes sparser here.

Twenty-seven pages in Volume 4 again discuss the Baltic region, mostly its military history. Three pages contain the usual lists of Nazi atrocities and final-solution plans. One and one half pages are devoted to anti-German opposition allegedly inspired by the Communist party. It is evident that the question of the proper line on bourgeois nationalist collaborators had yet to be resolved. Only one paragraph is devoted to this topic, with a rather safe socioeconomic explanation given for the collaboration: "The activity of the bourgeois nationalists was aided by the fact that kulakism had not been wholly liquidated in the Baltic Republics by the outbreak of the war. It became the base of the fascist occupation regime."[26]

Military Memoirs

A particular genre of Soviet historiography on the war is formed by military memoirs, which began to appear in the late 1950s, continued at a trickle through 1962–1963, and became a flood by 1963, once the Khrushchev-Zhukov struggle had been resolved.[27] They counter the dominant tendency to extol the role of the party and its Central Committee to the point of almost excluding the military professional themselves. These memoirs often are intent on setting the record straight. At times, they offer bold, frank, and unorthodox evaluations and serve as new, rewarding sources for historians who had earlier felt stifled by the historiographical line of the moment.[28] Marshal Zhukov's chapters on the opening days of the war provide very enlightening information. A figure like General Piotr Grigorenko in his *samizdat* letter to the editors of *Voprosy istorii KPSS*[29] is able to draw upon various statements from military reminiscences in his support of Nekrich.

These military memoirs shed some light on such questions of the Soviet Union at war as the responsibility for the 1941 and 1942 disasters as well as for the 1945 victory. They are obviously useful for military history. But they contain little on specific political questions or on diplomacy—areas in which Baltic events have acquired their peculiar identity in the Soviet historiography on World War II.

Memoirs and other works by Soviet Baltic military figures, such as Lembit Pern, Vladas Karvelis, and Vincas Vitkauskas, form part of the trend for military memoirs.[30] Since the Soviet Baltic military men were relatively insignificant in the Soviet military establishment, however, these memoirs provide little beyond the history of military operations.

Books extolling individual heroism during the war are frequently published to keep alive the memory of the war. Some of these, published in Moscow, occasionally deal with Baltic events. In the late 1960s Russian-language editions of such books began to emanate also from Baltic publishing houses.[31]

In addition to the military memoirs and accounts of heroism there is a large body of works on Soviet partisan activity. The importance given to them is clearly an attempt to stress the pro-Soviet identity of the wartime population. They are intended to dispel alleged Western skepticism about the partisan movement[32] and possibly to counter the various studies on "treasonable" activity that appeared in the 1960s.[33] Yet they appear to be attempts to exploit fully something that is marginal at best. Thus of the awards given to Komsomol groups during the war, as listed in the popular Russian collection *Fiery Years*, none seems to have gone to Baltic groups. Coverage of activity in the Baltic region in this book is scant. A 1943 report on the activity of the Estonian Komsomol, which claimed to have 800 members operating as partisans, contains a disproportionately high number of Russian names among the activists.[34]

The Last Year of Independence

The two Stalin-Hitler pacts of August and September 1939 have become extremely sensitive topics that are usually ignored or glossed over in Soviet historiography. Those who do mention them seldom go into detail, merely reiterating the Soviet line that they were made necessary by the Western attempt to provoke a war between the Soviet Union and Germany. *Pravda*'s statement of September 23, 1939, as given in the comprehensive history of the war, is about as detailed an explanation of the secret clauses of the August pact as has been given the Soviet people. The Kremlin has never admitted that the pact was part of a secret protocol:

> In these circumstances, the Soviet Union could not aid Poland whose government categorically refused it. The only thing which could still be done was to save Western Ukraine, Western Belorussia, and the Baltics from the German yoke. The Soviet government thus secured an obligation from Germany not to go beyond the rivers Pissa, Narew, Bug, Vistula, and San.[35]

This covered Poland only. The secret arrangements in the Baltic area have never been mentioned, though there are occasional hints of an author's awareness of the secret clauses. Vilnis Sīpols, a Latvian historian, for instance, stresses the fact that Latvia was able to escape a German attack in September 1939 because the Soviet Union was interested in the inviolability of the Baltic States: "In concluding a treaty of non-aggression with the USSR in August, 1939, Germany was obliged to take cognizance of this position of the Soviet government."[36] The public articles of the pact do not mention the Baltic States.

The Latvian academician Aleksandrs Drīzulis, however, seems to be unaware of or oblivious to the secret clauses of the pact. In his study of fascism in Latvia, his best defense for the pact—a topic that he cannot avoid—he repeats Stalin's famous *apologia*, given in the radio speech of July 3, 1941.[37] The pact was one of peace, Stalin said, and no peaceloving nation could have afforded to turn it down even when offered by a state led by such as Hitler and Ribbentrop. Although Drīzulis' bibliography contains numerous Western sources, *Nazi-Soviet Relations* is not one of them.

Some of the authors who have surreptitiously published *samizdat* studies in the West and are on the whole surprisingly well informed about sources show no awareness of the secret clauses. Roy Medvedev, author of a monumental history of Stalinism, holds that though the public portions of the pact can be defended from a point of view of state interest, it is quite another matter to apply such a defense to the secret protocols. But he seems to be aware only of the secret articles of the boundary and friendship treaty of September 29, 1939, which he labels unprincipled.[38] General Grigorenko in his letter of defense of Nekrich also takes the position that the friendship and boundary treaty cannot be explained away, though he does not go into detail, and it is not evident whether he has seen the text of the secret clauses.[39] He may be erroneously considering the line of demarcation announced in *Pravda* on September 23, 1939, to be the secret part of the treaty.

To counter Western inferences of aggressive Soviet intent in the Baltic in 1939 and 1940, the Soviet government usually points to the supposedly serious English negotiations with German Ambassador Herbert von Dirksen on the eve of the war, which were published by the Soviet government in retaliation for *Nazi-Soviet Relations*, but never goes into enough detail to refute Western accusations.[40]

The standard leitmotiv of Soviet historiography on the Baltic area in 1939–1940 has been the alleged pro-German orientation of the Baltic States in an international situation in which Western powers endeavor to channel German aggression against the Soviet Union.[41] One variant has the "reactionary" Baltic governments themselves actively moving toward a conflict with the Soviet Union.[42] There is talk of the bourgeois Estonian government's waiting to stab the Soviet Union in the back[43] as if that were physically feasible. German Generals Walter Brauchitsch and Franz Halder are supposed to have urged the Lithuanians to move on Vilnius in September 1939 so as to draw Lithuania into a conflict with Moscow.[44] Presumably, only the British-French declaration of war on Germany stopped the Lithuanian action.[45] Another variant has the

Western powers preparing to use the Baltic States for an anti-Soviet crusade. The trip of the American ambassador to the Soviet Union, Lawrence Steinhardt, to Riga in early February 1940 is viewed as part of such a secret plan.[46]

And according to the most frequently used variant, Western powers refused to extend joint guarantees to the Baltic States because they wanted to leave the Baltic region open as a corridor of aggression against the Soviet Union.[47]

Nekrich's work on English foreign policy on the eve of the war is a good example of a transition from Stalinist scholarship to a rather sophisticated treatment of the question of the Baltic States in the fall of 1939. His monograph on British policy in Europe between Munich and the outbreak of the war was published in 1955 and probably written at least a year earlier.[48] The Nazi-Soviet pact is entirely left out, but the thesis that the West attempted to spark a war between Germany and the Kremlin is stressed. The Baltic winters are mentioned very briefly in connection with the negotiations of the summer of 1939, while an entire section of a chapter is devoted to the struggle of the English Communist party against His Majesty's government's antipopular foreign policy.

In 1962 Nekrich wrote an article that covers the period from the outbreak of the war through January 1940.[49] Although the scope of the article is wide, encompassing Scandinavia as well, a fairly long section is devoted to the Baltic republics. Having apparently done research in the Estonian archives, he bases his examples of trends in all three countries on events in Estonia. As a result, his account of the Estonian government deliberations on the acceptance of the mutual-assistance pact and his coverage of all the perceived options available at the time are rather straightforward. Not surprisingly, Nekrich justifies Soviet policy by attempting to demonstrate that the Baltic quarter had presented a danger to Moscow for a long time. He asks the rhetorical question: "Could the Soviet Union calmly wait for Germany to strengthen itself in this area?" His starting point discusses the supposed role of the Western powers in maintaining the Baltic States as a center for anti-Soviet policies. Even a former Estonian state elder, Jaan Tõnnison, is quoted to prove the existence of this anti-Soviet stance of Estonia throughout the interwar period.

Western cynicism in dealings with the Baltic countries is also emphasized in Nekrich's article. The Chamberlain group in England, which was making use of these countries to provoke a conflict between Moscow and Germany, was quite ready to abandon them should circumstances change, he says. The Latvian foreign minister Vilhelms Munters' public expression of the abandonment of Poland is cited in support of this thesis. Even Great Britain's refusal to recognize the new Soviet republics in the Baltic in the summer of 1940 is viewed as being motivated solely by British interest in the Baltic gold deposits, which it allegedly planned to use as compensation for British property nationalized by the people's governments. This line of reasoning was elaborated in 1957 by G. A. Deborin, who viewed British-American defense of the interests of the Baltic peoples as consisting of a seizure of their ships and gold.[50] Such a stress on the absence of concrete Western aid to Poland in 1939 and Western mendacity on an alleged inability to provide such aid[51] was perhaps part of a wider campaign to dampen any popular pro-Western feeling. Soviet scholars have generally emphasized the allegedly pro-German orientation of the Baltic governments in every imaginable way. Nekrich, for example, cites a July 1939 note by the English consul in Tallinn expressing concern over the increasing German orientation of the Estonian government.[52] At times even such rather irrelevant material as a newspaper article in the Lithuanian Christian Democratic daily *XX Amžius*, expressing contentment over the good relations with Germany after the Klaipėda *Anschluss*, is used as evidence of pro-fascism.[53] One wonders what a similar use of *Pravda* from the period of the Nazi-Soviet pact might demonstrate.

In connection with the pro-German orientation of the three Baltic governments, considerable attention is paid to the alleged September 1939 offer by the Lithuanian president Antanas Smetona to turn Lithuania into a German protectorate. Augustinas Povilaitis, the chief of the Lithuanian Security Service, supposedly paid two secret visits to Germany for this purpose.[54] His talks with the Germans, held at Soppot near Danzig, were revealed in 1944, before the U.S. Army had seized the German Foreign Ministry Archives in the Harz Mountains.[55] The Soviet scholars seem unaware, at least officially, of the existence of the secret clauses in the Nazi-Soviet pact.[56] Since these Soppot talks were held before September 20, 1939, they antedate the friendship and boundary treaty that transferred Lithuania from the German to the Soviet sphere of interest. Therefore, it is evident that Germany was merely taking steps to implement its settlement with the Soviet Union, as determined the previous month.

An awareness of the significance of this date sequence also clarifies some otherwise rather cryptic events mentioned by Robertas Žiugžda in his article "A Helping Hand at a Terrible Time."[57] He refers to German plans for concluding a military alliance with Lithuania which "belonged to the German sphere." The Lithuanian foreign minister Juozas Urbšys, whom the Germans had invited to visit Berlin, was asked to defer the trip for a few days—presumably because of the minister's stress of Lithuanian neutrality in a recent speech. Urbšys never did go to Berlin, and, continues the article, Ribbentrop, during a subsequent visit to Moscow, was "forced to desist, albeit temporarily, from aggressive intentions towards Lithuania." Lithuanian independence was thereafter supposedly secured by the mutual-assistance pact with the Soviet Union.

Lithuanian attempts to impose a German protectorate on themselves are ascribed to later periods as well,[58] though the *Kulturverband* plot discussed by J. Žiugžda never reappears. One author, without going into detail, even suggests that the mission sent to convince President Smetona to return from Germany on June 16, 1940, also had as an aim negotiations for the receipt of German military aid.[59]

The Summer of 1940

Contemporary Soviet Baltic works have adopted a more balanced view of the brotherly help received from the Soviet Union in 1940. For one, this topic has lost some of its 1949 preeminence. Too, frequently there is a separation of internal difficulties, considered to be a precondition for the revolutionary situation during which the fascist regimes were toppled, from international questions, which led to the introduction of additional Soviet units in mid-June 1940. Soviet troop deployment is viewed as having been necessitated by the bad faith showed by the Baltic governments in secretly participating in anti-Soviet negotiations, the series of provocations against Soviet garrisons, the increase in training and anti-Soviet indoctrination of their reserves, their pro-Finnish attitudes—in short, by all of the well-known misdeeds that Molotov conjured up in 1940.[60] The danger of German aggression was also increasing. The region had been a fertile ground for German espionage, and German repatriates of 1939 had begun to show a curious interest in returning. The fact that Germany had not attacked the Baltic States in the fall of 1939 did not mean that she would not do so in the summer of 1940. Together with the Soviet mistrust of the Baltic fascist leaders of that time this led to the ultimatums of June 1940 and to the introduction of the additional Red Army units, according to Soviet historians.

The Stalinist formula for a 1940 revolutionary situation in the Baltic states, already discussed, also continues to appear in various forms in post-Stalinist historiography. While the Baltic governments persisted in their anti-Soviet stance, the populations of these states, the great movers of history, exhibited virtually age-old, predetermined pro-Soviet tendencies. A 1961 article by V. V. Gushchin, "The Struggle of the Working Class of Lithuania against the Anti-Popular Foreign Policy of the Bourgeois Government (1939–1940),"[61] is a prime example of the extended insinuating tone that the worst in Soviet historiography is capable of producing. Though spiced with archival research in Moscow and Lithuania, this polemical work is obviously part of the never-ending struggle against émigré "falsifiers."

Most of the current Soviet scholars separate external and internal events. The Estonian Peeter Larin goes even further: his discussions of the external and internal situations are separated by a section on Nazi plans to exterminate the Estonian people.[62] Others view the events as connected temporally,[63] but do not stress their causal relationship.[64] The latest edition of the *History of the Latvian SSR*, echoing a thesis elaborated earlier by the Estonian historian Viktor Maamägi,[65] presents the socialist revolutions in the Baltic States as being among the first proletarian victories won without an armed struggle. The presence of the Red Army is understood to have been of crucial importance, since it prevented the bourgeoisie from using military force to undo the revolutions and from requesting foreign aid, as had happened in 1918–1920. Indeed, the revolutionary agitation, official Latvian historians maintain in this work, was sparked by police attacks on the workers who had come out to greet the Red Army. The Lithuanian historian Vytautas Kancevičius considers the essential element in the Lithuanian revolution to be a tilt of the balance of power between classes in favor of the "people."[66] However, the entry of the Red Army is viewed as "the objective situation which raised the anti-fascist tendencies of the masses and which led them to act against the old regime." Possibly due to the Soviet propagandist emphasis on the military in the 1970s, a more recent study by Kancevičius[67] seems to accentuate somewhat the positive and beneficial role of the Red Army. Kancevičius also appears to be indirectly praising the bourgeois Lithuanian Army for not following Smetona into Germany.[68] But once the revolution has succeeded, the Red Army, together with all other Soviet activity, dissapears from Kancevičius' account. The subsequent reorganization is pictured as a purely internal matter.

Another recent Lithuanian critique of the Western interpretation of the 1940 events is extremely vague on the specific role of the Red Army.[69] Its author, H. Šadžius, perfunctorily labels as lies various Western contentions that the "revolution" was forced by the Soviet Union. In a rather crude way, he also tries to disprove bourgeois claims that the 1940 Socialist revolution in Lithuania had no basis in extant class antagonisms and that the 1939 mutual-assistance pacts were concluded by the Baltic governments under duress.

Ambassador Ivan Maiskii's cynical account of his meeting with Lord Halifax on August 15, 1940, to request the termination of the Baltic missions in Great Britain presents a curious interpretation. When confronted by Halifax with the charge that Soviet actions in the Baltic States had constituted aggression, Maiskii comes up with the analogy of the Siberian peasant Ivan. During Ivan's illness, his neighbors steal his possessions. After recovering, he forcibly takes back that which had been stolen. "So now, Lord Halifax, who was the aggressor in your opinion, the peasant Ivan or his neighbours?"[70]

The events of 1940 acquire a somewhat different meaning in the work of the Lithuanian historian Kostas Navickas. According to him, since its bourgeois government had sought to transform Lithuania into an "illegal" colony of Hitlerite Germany—an act detrimental both to the interests of the Lithuanian nation as well as to the security of the Soviet Union—"the new security measures [June 1940 ultimatums] of the government of the USSR were wholly justifiable even from the point of view of bourgeois international law."[71] He does not elaborate. In a subsequent work he offers an original, though not credible, explanation that stands out in the gray mass of Soviet uniformity. The need to incorporate Lithuania into the Soviet Union, he says, has an international cause. Under other circumstances Lithuania could have become a people's republic, tied to the Soviet Union only internationally. It was the imminence of the German threat that necessitated closer relations with the Soviet Union.[72]

The First Year of Soviet Power

Apart from general encomiums on the great benefits of the Soviet system to the Baltic peoples, Soviet Baltic historiographers have paid little attention to the first year of Soviet rule. One of the few Soviet studies of the nationalist opposition to the Soviet regime during the year following June 1940 is an article by A. Žagars[73] in a collection dealing mostly with such relatively safe topics as the heroism of Red Latvian partisans, Nazi economic exploitation of Latvia, and military history. Žagars' thesis— that ingrained bourgeois views and attitudes cannot be changed within one year—also serves to explain wartime collaboration with the Germans. He begins by listing eight factors that faciliatated victory of the proletariat in Latvia in 1940. Among these are the character of the Communist leadership (always positive), internal difficulties, both economic and political, and the split within the bourgeois camp caused by the 1934 suppression of diversified political activity. As the last of these eight factors he lists the presence of the Red Army, taking pains to explain that it was not crucial and that events would have taken a similar turn without its positive presence. Žagars' factors do not differ from those elaborated by Maamägi.

The *Aizsargi* (volunteer militia of the Latvian republic) are viewed as the heart of the anti-Soviet movement in Latvia. Some had managed to hide their weapons for use against the Soviet regime after the German attack. A surprising element in Žagars' article is the admission of the extent of anti-Soviet feeling in Latvia after June 1940. Because of the extensive indoctrination campaign of 1939–1940, the army, although made up largely of workers and peasants, was hostile to the Soviet order.[74] The nationalization of small shops and other economic units in the fall of 1940 increased the ranks of the dissatisfied. The intelligentsia consisted mostly of the bourgeoisie and kulaks, a significant number of whom opposed Soviet power. Bourgeois teachers organized anti-Soviet demonstrations in the fall of 1940, and many students who loathed the Soviet system later joined the Hitlerites. But lest the Soviet reader get an improper view of Latvian chauvinism, Žagars mentions that it was not only the Latvian schools that were anti-Soviet troublespots: "In the Russian schools a significant proportion of the instructors were connected with various Russian White Guard organizations, and the Jewish schools were objects for the Jewish bourgeoisie in attempts to turn them into foci of Zionism that nurtured the idea of 'Jewish exclusivity.'"[75]

In Žagars view, the Latvian bourgeois underground had no program other than its anti-Sovietism and a desire for a return of nationalized property. It served German intelligence in small groups. Žagars' account makes one question the officially announced results of the July 1940 and January 1941 elections. If opposition was so widespread that it could, in some cases, induce peasants to refuse proffered kulak land or make it possible to carry out sabotage against rural polling places, have not the election results perhaps been inflated? Žagars does not even bother to provide the 1940 election statistics, and limits himself to a statement that they reflected the overwhelming desire of the workers and peasants. A figure of 98% in favor of Soviet candidates is provided for the subsequent January 1941 elections. But it remains unconvincing in view of the admitted existence, among other opposition groups, of 60,000 *Aizsargi*.

The June 1941 deportations from the Baltic countries could be ignored as long as other problems connected with the war situation received only scant attention. The Khrushchevite line in historiography toward more open and sophisticated explanations made it necessary to take up the deportations as well. They were usually justified in terms of imminent danger from Germany. On June 15, 1941, however, the Soviet government made its famous no-war-threat declaration in *Pravda*. The TASS communiqué, which was extensively used by Khrushchev's war historians as the most damning piece of evidence of Stalin's shortsightedness and inability to face the facts, denied that Germany had presented territorial and economic claims on the Soviet Union. It stated categorically that "Germany is . . . unswervingly observing the conditions of the Soviet-German Non-Agression Pact, just as the USSR is doing. Therefore in the opinion of Soviet circles, the rumours of Germany's intentions to tear up the Pact and to undertake an attack on the USSR are without any foundation."[76] If so, fear of German attack cannot explain the deportations. Actually, Khrushchev's general line on Stalin's leadership before and during the war tends to relegate the June 15, 1941, declaration to oblivion.

Another view of the deportations, elaborated among others by Maamägi,[77] stresses an intensification of the class struggle as the cause. It is admitted that under the conditions of the personality cult mistakes in carrying out the resettlement were made. It was done in haste, the reasons for it were not properly explained to the people, and misidentifications at times led to the exile of the wrong persons. Bourgeois nationalists took advantage of these mistakes to spread rumors that the Baltic populations would be systematically resettled.[78] But weighed on the overall Soviet scale of historical values, says Maamägi, the deportations were "progressive" and served the state well on the eve of the war in that they deprived the Nazis of a significant portion of their potential fifth column.[79]

The German Occupation

Nazi atrocities are one of the easiest and safest areas for Soviet historiographic research on World War II. Not surprisingly, therefore, they dominated the scant Stalinist body of works on the war years in the Baltic region and still continue to receive attention.

In early 1960s atrocity-oriented publications increased greatly in connection with a series of well-publicized trials of war criminals. Some of the defendants were émigrés being tried in absentia because their countries of exile had refused to extradite them. Most of this propaganda-laden material had little scholarly value, though it was indicative of the contemporary trend.[80]

The treatment of wartime Baltic atrocities is connected with the question of the role of the Baltic nationalists during 1940–1941. The earliest mention of these nationalists implicitly attempted to mark them as collaborators, hence to incriminate them in the atrocities that the German occupation was noted for. A rigid picture was painted of "bourgeois nationalists" and "fascists" striving to turn their countries into German colonies prior to the mutual-assistance pacts, continuing such activity during the winter and spring of 1940, going underground during the first year of Soviet power, and surfacing after the German attack to concretize their fondest dreams. The Lithuanian series of documents, *Faktai kaltina* (*Facts Accuse*), consisting thus far of nine volumes published between 1960 and 1968,[81] ties together prewar right-wing activity (official and unofficial), wartime collaboration and atrocities, and postwar anti-Soviet resistance as different facets of one and the same subject for investigation.

While Žagars focused his investigation on the internal aspects of anti-Sovietism in Latvia, Lithuanian researchers since 1960 have tended to stress the foreign connections of the opposition in Lithuania. One of the earliest Lithuanian studies was an article by Aldona Gaigalaitė.[82] She approached the problem through the most extreme right-wing group in prewar Lithuania, the Iron Wolf, attempting to tie the pro-Nazi aims of this group to other groups and thus demonstrate the similarity of aims among all nationalist groups and to define these in terms of the extreme right wing. Her most scathing indictment is that the leaders of the Lithuanian Activist Front (the underground anti-Soviet opposition headed by the former Lithuanian minister in Berlin, Kazys Škirpa), allegedly knew that the German government was opposed to the creation of an "independent" Lithuania in the event of a Russian-German conflict, but hid this knowledge from their rank and file followers and thus deceived them. This implicit exoneration of the anti-Soviet Lithuanian rank and file remains, to my knowledge, rare among the Manichean Soviet explanations of nationalist anti-Soviet activity in the Baltic area. Her portrayal of the Lithuanian insurrection of June 23, 1941, which followed the German attack on the Soviet Union, is also notable for its detail, candor, and realism, which seem to be absent from later Soviet accounts.

Gaigalaitė's article was followed up by J. Dobrovolskas.[83] His level of scholarship and research equals that of Gaigalaitė, but his tone is polemical and his estimates of anti-Soviet discontent more conservative. The theme of treason—pro-German activity in view of a full knowledge of Nazi plans for Lithuania—is continued here, though without any of the extenuating circumstances of ignorance on the part of the rank and file. This theme has become standard in Soviet Lithuanian literature on the question.

The wish to demonstrate that the nationalists consciously collaborated with the Germans in the face of minimal popular support probably also underlies the publication of a whole series of edited and abridged documents relating to collaboration.[84] The most interesting among them is the last speech by the acting prime minister of the Lithuanian Provisional Government of 1941, Juozas Ambrazevičius, on August 5, 1941, the day the Provisional Government, unable to reach a *modus vivendi* with the Germans, suspended its activities. Though Ambrazevičius refers to attempts at military and diplomatic cooperation, the document also discloses a strong streak of nationalism and independence in the aims of the Provisional Government. There is no evidence that this was a group of German stooges and that its relationship to forces of occupation had been one of a puppet to its master. This and other documents in the collection hint that the level of collaboration during the initial period of German occupation was in fact much lower than that suggested by the editors of the collection.

Bourgeois nationalism in Lithuania is briefly discussed by J. Butėnas in a short, undocumented article in Russian.[85] In a manner typical of much of Soviet popular historical writing, the terms "bourgeois nationalist" and "fascist" are used synonymously when convenient and in separate senses when not. For instance, it is difficult to see why a "fascist" organization, the Iron Wolf, had to operate underground during the years of "fascist" rule by President Smetona. Butėnas' explanation of why Lithuanian nationalists joined the army of General Plechavičius in 1944 is also detrimental to his main thesis. That the army's rank and file fled to the woods to avoid being removed from Lithuania might indicate other motives and ideals than a desire to save Nazism from collapse, a fact that the author is unable or unwilling to mention. Even though Butėnas alludes to substantial disagreements and conflicts between the bourgeois nationalists and the Germans, he has no reservations about placing the responsibility for all occupation evils in Lithuania on the nationalists.

A similar theme runs through Jonas Aničas' works on the Catholic Church in Lithuania during the German occupation.[86] He considers both the Catholic hierarchy and the Catholic lay activists to have been openly pro-German. If they assumed an anti-German posture, it was merely to deceive the populace. Their prominence in the 1941 Provisional Government, he claims, stems from their anti-Smetona stance, which made them more acceptable to the masses. Aničas also attempts to connect the Lithuanian Catholic Church to the extermination policy of the Germans, though he admits that there were exceptions among the clergy in this respect. His only "evidence" is the "Regulations on the Status of Jews" of August 1, 1941, which were supposedly promulgated over the signature of the Provisional Government. First, these regulations *per se* are not a document, decreeing a policy of extermination. Second, they were issued in August when, as Aničas himself admits, the Nazi *Zivilverwaltung* already controlled the entire administrative apparatus. Third, since the Provisional Government did not promulgate any anti-Jewish legislation in June and July, it is questionable whether signatures allegedly affixed to this document are authentic. The rest of Aničas' account imputes an overt or covert Catholic collaboration with the Germans, mainly, it appears, because they failed to oppose the occupants militarily. Soviet historians generally attribute any act of opposition to the German occupation in Lithuania to the leadership of the underground Communist party, though this party at that time was very weak and inconsequential.

A somewhat less harsh evaluation is presented by Juozas Bulavas in his study of the German occupation administration in Lithuania. It is impossible, Bulavas claims, to issue a blanket condemnation of all local organs during the occupation, since many worked in the interests of the local population under existing conditions.[87]

Unlike some Latvian scholars who hold that the Latvian nationalist "opposition" to the Germans in fact strengthened the German occupation (see below), Bulavas states that the only practical activity of the anti-German Lithuanian nationalists was the publication of underground newspapers. Their treason to the nation consists not so much in collaboration as in flight to the West in 1944 after having frightened many into going along with them. The implication is that they left Lithuania in ruins and smoke, placing personal and/or material comfort before national interests.

A slightly new twist in differentiating between the bourgeois nationalist strands during the occupation appears in the latest Russian-language work by Aleksandrs Drīzulis—a massive and luxurious tome on the wartime struggle of the Latvian people.[88] The greater part of the volume is devoted, as can be expected, to previously developed and approved themes, such as resistance and military heroism. The short section on the bourgeois nationalists make the admission, already noted in the 1966 three-volume Baltic war history, that some of the bourgeois were not exactly Nazis. The distinction between the two is rendered academic, though, by concluding that the end result was a general weakening of opposition to the German occupants. It is clearly implied that a bourgeois nationalist opposition was tolerated by the Germans as a practical measure in keeping the opposition down. When this failed to achieve the intended result, Alfreds Valdmanis' "opposition" was closed, as was the Latvian National Council.

A halfhearted attempt is made to overcome a seeming contradiction between a statement that the Germans left the Latvian National Council alone and the fact that one of its members, Konstantins Čakste, died at the Stutthof camp. Perhaps the author hoped to resolve this contradiction by accusing another member of the Council, Bruno Kalniņš, a Social Democratic activist now in exile, of having been a German agent. Similarly, the army of General Jānis Kurelis is described as having been useless and unpopular, yet it apparently was sufficiently irksome to the Germans for them to bother condemning some of its members to Stutthof.

A General Baltic History of the War Years

A Baltic equivalent of the large multivolume all-Union official history of the war is the three-volume *The Struggle for the Soviet Baltic During the Great Fatherland War*. Published in 1966 by the Military Scientific Society at the Riga District Soviet Army Officers' Club, it was written by a large collective, in which Russians, probably experts in military history, seem to predominate.[89] Like the large all-Union history, most of it is devoted to military history. Volume 1 covers, in its first few sections, the events preceding the German-Soviet hostilities in a rather cursory fashion, usually merely summarizing previous pronouncements. The Non-Aggression Pact with Germany, which directly affected the Baltic, is discussed in one paragraph. By page 23 of the 369-page volume the political events of 1940 have been fully described. The most interesting section of this work comes at the end of Volume 3, when 49 of the 319 pages in the volume are devoted to the chapters entitled "The Anti-Popular Activity of the Bourgeois Nationalists of Lithuania, Latvia, and Estonia" and "Against the Falsifiers of History." After a reiteration of the theme of the bourgeois nationalists as crypto-German agents even before September 1939, and after a brief treatment of the events of 1940, there follows a section obviously based on the research of Žagars concerning the ability of the nationalist bourgeoisie to preserve a limited economic position and some influence on the population even after the workers' victory. In view of this, the 1940 election figures, published straightforwardly in Volume 1, are not repeated here.

Also discussed is anti-Soviet émigré activity before the outbreak of German-Soviet hostilities. Although a group of Estonians is reported to have operated out of Helsinki, the only successful counterrevolutionary organizations are found to have existed in Lithuania. When war started, these groups supposedly perpetrated concrete diversionary acts, though the Lithuanian Provisional Government is made to appear to be a mere branch of the German military administration. Nothing is said about diversionary acts in Latvia. However, a hint of the magnitude of the anti-Soviet reaction comes through in a citation from the 1943 secret report by the Latvian Komsomol hero Imants Sudmalis to the Latvian Communist party—in the first days of the war, he reports, 3000 "bourgeois nationalists" were active in Liepāja. An attempt is made to discredit the membership of the occupation police in Latvia, which was composed largely of former military personnel of the bourgeois army. The author characterizes it as containing many former criminals: on November 22, 1941, of the 227 members of the Daugavpils Prefecture, 28 had been previously convicted. "Previously" is not defined, though political criminality seems to be implied. The section on Estonia is the shortest and most general. There is little on the politics and motives of the nationalists—just a list of persons in the occupation government and police, their functions, and their alleged crimes.

Although this history continues to identify nationalist interests with Nazi interests during the occupation, an attempt at differentiating between them is made at one point in regard to Latvia and Lithuania. According to this version, some of the collaborators, aware of the popular hatred of the Germans, began to feign an opposition to them in order to gain the confidence of the peasants and the intelligentsia. The Valdmanis group in Latvia is given as an example. They were evidently ready to offer the Germans everything in return for being allowed to manage the exploitation of Latvia. Others among the bourgeoisie, working toward the 1919 variant of control over the population with British-American aid, advocated passivity until the crucial moment. They neither opposed nor aided Soviet partisans. While virulently slandering the Soviet Union, their illegal press only mildly criticized the Germans. One of the Latvian leaders of this ilk, Bruno Kalniņš, is supposed to have admitted that the net effect of his opposition activity was to aid the German forces in their campaign against Red partisans.[90] Their political predilections notwithstanding, a clear attempt is nevertheless made to link all shades of bourgeois nationalism with the Germans.

The chapter on the falsification of history brings wartime events into a current political forum. Its author claims that certain West German elements and émigrés are waging a propaganda war against the peoples of the Soviet Union and are purposely distorting the history of the war. The myth, from the Soviet viewpoint, that the Balts had greeted the *Wehrmacht* as a liberation force is very inadequately countered by quoting a former *Wehrmacht* propaganda chief, of an unspecified date, to the effect that the indigenous population of the occupied areas was not inclined to collaboration and by citations from émigré publications demonstrating lack of enthusiasm for service in the Latvian SS. The bourgeois "falsifiers of history" are castigated for ignoring the Red Baltic units. Although Goebbels' propaganda had depicted these as being composed of Russians, the author explains that 88.5% of the 8th Estonian Rifle Corps, at an unspecified date, consisted of Estonians. No figures are given for the 130th Latvian Corps or for the 16th Lithuanian Division.

At one point, in his attempt to expose bourgeois falsifiers, the author of the sections on collaboration strains the reader's credibility. An émigré publication entitled *The Estonian State and People in World War II*,[91] he says, lists among Estonia's fighters for freedom the German general commissioner Karl Litzmann, convicted by a Soviet court, the war criminal Ain Mere, and even Heinrich Himmler. Among the "historians" of the émigré collection, the Soviet author notes twelve former Gestapo officials, twenty former secret Gestapo agents, sixteen former SS men, nineteen spies serving in a general way the intelligence services of ten states, and five former German intelligence agents.[92]

The émigré falsifiers, it is claimed, do not deny fascist bestiality in destroying the peaceful Lithuanian village of Pirčiupis, but somehow they insidiously manage to lay the blame for the massacre of the peasants on Soviet partisans. No details are provided of the mechanics of this depraved bourgeois reasoning. One might quite logically deduce from the statements given that the émigrés are talking about a joint expedition by Nazis and Soviet partisans to exterminate the village![93]

The chapter ends on an emotional note with an attack on the Estonian émigré historian Evald Uustalu for his statement that the capitulation of Germany brought no joy to Estonia. Is he unaware, asks the Soviet author, of the fate Hitler had in mind for the Estonian people? And that Hitler's plans were frustrated by the might of the Red Army?[94]

Overall, this sole Soviet attempt to deal with the wartime Baltic states suffers from some problems that can naturally be expected to occur from an effort of this nature. The three-volume work shows little evidence of original scholarship. The rather rough hems of a compilation from varied and diverse sources in the three Baltic republics are readily evident. Since apparently few of the authors were competent in all three Baltic languages, they were forced to depend on Russian translations or summaries for at least part of their source material. As result of the earlier dearth (apart from military history)[95] of Russian-language material on Estonia at war, there is an overemphasis on Lithuania and Latvia.

Conclusion

The history of Soviet historiography on the Baltic States during World War II, like all Soviet historiography, reflects the vagaries of Soviet politics. First comes the relative silence of the Stalin period, interrupted only by the need to answer outside attacks. The establishment of one standard line follows in the late 1950s and early 1960s, accompanied by elaborations on specific points and attempts to refute embarrassing facts made public by émigrés.

As any body of historical writing, Soviet historiography on the Baltic area in World War II is uneven. Works of the caliber of Nekrich's are of real value. But in view of the inaccessibility of the relevant archives to foreigners, any Soviet work of a semiacademic and even popular nature can acquire a scholarly value that it would not have otherwise possessed. Much remains to be unveiled and discussed. The Baltic archives doubtlessly have much to reveal, and even when seen through the prism of Soviet historical scholarship, such revelations often provide a valuable contribution, particularly in the form of document collections.

In regard to some topics, only the tip of the iceberg seems to have been touched. Compared to what was available in print ten years ago, however, much has been done. The Brezhnev cultural chill, apparent in regard to such general questions of the war as the Nekrich affair, is little in evidence in Soviet historiography on the narrow topic of the Baltic area in wartime. But, then, Soviet writing on this theme has usually been cautious. Under these circumstances, the rate of studying specific new themes and revealing details in Soviet historiography on the Baltic States at war is likely to remain unchanged.

Notes

AA   Auswärtiges Amt, Archives of the German Foreign Ministry on Microfilm in the National Archives of the United States

ARA   American Relief Administration

AVPR   Arkhiv Vneshnei Politiki Rossii (Moscow)

BBC   British Broadcasting Corporation

CP   Cabinet Papers

DBFP   *Documents on British Foreign Policy* (London)

DGFP   *Documents on German Foreign Policy 1918–1945*, Aussenministerium, Germany

DNDTF   *Darstellungen aus den Nachkriegskämpfen deutscher Truppen und Freikorps*, Forschungsanstalt für Kriegs- und Heeresgeschichte, Germany

DZA   Deutsches Zentralarchiv

FO   Foreign Office Papers

FRUS   *Foreign Relations of the United States*

HA   Hoover Institution, Archives (Stanford, Calif.)

IDA   Istoriko-Diplomaticheskii Arkhiv

LCVA   Lietuvos TSR Centrinis Valstybinis Archyvas (Central State Archive of the Lithuanian SSR)

LCVIA   Lietuvos TSR Centralinis Valstybinis Istorinis Archyvas (Vilnius) (Central Historical State Archive of the Lithuanian SSR)

LMARS   Lietuvos TSR Mokslų Akademijos Mokslinės Bibliotekos Rankraščių Skyrius (Manuscript Division of the Library of the Academy of Sciences of the Lithuanian SSR)

LSS   Latvijas Sūtniecība Stokholmā (Archives of the Latvian Legation in Stockholm)

MP	*Maanõukogu Protokollid* (Tallinn, 1935)
NA	National Archives of the United States (Washington, D.C.)
PRO	Public Record Office (London)
TsGVIA	Tsentralnyi Gosudarstvennyi Voenno-Istoricheskii Arkhiv SSSR (Moscow)
VURS	Vilniaus Universiteto Bibliotekos Rankraščių Skyrius (Manuscript Division of the Library of the University of Vilnius)
VVDN	*Verhandlungen der Verfassungsgebenden Deutschen National-versamlung*

Introduction: The Baltic Peoples in Historical Perspective

1. Royal Institute of International Affairs, *The Baltic States* (London, 1938).

2. Georg von Rauch, *Geschichte der baltischen Staaten* (Stuttgart, 1970; English translation, Berkeley, Calif., 1974).

3. August Rei, *The Drama of the Baltic Peoples* (Stockholm, 1970), 339ff; Seppo Myllyniemi, *Die Neuordnung der baltischen Länder, 1941–1944* (Helsinki, 1973), 72–86; Zenonas Ivinskis, "Lithuania During the War: Resistance Against the Soviet and the Nazi Occupants," in V. Stanley Vardys, *Lithuania Under the Soviets* (New York, 1965), 61–84; Martin Broszat, "Die nationale Widerstandsbewegung in Litauen im Zweiten Weltkrieg (1941–1944)," in *Gutachten des Instituts für Zeitgeschichte* (Munich, 1958), 239–79.

4. Text of a speech by Ambrazevičius in a meeting with the newly appointed Generalkommissar of the German occupation regime on August 5, 1941. See *Documents Accuse* (Vilnius, 1970), 96. Verbatim, Ambrazevičius said: "Having no means, the Government could not positively influence any outrages, e.g. the executions of Jews in Kaunas and in the Provinces." Ibid.

5. The exact wording is: "I do not envy the leaders of those days to whom history presented a choice among Hitler, Stalin, and death, each choice not necessarily excluding the other two." See Tomas Venclova, "Evrei i litovtsy," originally published in the Jewish *samizdat* journal *Tarbut* as a supplement to the issue "Evrei v SSSR." It has been reprinted in *Nasha strana* (Tel Aviv), September 3, 1976.

6. Further see V. Stanley Vardys, "The Partisan Movement in Postwar Lithuania," *Slavic Review* (1963), 499–522.

The Estonian *Maapäev* during 1917

1. The use of the word "autonomy" in connection with the law of March 30, which this paper disputes, is quite common. See, for example, Evald Uustalu, *The History of*

Estonian People (London, 1952), 155. In a later work, however, Uustalu has qualified his use of the word "autonomy" to describe the *Maapäev*: "Its broad competence made it, however, in a certain sense, into an autonomous organ." See "Die Staatsgründung Estlands," in J. von Hehn, H. von Rimscha, and H. Weiss, eds., *Von den baltischen Provinzen zu den baltischen Staaten, 1917–1918* (Marburg/Lahn, 1971), 275. August Rei also uses the word "autonomy": "By the Law on Estonian Autonomy, issued on April 12th, 1917, the Estonian people acquired an autonomous self-government with fairly extensive authority." See *The Drama of the Baltic Peoples* (Stockholm, 1970), 4. Artur Mägi refers to "the law of Estonian autonomy" in his monograph *Das Staatsleben Estlands während seiner Selbständigkeit: I. Das Regierungssystem* (Uppsala, 1967), 21. Finally, Elmar Järvesoo has recently used the phrases "autonomous self-government" and "provisional autonomy law" to refer to the law of March 30. See "Estonia's Declaration of Independence in 1918," in A. Ziedonis, Jr., W. L. Winter, and M. Valgemäe, eds., *Baltic History* (Columbus, Ohio, 1974), 162. The commonly accepted Soviet Estonian interpretation has, on the other hand, downgraded the functions assigned to the *Maapäev* to such an extent that it is described as a consultative body attached to the *guberniia* commissar. See V. Maamägi et al., eds., *Eesti NSV ajalugu* (Tallinn, 1971), 3:25. This interpretation has, however, recently been revised by K. Siilivask, who notes correctly that according to the law of March 30 both the *guberniia* commissar and the *Maapäev* were given authority over self-governmental and administrative matters in Estonia. See *Veebruarist Oktoobrini 1917* (Tallinn, 1972), 142. The claim that the declaration of November 15 was a declaration of independence is made explicitly by A. T. Kliiman: "This day is the day of independence for the Estonian state." See "28 November," in H. Kruus and J. Ots, eds., *Vabaduse tulekul* (Tartu, 1938), 1:21. It is also put forward by Ants Piip, "Maanõukogu 1917. a.," *Vabaduse tulekul*, 17–19, in the only serious study of the activities of the *Maapäev* to date. The standard objections of Soviet Estonian historians to the elections are listed in Maamägi, 35–36. These objections follow the basic charges made against the elections by the Estonian Bolsheviks in 1917—that the elections were indirect in nature and that the small towns were overrepresented in the *Maapäev*.

2. The North Baltic Committee had been formed in 1915 on the initiative of Tõnisson. It performed functions in southern Estonia (northern Livland) that the Unions of the Zemstvos performed elsewhere in Russia. It thus filled a vacuum in the Baltic area since the Livland *Landtag* was unwilling and probably would also have been unable to carry out a meaningful mobilization of society in support of the war effort. The meetings of the North Baltic Committee also served as forums where Estonian national aims would be discussed. See Jaan Tõnisson, "Autonoomialt—iseseisvusele," *Vabaduse tulekul*, 55–56; "Eesti autonoomia tuleku päevilt," in E. Laaman, ed., *Mälestused iseseisvuse võitluspäivilt* (Tallinn, 1927), 1:8.

3. Tõnisson, *Vabaduse tulekul*, 56–58; Tõnisson, *Mälestused*, 9. A reproduction of the document authorizing Raamot to conduct this inquiry can be found in Eduard Laaman, *Eesti iseseisvuse sünd* (Tartu, 1936; rpt. Stockholm, 1964), 87.

4. For accounts of the conference see Tõnisson, *Vabaduse tulekul*, 58–60; also Karl Ast's report in *Pealinna Teataja*, 15/28 March 1917. The proposal that came out of the Tartu conference is outlined in *Pealinna Teataja*, 17/30 March 1917.

5. *Sbornik ukazov i postanovlenii Vremennago Pravitel'stva* (Petrograd, 1917), 1:155–58. Estonian-language translations can be found in most Estonian newspapers of the period; also *Suur Sotsialistlik Oktoobrirevolutsioon Eestis: Dokumentide ja materjalide kogumik*

(Tallinn, 1957), 102–4. An English translation is given in Robert P. Browder and Alexander F. Kerensky, eds., *The Russian Provisional Government 1917* (Stanford, 1961), 1:300–301. The Browder-Kerensky translation contains the careless addition of a whole phrase [section III, article 5d: "assessment of general zemstvo taxes on the basis of existing laws"] that is not to be found in the original document.

6. Reinhard Wittram, "Die baltische Frage als Problem der russischen provisorischen Regierung," *Von den Baltischen Provinzen*, 74–75.

7. Article 5 of section III states: "The *guberniia* commissar, jointly with the provisional *guberniia zemskii soviet* shall have authority over: a) the management of local self-governmental affairs and of the zemstvo economy in the *guberniia*, b) the management of general administrative affairs . . . , g) the preliminary working out of questions concerning the composition of a draft of provisional regulations on the administrative order of the Estonian *guberniia* and of a statute on local self-government on the basis of universal, without distinction as to sex, equal, secret, direct, and proportional vote." Furthermore article 10 of section III states: "The *guberniia* and the *uezd zemskii soviets* are given the right to establish individual or collegial executive organs." *Sbornik ukazov*, 256–57.

8. N. Maim, "Eestimaa avaliku korra muutmise aktid vene siseministeeriumi peavalitsuses 1916. ja 1917. a.," *Vabaduse tulekul*, 74–75. Maim was an official of the Main Administration and was able to follow and participate in the bureaucratic politics leading to the implementation of the March 30 law.

9. Ibid., 76–77; see also Ants Piip, *Mälestused iseseisvuse võitluspäivilt*, 61–62. Maim was able to warn the Estonian delegation to the hearings of Veselovskii's intention; the Estonian delegates were then able to outmaneuver Veselovskii and shift the discussion back to the March 30 law.

10. Note to article 15 of "Pravila o vvedenii v deistvie postanovleniia Vremennago Pravitel'stva, 30 Marta, 1917 goda." The law and rules of implementation of the March 30 law were published as a special supplement to the *Estliandskiia gubernskiia vedomosti*, 5 July 1917.

11. This is the conclusion of K. Siilivask, who has examined the election protocols of about one-half of the *valds* in Estonia. *Veebruarist Oktoobrini 1917*, 269.

12. In the Viljandi *maakond*, for example, the Socialists were able to elect three of the five deputies to the *guberniia Maapäev* and ten of the fifteen to the *maakond* council. *Sakala*, 28 June/11 July 1917.

13. *MP*, no. 13, 20 July, 43; no. 14, 21 July, 45.

14. *MP*, no. 19, 2 August, 63–64; no. 30, 11 August, 102–5; no. 39, 25 September, 148. At a congress of educational curators in Petrograd the curator for the Baltic region, Grabar, opposed the reform that was adopted to hand over the administration of schools to self-governmental institutions. *Tallinna Teataja*, 14/27 August and 23 September/6 October 1917.

15. *Tallinna Teataja*, 9/22 May 1917; 10/23 June 1917; 8/21 September 1917.

16. *MP*, no. 30a, 25 August, 109.

17. *MP*, no. 30b, 25 August, 111.

18. Ibid., 113.

19. According to Artur Mägi the final party lineup of the 62 members was as follows: 5 Bolsheviks, 9 Estonian Social Democrats, 8 Estonian Socialist Revolutionaries, 11 Laborites (of whom 7 were Radical-Socialists), 7 from the Democratic party, 4 Radical Democrats, 13 from two Agrarian parties, 3 independents, and 1 German and 1 Swedish

minority representative. *Das Staatsleben Estlands*, 22.

20. *MP*, no. 39, 25 September, 148.

21. *MP*, no. 39, 25 September, 147.

22. *MP*, no. 40, 26 September, 153.

23. By October, however, the *maakond* councils were no longer receiving funds for the police from Petrograd on a regular basis. *MP*, no. 51, 7 October, 220.

24. *MP*, no. 56, 12 October, 245–47. The full budget adopted by the *Maapäev* may be found in *MP*, no. 57, 13 October, 253–58.

25. *Suur Sotsialistlik Oktoobrirevolutsioon Eestis*, 431–32.

26. Tõnisson, *Vabaduse tulekul*, 66.

27. *MP*, no. 59, 15 November, 273–74.

28. The Committee of Elders, which consisted of representatives from all Estonian political parties with the exception of the Bolsheviks, and the administrative board of the *Maapäev* voted in favor of Estonian independence being proclaimed at the earliest opportune moment at its meeting of December 31, 1917. The protocol of the meeting can be found in *Mälestused iseseisvuse võitluspäivilt*, 392–94.

29. *Sotsialdemokraat*, 17/30 November 1917.

30. The Bolsheviks justified their stopping the elections in the following terms (*Suur Sotsialistlik Oktoobrirevolutsioon Eestis*, 661): "The convening of the Estonian Constituent Assembly was to be a signal to the bourgeois secret societies to begin an armed rebellion. For that reason the Executive Committee of Estonian Working People's and Soldiers' Soviets decided to stop the elections to the Estonian Constituent Assembly and take extreme measures for the defense of the revolution." Of the votes cast in the elections the Bolsheviks received 37% (compared to 39.9% in the elections to the Russian Constituent Assembly in November 1917). The largest gains were registered by the Estonian Labor party, which received 29.8% of the vote (compared to 21.4% in the November elections). The Democratic bloc received 23.4% (compared to 22.4% in November). For statistics on the election see A. Helbe, "Esseeride tegevusest Eestis Oktoobrirevolutsiooni võidu ja Nõukogude võimu kindlustamise perioodil," *Eesti NSV ajaloo küsimusi*, 6, Tartu Riikliku Ulikooli Toimetised, 258 (Tartu, 1970): 376–94.

The 1919 German Campaign in the Baltic: The Final Phase

1. For details and an analysis of the Spring Campaign see Charles L. Sullivan, "The German Role in the Baltic Campaign—Spring 1919," *Baltic Review* 36 (October 1969): 40–62.

2. *DBFP*, 1st ser. (1949), III, 9–10; Emanuel du Parquet, *Der Drang nach Osten: L'Adventure Allemande en Lettonie* (Paris, 1926), 104–5.

3. HA, ARA, Documents, 1918–1922, XVII, 155–56; Sir Stephan Tallents, *Man and Boy* (London, 1943), 337; HA, Thomas J. Orbison Papers, "The Diary," 9 July 1919; Karl von Plehwe, *Im Kampfe gegen die Bolschewisten* (Berlin, 1926), 23.

4. *Deutsche Zeitung* (Berlin), 28 June 1919; *Die Ostwacht* (Allenstein), 2 July 1919; Karl Brammer, *Verfassungsgrundlagen und Hochverrat, nach stenographischen Verhandlungsberichten und amtlichen Urkunden des Jagow-Prozesses* (Berlin, 1922), 13–16.

5. U.S., *Senate Documents*, 66th Cong., 1st sess., 1919, XV, no. 105, 22–24; HA, ARA, XVII, 342–44.

6. Rüdiger von der Goltz, *Meine Sendung in Finnland und im Baltikum* (Leipzig, 1920), 219–20; Kurt Stavenhagen, *Die eigene Scholle in der Baltenmark* (Stuttgart, 1919), 1–20.

7. *Freiheit* (Berlin), 9 July 1919; *Die Trommel* (Jelgava-Mitau), 4 August 1919; Josef Bischoff, *Die letzte Front* (Berlin, 1935), 150–52, 174; Goltz, *Meine Sendung*, 235; Rüdiger von der Goltz, *Als politischer General im Osten, 1918-1919* (Leipzig, 1936), 136–37.

8. Pavel Mikhailovitch Awaloff-Bermondt, *Im Kampfe gegen den Bolschewismus* (Glückstadt, 1925), 142–54; Nikolai von Budberg, *Im Schatten der Toten* (1958), 39–41; *Leipziger Volkszeitung*, 27 March 1919; Wilhelm von Rosenberg, *Hinter den Kulissen der russischen Konterrevolution* (Hamburg, 1920), 9–11.

9. *DNDTF* (Berlin, 1937), III, 51–53; Goltz, *Meine Sendung*, 224–25; Gustav Noske, *Von Kiel bis Kapp* (Berlin, 1920), 179; Kurt von Braatz, *Fürst Anatol Pawlowitsch Lieven, Im Kampfe gegen den baltischen Separatismus, russischen Bolschewismus, und die Awaloff-Bermondt Affäre* (Stuttgart, 1926), 113–16.

10. *VVDN* (Berlin, 1920), vol. 327, 46th sess., 4 July 1919, 1298.

11. *DBFP*, 1st ser., III, 19–20; *DNDTF*, III, 40–42.

12. Goltz, *Meine Sendung*, 232; Bischoff, 176; Von Seeckt Papers, Hoover Institution, Item 140, dated 6 January 1920.

13. *FRUS, The Paris Peace Conference*, VII, 430; *DZA* (Potsdam), Waffenstillstandkommission, no. 279, sheets 128, 244, as cited by Günther Rosenfeld, *Sowjetrussland und Deutschland, 1917–1922* (Berlin, 1960), 222; *DBFP*, 1st ser., III, 80–81.

14. Sullivan, "The German Role," 48–51.

15. *VVDN*, vol. 328, 67th sess., 26 July 1919, 1962–70; *Baltische Heimat* (Riga), 19 July and 31 July 1919, 10 August 1919.

16. *Freiheit*, 5 July and 9 July 1919; *Vorwärts* (Berlin), 8 July 1919; *VVDN*, vol. 326, 46th sess., 4 July 1919, 1295–96; vol. 328, 64th sess., 23 July 1919, 1855; 67th sess., 26 July 1919, 1959–70.

17. *Latvijas Sargs* as quoted by *Rigasche Zeitung*, 9 July 1919; *Jaunakas Ziņas* [*sic*] as quoted by *Baltische Heimat*, 4 July 1919.

18. Goltz, *Meine Sendung*, 91–93; C. Jay Smith, *Finland and the Russian Revolution, 1917-1922* (Athens, Ga., 1958), 115–16.

19. It should be noted that this stage of the campaign took place during the period in which the German High Command was undergoing a process of dissolution under the terms of the Peace Treaty. The old High Command ceased to exist on the very day the Treaty of Strazdumuiža was signed. Its temporary replacement, the *Kommandostelle Kolberg* (*KSK*), was not able to oversee the operations of the *OKN* with any degree of authority, a fact that had much to do with the ability of the leaders of the "Bermondt Scheme" to cover their real plans until later in the fall. See Waldemar Erfurt, *Die Geschichte des deutschen Generalstabs von 1918 bis 1945* (Göttingen, 1957), 52–55.

20. *DBFP*, 1st ser., III, 80–81.

21. Otto Wilhelm Heinrich Wagener, *Von der Heimat geächtet* (Stuttgart, 1920), 36–45; Goltz, *Meine Sendung*, 214–15, 235; Goltz, *Als politischer General*, 134–36.

22. *Die Trommel*, 26 July 1919.

23. Goltz, *Meine Sendung*, 233–34; *DBFP*, 1st ser., III, 34–38; Tallents, 346–48; Sir Hubert Gough, *Soldiering On* (New York, 1957), 199.

24. Cordt von Brandis, *Baltikumer, Schicksal eines Freikorps* (Berlin, 1939), 213–16; Goltz, *Meine Sendung*, 236; *DNDTF*, III, 56

NOTES

25. Goltz, *Als politischer General*, 136–37, 141, 164; Bischoff, 152; Otto-Ernst Schued-dekopf, *Das Heer und Republik* (Hanover, 1955), 100–101.

26. *Baltische Blätter*, no. 25 (9 August 1919): 177; *Baltische Heimat*, 14 August 1919.

27. *DBFP*, 1st ser., III, 23, 40; *Paris Peace Conference*, VII, 303, 428–33.

28. Rosenfeld, 223–24; *DNDTF*, III, 61; Rene de Vanlande, *Avec Général Niessel en Prusse et en Lithuanie; La dernière defaite allemande* (Paris, 1921), 33, 39; Wipert von Blücher, *Deutschlands Weg nach Rapallo* (Wiesbaden, 1951), 76–77; Wagener, 2, 43; Erfurt, 57; Hauptmann von Medem, *Stürmer von Riga, Geschichte eines Freikorps* (Berlin, 1935), 91–95.

29. Goltz, *Meine Sendung*, 299–303.

30. "Aus den Groener Dokumenten," *Deutsche Rundschau*, 1950, nos. 7–12, as cited by Rosenfeld, 223; Goltz, *Meine Sendung*, 241–42; *DNDTF*, III, 61.

31. *DZA* (Potsdam), Büro des Reichspräsidenten, no. 51, item 53, as cited by Rosenfeld, 224; Goltz, *Meine Sendung*, 242–43; *VVDN*, vol. 330, 94th sess., 9 October 1919, 2959.

32. Bischoff, 189–90; *DNDTF*, III, 59–61; Brandis, 224; *Baltische Heimat*, 26 August and 27 August 1919.

33. Bischoff, 190; Ernst von Salomon, "Der Weg vom Freikorps zur freiwilligen russischen Westarmee," *Das Buch vom deutschen Freikorpkämpfer* (Berlin, 1938), 191.

34. The general stayed on with the full understanding of the German government, according to Foreign Minister Müller. See *VVDN*, vol. 330, 94th sess., 9 October 1919, 2959; *Berliner Tageblatt und Handels-Zeitung*, 27 August 1919.

35. Bischoff, 201; *Freiheit*, 5 September 1919.

36. Wagener, 46–47; Brandis, 211.

37. *Hamburger Nachrichten*, 6 September and 7 September 1919; *Berliner Tageblatt und Handels-Zeitung*, 6 September 1919.

38. Hardly a session went by between July and October without some mention of the activities of the *Baltikumer*s. Extended debates took place on July 4, July 23, July 26, July 28, October 8, October 9, and October 10.

39. *DBFP*, 1st ser., III, 120–25. Curzon thought that von der Goltz had 120,000 men under arms, about triple the actual figure.

40. Goltz, *Meine Sendung*, 266–67; *DNDTF*, III, 71–72; *Baltische Heimat*, 18 September 1919.

41. Bischoff, 251–56.

42. *DNDTF*, III, 75; Goltz, *Als politischer General*, 150; Goltz, *Meine Sendung*, 270–71; For Noske's duplicity in this matter see *DBFP*, 1st ser., III, 127–28.

43. *Paris Peace Conference*, VIII, 231–32, 254–63, 342, 406–7, 416–17, 419–20.

44. Wagener, 57–58; *Baltische Blätter*, no. 34 (11 October 1919), 250–51; Goltz *Als politischer General*, 151; Goltz, *Meine Sendung*, 268, 271; Bischoff, 213; *DNDTF*, III, 83–87.

45. *Paris Peace Conference*, VIII, 517–19; Bischoff, 212–15; Wagener, 58–59.

46. Awaloff-Bermondt, 224–25; *DNDTF*, III, 88–89; *Rigasche Rundschau*, 11 November 1919.

47. *DBFP*, 1st ser., III, 155–56. By the end of the month the British had eliminated German shipping from the Baltic Sea. Some 58 ships lay idle at Stettin; the Pomeranian fishing fleet had been swept from the sea. See *Deutsche Tagezeitung* (Berlin), 17 through 25 October 1919; *Deutsche Soldaten-Zeitung* (Jelgava), 26 October and 29 October 1919.

48. Alfred Erich Senn, *The Emergence of Modern Lithuania* (New York, 1959), 185–88.

49. Wagener, 99–115; Orbison Diary, 11 November 1919; Bischoff, 233; *DNDTF*, III, 109–10.

50. *DNDTF*, III, 128–31; Wagener, 126, 135; Georg von Rauch, *The Baltic States* (Berkeley, Calif., 1974), 68–69.

51. Ernst von Salomon, *Die geächteten* (Berlin, 1930), 167–71; Erich Balla, *Landesknechte wurden wir . . . Abenteuer im Baltikum* (Berlin, 1932), 226–31; Friederich Wilhelm von Oertzen, *Kamerad, reich mir die Hände, Freikorps und Grenzschutz, Baltikum und Heimat* (Berlin, 1933), 132–39; Walter Duranty, *I Write As I Please* (New York, 1935), 38–40.

52. *FRUS, Paris Peace Conference*, IX, 604; *DBFP*, 1st ser., III, 248; Wagener, 159.

53. Goltz, *Als politischer General*, 160–61.

54. Gustav Noske, *Erlebtes aus Aufstieg und Niedergang einer Demokratie* (Offenbach, 1947), 126–27; *DBFP*, 1st ser., III, 248.

55. Bischoff, 242–47; Vanlande, 152; Wilhelm Hoegner, *Die verratene Republik* (Munich, 1958), 59–66; Ernst von Salomon, *Putsch und Verschwörung* (Frankfurt a.M., 1938), 4–5; *The Times* (London), 19 March, 20 March, 22 March, and 24 March 1920.

56. Hans zur Megede, "Die baltische Tragödie," *Der Schulungsbrief*, 1, no. 4 (June, 1934): 20–28.

The *Land Oberost* and Its Place in Germany's *Ostpolitik*, 1915–1918

1. Some insignificant groups in Germany did oppose annexation. See Egmont Zechlin, "Die Zentralorganisation für einen dauernden Frieden und die Mittelmächte," *Jahrbuch für Internationales Recht* 2 (1962): 448–511.

2. S. Grumbach, *Das annexionistische Deutschland* (Lausanne, 1917), 126.

3. According to Erich Ludendorff's evidence, the military command's policy in the *Land Oberost*, obviously annexionistic, had always had the endorsement of the *Reichskanzler*. See *Meine Kriegserinnerungen, 1914–1918* (Berlin, 1919), 426. G. Ritter writes that Bethmann Hollweg agreed to the annexation only after April 5, 1916; *Staatskunst und Kriegshandwerk*, vol. 3. *Die Tragödie der Staatskunst: Bethmann Hollweg als Kriegskanzler* (Munich, 1964), 143.

4. Werner Basler, *Deutschlands Annexionspolitik in Polen und im Baltikum* (Berlin, 1962); *Borba za sovetskuiu vlast' v Pri-Baltike* (Moscow, 1967); B. Sīpols, *Za kulisami inostrannoi interventsii v Latvii 1918–1920* (Moscow, 1959); A. S. Stražas, *Germanskaia politika kolonizatsii i germanizatsii Litvy v pervie gody pervoi mirovoi voiny* (Leningrad, 1958). Western works include Ulrich Le Coutre, *Die Probleme des Baltikums und die Mächte 1918–1919* (Kiel, 1962); Gerd Linde, *Die Deutsche Politik in Litauen im Ersten Weltkrieg* (Wiesbaden, 1965); "Um die Angliederung Kurlands und Litauens," *Jahrbücher für Geschichte Osteuropas* 1 (1962); Bernhard Mann, *Die baltischen Länder in der deutschen Kriegszielpublizistik 1914–1918* (Tübingen, 1965).

5. F. F. Epstein, "Neue Literatur zur Geschichte der Ostpolitik im Ersten Weltkrieg," *Jahrbücher für Geschichte Osteuropas* 14 (1966): 81.

6. Our sources are based mainly on the following: (*a*) *Dokumente der deutschen Militärverwaltung*—a great number of handwritten and typed thoughts, notes, orders, and district reports of officials at various administrative levels that in 1954 were found in LCVIA, F. 641, in a disorderly mass. These documents reflect the constant collaboration

between the central government and the senior officials of the "German military administration Ober Ost." Drafts of the district reports of lower-level officials show that the printed version often was "embellished." Especially informative are the calculations for the postwar state of "Neuland," which was to include all the territory of the "Land of the Commander in Chief Ost." (b) Documents of the Lithuanian Cabinet of Ministers, the War Ministry, and others in LCVA, 1918–1920, F. 383/58, 384/59, 923/465, etc.). These documents contain the minutes of the *Taryba*, notes and outlines relative to negotiations with the military administration and the government of the Reich, and others. (c) LMARS, XVII, 44, 45, MB-V, etc., which contains documents from the archives of the German military administration, documents of the Lithuanian Scientific Society, and a number of private archives. Among these are all the documents of the so-called Organization Committee, which convened the conference that elected the *Taryba*. (d) VURS, R.S. 2340, F. 493, etc., which contains a number of highly informative documents on the municipalities organized on a democratic basis after the departure of the Russian forces and before the arrival of the Germans. (e) AVPR, F. Osob—politotdel, Kanceliariia—"Voina," Missiia v Berne, etc. These documents contain considerable information on a number of questions, such as the political and settlement activities of the Baltic Germans, war aims, and attitudes toward nationalism in the Baltic provinces. (f) TsGVIA, F. 2003, 2005, 2007, 2031, etc., which contains reports on negotiations and contacts in neutral states concerning Baltic questions and factions in the Lithuanian, Latvian, and other national movements. Of special interest are the documents about the partisan movement in the occupied territories, which was organized, and later disbanded, by the Russian General Staff. (g) The German archives were brought to Moscow at the end of World War II, kept in the IDA, and later returned to East Germany. The exchange of personal and official letters between Bethmann Hollweg and the ambassadors in the *Bundesstaaten* on the question of the Lithuanian and Courland crowns are located here. (h) DZA (Merseburg), Hist. Abt. II, contains numerous documents relating to the political future of Lithuania and Courland as planned in the spring and summer of 1918.

7. Gert von Pistohlkors (Göttingen) criticizes Leonard Lundin. "Political Problems of the German Balts before World War I," Third Conference on Baltic Studies in Scandinavia (Stockholm, 1975).

8. Otto Kessler states that 20,000 German peasants were settled in Courland during the nine years before the war. *Die Baltenländer und Litauen* (Berlin, 1916), 114.

9. Komaroff-Kurloff, *Das Ende des russischen Kaisertums* (Berlin, 1920). TsGVIA, F. 2005, op. 1, d. 101, 1. 236; see also secret information of the Russian General Staff of October 5, 1914 (11, 12, 16–17); police report of October 23, 1914 (53); report of the Deputy Minister of Interior Affairs, Commander of the Special Gendarme Corps, Major-General Dzhunkovskii, of September 20, 1914 (70–72); cf. V. S. Diakin, "Pervaia mirovaia voina i meropriiatiia po likvidatsii tak nazivaemogo "nemetskogo zasiliia," *Nauchnaia sessiia po istorii pervoi mirovoi voiny*, Sektsiia 11 (Moscow, 1964), 1–5.

10. TsGVIA, F. 2005, op. 1, d. 101, 1. 49, 301, 307.

11. Rüdiger von der Goltz, *Meine Sendung in Finnland und im Baltikum* (Leipzig, 1920), 36.

12. Cf. K. Žukas, *Žvilgsnis į praeitį, žmogaus ir kario atsiminimai: medžiaga istorikams* (Chicago, 1959), 23, 99–100.

13. *Statistinės žinios apie Lietuvą ligi karui 1914* (Kaunas, 1919), 56–59. Data on the area's population from the same source and from LCVIA, F. 641, op. 1, etc.

14. Kessler, 40; TsGVIA, F. 2005, op. 1, d. 101, 1. 248.

15. Ritter, 89, 142, 604.

16. Cf. Egmont Zechlin, *Die deutsche Politik und die Juden im ersten Weltkrieg* (Göttingen, 1969), 125.

17. Henry Cord Meyer, *Mitteleuropa in German Thought and Action* (The Hague, 1955), 255.

18. André Scherer and Jacques Grünewald, *L'Allemagne et les problèmes de la paix pendant la première guerre mondiale. Documents extraits des archives de l'Office Allemand des Affaires Étrangères* (Paris, 1961), 2: 37.

19. AVPR, F. Osobpolitotdel, op. 474, d. 137, 1. 4 (Zapiska russkogo politicheskogo agenta v Shveitsarii, January 20, 1916).

20. M. Urbšienė, *Vokiečių karo meto spauda ir Lietuva* (Kaunas, 1939), 42–43.

21. *Kurjer Poznański*, no. 154, 9 July 1918; *Nowa Reforma*, no. 214, 13 May 1918; *Verhandlungen des Reichstags*, Stenographische Berichte, B.331 (Berlin, 1918), 4309.

22. LCVIA, F. 641, ap. 1, b. 967 (Verwaltungsordnung); b. 883a, 167; Ludendorff, 158.

23. A. S. Stražas, "Kolonial'nyi rezhim germanskikh imperialistov v Litve (1915–1918)," *Voprosy istorii* (1958, no. 12), 76–77.

24. *Das Land Oberost: Deutsche Arbeit in den Verwaltungsgebieten Kurland, Litauen und Bialystok-Grodno*, herausgegeben im Auftrage des Oberbefehlshabers Ost, bearbeitet von der Presseabteilung Ober Ost (Stuttgart and Berlin, 1917), 79.

25. C. Rivas, *La Lituanie sous le joug allemand 1915–1918. Le plan annexioniste allemand en Lituanie* (Lausanne, 1919), 513; cf. Pr. Žadeikis, *Didžiojo karo užrašai* (Klaipėda, 1921), 1 : 6.

26. A. Stražas, "Die deutsche Militärverwaltung Oberost Prototyp der geplanten Kolonialadministration 'Neuland' (1915–1918)," *Wissenschaftliche Zeitschrift der Pädagogischen Hochschule "Dr. Theodor Neubauer," Erfurt—Mühlhausen, gesellschafts—und sprachwissenschaftliche Reihe* 8 (1971):1H.

27. LCVIA, b. 52, 1. 137; b. 53, 1. 2, etc.; Ludendorff, 145.

28. E. Direnberger, *Oberste Heeresleitung und Reichsleitung 1914–1918* (Berlin, 1939), 37.

29. M. Ragana, *La Lituanie sous la botte allemande* (Paris, 1917), 16.

30. LMARS, MB-V, 1. 11.

31. Prof. Dr. Dr. Bredt, *Der Deutsche Reichstag im Weltkrieg: Das Werk des Untersuchungsausschusses der Verfassungsgebenden Deutschen Nationalversammlung und des Deutschen Reichstages*, 4. Reihe, *Die Ursachen des deutschen Zusammenbruches im Jahre 1918*, B.8 (Berlin, 1926), 159.

32. Cf. Gerd Linde, "Um die Angliederung Kurlands und Litauens," *Jahrbücher für Geschichte Osteuropas* 10 (1962, no. 4): 566.

33. For information on personnel see Alfred Kruck, *Geschichte des Alldeutschen Verbandes 1890–1939* (Wiesbaden, 1954), 137, 179; Robert Stupperich, "Siedlungspläne im Gebiet des Oberbefehlshabers Ost (Militärverwaltung Litauen und Kurland) während des Weltkrieges," *Jomsburg* (1941, no. 5), 362; LCVA, F. 384/59, ap. 3, b. 26, 11. 189–91.

34. LCVIA, F. 641, ap. 1, b. 883, 1. 14, 22, 23 (Ergebnis der Besprechungen am 17 und 18 April 1916).

35. Ibid., F. 641, ap. 1, b. 697, 697b (Finanzberichte, Oberost). Further on the situation, see ibid., b. 975, 1. 17; 971, 1.90; 1. 18–22.

36. A. Stražas, "Hamburgo karo tikslai ir jo ekspansija į Pabaltijį 1914–1918 m.," *Istorija* 10 (1969).

37. LCVA, F. 384/59, ap. 3, b. 1, 1. 191.

38. From the speech of a Polish deputy in the *Reichstag* on July 5, 1918, *Kurjer Poznański*, no. 154, 9 July 1918.

39. Data on economic and financial policies in LCVIA, F. 641, ap. 1, b. 978 (Verordnungsblatt, no. 1, 28 January 1916, 1–2; Verordnungsblatt no. 15, 30 June 1916, 190); no. 5, 12 March 1916, 57; b. 53, 1. 209; b. 978. On currency and the black market, see LCVA, F. 923, ap. 1, b. 9, 1. 3 (minutes of a sitting of the Lithuanian Council of Ministers, 14 November 1918); CGVIA, F. 2003, op. 1, d. 1657, 1. 469.

40. LMARS, 156 MB-5 1. 19.

41. According to the Russian Ministry of Foreign Affairs, the number of Lithuanians in the United States was only 610,000 (AVPR, F. Osobpolitotdel, op. 474, d. 138, 1. 35).

42. Antoine Viscont, *La Lituanie et la guerre* (Geneva, 1917), 145.

43. K. Pakštas, "Lietuvių amerikiečių kovos dėl Lietuvos nepriklausomybės," *Židinys* (1938, no. 5–6): 640.

44. A. Dambrauskas, *Mano užrašai* (unpublished part), VURS, K.U.F., b. 1089, 215.

45. F. Fischer, "Deutsche Kriegsziele, Revolutionierung und Separatfrieden im Osten," *Historische Zeitschrift* 188 (1959): 295; cf. Alfred Erich Senn, *The Russian Revolution in Switzerland* (Madison, Wisc., 1971), 61; cf. Roy E. Heath and Alfred Erich Senn, "Edmont Privat and the Commission of the East in 1918," *Journal of Baltic Studies* 6 (1975, no. 1): 9, 15.

46. F. Norus and J. Žilius, *Lithuania's Case for Independence* (Washington, 1918), 71. According to the Russian Ministry of Foreign Affairs, 120,000 Lithuanians lived in Lithuania Minor (AVPR, F. Osobpolitotdel, op. 474, d. 138, 1. 35).

47. A. Steponaitis, *Atsiminimai 1914–1919* (Kaunas, 1940), 76.

48. AVPR, F. Osobpolitotdel, op. 474, d. 147, 11. 12–13.

49. TsGVIA, F. 2003, op. 1, d. 1657.

50. Data on Bibikoff, Pokrovskii, and Gabrys in AVPR, F. Osobpolitotdel, op. 474, d. 143, 11. 6–8; d. 103, 1. 3; d. 139, 1. 14. F. Missiia v Berne, op. 843/3, d. 807, 11. 6–7.

51. *Santara*, 5 May 1917.

52. AVPR, F. Osobpolitotdel, op. 474, d. 77, 1. 23: Circular telegram of October 25, 1917, from Tereshchenko to ambassadors. On Gabrys, F. Osobpolitotdel, op. 474, d. 134, 1. 17; d. 143, 1. 12^v–13 (the exact date is not given).

53. LCVIA, F. 641, ap. 1, b. 53, 1. 76.

54. TsGVIA, F. 2007, dd. 67, 68, etc.

55. A. S. Stražas, "Borba litovskogo naroda protiv germanskikh kolonizatorov 1915–1917," *Voprosy Istorii* (1959, no. 10).

56. *Czas*, no. 644, 23 December 1916.

57. LCVIA, F. 641, ap. 1, b. 964, 1. 42 (Dienstanweisung für die Inspekteure).

58. AVPR, F. Osobpolitotdel, op. 474, d. 56, a. 36 ("Patent" of 12 September 1917).

59. F. Fischer, *Griff nach der Weltmacht* (Düsseldorf, 1961), 617–18.

60. Scherer, *Grünewald*, Documents 91, 98, 100.

61. A. Thimme, "Gustav Stresemann, 297–298, Legende und Wirklichkeit," *Historische Zeitschrift* 181 (1956).

62. TsGVIA, F. 2003, op. 1, d. 1657, 1. 468.

63. Fischer, "*Deutsche Kriegsziele*," 277.

64. A. Stražas, "1917 m. Popiežiaus taikos nota ir lietuvių nacionalistų paslaugos

Vokietijos imperializmui," *Istorija* 3 (1962); Scherer, *Grünewald*, 309.

65. LCVIA, F. 641, ap. 1, b. 966; see A. Stražas, "Militärverwaltung."

66. A. Stražas, "Protivorechiia v germanskom soiuze i vopros o prestolakh Litvy i Kurliandii v gody pervoi mirovoi voiny," *Istoriia* 11 (1970).

67. See A. Strazhas, "Der litauische Landesrat als Instrument der deutschen Ost-politik, 1917–1918," *Jahrbücher für Geschichte Osteuropas* 25 (1977).

68. "Erläuterung zu dem Entwurf eines Bündnisvertrags zwischen dem Deutschen Reich, dem Herzogtum Kurland, dem Grossfürstentum Litauen," DZA (Merseburg), Ministerium des Innern, Rep. 77, Tit. 49, no. 52, 50; Gerd Linde, "Um die Angliederung Kurlands und Litauens," *Jahrbücher für Geschichte Osteuropas* 10, (1962, no. 4).

69. *Verhandlungen des Reichstags*, B. 311, 4435.

70. Bredt, 273; Fischer, *Griff nach der Weltmacht*, 608.

71. Direnberger, 57.

72. E. Zechlin, "Friedensbestrebungen und Revolutionierungsversuche," *Aus Politik und Zeitgeschichte*, 15 May 1963, 19; A. S. Stražas, "'Zemlia Oberost' i germanskie tseli voiny na vostoke v gody pervoi mirovoi voiny," *Voprosy istorii* (1964, no. 8).

73. IDA, F. M. N.63/P19, no. 141.

74. G. Stresemann, *Reden und Schriften, Politik, Geschichte, Literatur, 1897–1926* (Dresden, 1926), 2:329.

75. Fischer, "*Deutsche Kriegsziele*," 308.

76. K. H. Janssen, *Macht und Verblendung* (Berlin-Frankfurt-Zürich, 1963), 204.

The Rise of Authoritarian Rule in the Baltic States

1. *Komunistas* (Vilnius), no. 9 (1976): 56.

2. These and other data on parliaments from V. Stanley Vardys, "The Baltic Nations in Search of Their Own Political Systems," *East European Quarterly* (January 1974): 402ff.

3. A. Pankseev et al., *Zhiz'nenaia sila leninskikh printsipov partiinogo stroitel'stva* (Tallinn, 1975), 67, 68.

4. Royal Institute of International Affairs, *The Baltic States* (London, 1938), 105.

5. Aleksandras Merkelis, *Antanas Smetona* (New York, 1964), 328; Kazys Škirpa, in Antanas Rūkas, *Mykolas Sleževičius* (Chicago, 1954), 257ff.

6. Letter by Krupavičius, in Juozas Eretas, *Stasys Šalkauskis* (Brooklyn, N.Y., 1960), 116. See also Petras Maldeikis, *Mykolas Krupavičius* (Chicago, 1975), 196–206. While some military sympathizers and younger members aided the coup, the leadership was divided. Some, like the former president Aleksandras Stulginskis, warned of collaboration; others shared Krupavičius' feelings. Some Christian Democratic supporters, such as the leader of the dominant Catholic Action organization "Ateitis," Professor Stasys Šalkauskis, denounced the coup.

7. Text of M. Sleževičius' speech in Daugirdaitė-Sruogienė, *Lietuvos Steigiamasis Seimas* (New York, 1975), 190.

8. Stasys Šalkauskis' article in *Židinys*, nos. 6–7 (1926): 440, cited by Zenonas Ivinskis, *Politinis nepriklausomos Lietuvos gyvenimas* (London, 1969), 11.

9. Records of the meeting of Lithuanian bishops on October 6–8, 1926 (archival document).

10. Stasys Raštikis, *Kovose dėl Lietuvos* 1 (Los Angeles, 1956), 202.

11. *The New York Times*, 22 December 1926: 5.

12. Cited by Tõnu Parming, *The Collapse of Liberal Democracy and the Rise of Authoritarianism in Estonia* (London-Beverly Hills, 1975), 33.

13. Seppo Myllyniemi, *Die Neuordnung der baltischen Länder, 1941–1944* (Helsinki, 1973), 31.

14. Election data from an official Estonian statistical bulletin, cited in Parming, 44. A brief analysis of the newly adopted constitution appears in Henn-Jüri Uibopuu, "The Constitutional Development of the Estonian Republic," *Journal of Baltic Studies* 1 (1973): 18–22.

15. *The New York Times*, 14 March 1934: 12. On April 14 the newspaper reported (p. 9) that 200 fascist leaders had been placed on trial and charged with collusion with Berlin. Seven ringleaders were sentenced to prison terms. The importance of the Veterans in the conflict is discussed by Imre Lipping, in Arvīds Ziedonis et al., eds., *Baltic History* (Columbus, Ohio 1974), 209–16. See also Parming's study and Uibopuu's constitutional analysis as well as Seppo Myllyniemi, 29–31. According to Myllyniemi (German archives and von Rosenberg's diary), some leaders of the Veterans (Dr. Hjalmar Mäe) were in continuous contact with Dr. Peter Kleist in the German Foreign Ministry and discussed the policies that Estonia should pursue if the Veterans came to power. Mäe's plan included a customs and currency union with Germany as well as a common army and foreign policy.

16. Malbone W. Graham, *New Governments of Eastern Europe* (New York, 1927), 345.

17. Georg von Rauch, *The Baltic States: The Years of Independence* (Berkeley, 1974), 151.

18. Royal Institute, 54–55. For further information on the Thunder Cross movement see Myllyniemi, 31–32; Jürgen von Hehn, *Lettland zwischen Demokratie und Diktatur* (Munich, 1957), 25–26.

19. Royal Institute, 54; U.S. House of Representatives, Select Committee to Investigate Communist Aggression, *Third Interim Report* (Washington, 1954), 115.

20. Royal Institute, 55.

21. Arnolds Spekke, *History of Latvia* (Stockholm, 1957), 376. Myllyniemi suggests that Ulmanis, like Päts, acted only against the extreme nationalists, 31–32.

22. Declaration cited in Alfred Bilmanis, *A History of Latvia* (Princeton, 1947), 359; full text in Hehn, 64–66; *The New York Times*, 3 June 1934: IV, 3, commented that Ulmanis "ended [the] Nazi threat" and prevented the Nazis and the Socialists from "conspiring against each other to obtain control of the country by a coup d'état." The Latvian Supreme Court, however, did not find the accused Socialist leaders guilty of such conspiracy. Hehn, 40–41.

23. Documents 2952-PS and 2953-PS, *Trial of the Major War Criminals Before the International Military Tribunal, Nuremberg, 14 November 1945–1 October 1946* (Nuremberg, 1948), XXXI, 385–91. The German Foreign Ministry authorized grants of small amounts of money, but not weapons, for the founding of a National Socialist party and for organizing anti-Semitic activities in Lithuania. These documents do not explain who received these contributions of "some hundreds of marks." Voldemaras himself apparently was not involved in these machinations, since at that time he lived in exile in France, totally withdrawn from politics. The "Voldemarists" were merely using his name to attract followers.

24. Von Rauch, 154–61ff.

25. According to figures compiled by Alfred Bilmanis, *Baltic Essays* (Washington, 1945), 217–18.

26. For example, Romuald J. Misiunas has found the fascist influence in Lithuania to be very severely confined. See his "Fascist Tendencies in Lithuania," *Slavonic and East European Review* 48, no. 119 (January, 1970): 97ff.

27. Royal Institute, 36.

28. Bilmanis, *A History of Latvia*, 192.

29. See Ernst Albert Plieg, *Das Memelland, 1920–39* (Würzburg, 1962), 119–37; Martin Broszat, "Die Memeldeutschen Organisationen und der Nationalsozialismus," *Gutachten des Instituts für Zeitgeschichte* (Munich, 1958), 1:395–400.

30. *Encyclopedia Judaica* (1971), 11:382; *Lietuvių Enciklopedija* (1966), 35:291–92; *XX Amžius* (Kaunas), 12 April 1940:4. According to Max M. Lazerson, "The Jewish Minorities in the Baltic Countries," *Jewish Social Studies* 3 (1941): 275, in Lithuania the number of Hebrew-language schools grew quicker than in any other country in the world except Palestine. In 1938 Lithuania's Jews constituted 7.2% of the republic's population. The other minorities were smaller. The Germans had 4.1%, the Poles 3%, the Russians 2.3%, and 2.6% were classified as "others." See *Lietuvos statistikos metraštis 1939m* (Vilnius, 1940), 16.

31. Finance Department of the Ministry of Finance, *Receipts and Expenditures of the Republic of Lithuania for the Year 1938* (Kaunas, 1938), 53. The Jews were budgeted to receive a subsidy of Lt 105,500 (1 litas was approximately 20 United States cents); the Catholics—Lt 1,376,778; Evangelical Reformed believers—Lt 26,360; Evangelical Lutherans—Lt 88,000; Greek Orthodox Lt 60,360; Old believers—Lt 31,920; Karaites —Lt 400; Moslems—Lt 2400.

32. See Alfred Blaustein's collection of world constitutions, published by Oceana, the volume on special sovereignties and dependencies.

33. Parming, 59–60.

34. Rein Taagepera regards Konstantin Päts as a voluntary manager of the Estonian system toward a democracy by semi-authoritarian means. See "Civic Culture and Authoritarianism in the Baltic States, 1930–1940," *East European Quarterly*, no. 4 (January 1974): 411. Imre Lepping maintains that in 1937 Päts reached his own "outer limit" of democratization. Similarly, despite opposition to further democratization by the Nationalist party, I have maintained that in Lithuania the "liberalizing trend could not be reversed." See V. Stanley Vardys, ed., *Lithuania Under the Soviets* (New York, 1965), 38. This view is disputed by Leonas Sabaliūnas, *Lithuania in Crisis: From Nationalism to Communism* (Bloomington, Indiana, 1972), 214–15.

Ethnic Minorities in the Estonian and Latvian Parliaments: The Politics of Coalition

1. Demographic data from Georg von Rauch, *The Baltic States: The Years of Independence* (Berkeley, 1974), 81–86.

2. Latvia's Constituent Assembly had 150 members; the parliament had 100. The

Germans and the Jews each had six representatives in the Constituent Assembly, while the Russians had four and the Poles had one. In the four parliaments between 1922 and 1934 the Germans had six representatives, except in the second *Saeima*, which had five Germans. The Russians had three deputies in the first parliament, five in the second, and six in the remaining two. In the first parliament these consisted of one representative each from the Christian Union of Latvian Orthodox, the Party for Communal Activities, and the National Union. In the second parliament the Christian Union had two, the Party of the Orthodox had two, and the Party for Communal Affairs had one. In the third, the Party of Communal Affairs increased its number to two. This dropped again in the fourth parliament. The remaining seat fell to a new group, Union of Russian Farmers. Jewish representatives in the first *Saeima* consisted of two from *Agudas Isroel*, two from *Misrachi*, and one each from *Zeire Zion* and the Socialist Workers' party (*Bund*). In the second parliament, *Agudas Isroel* kept its two seats, while the others equally shared the remaining three. In the third parliament, *Agudas Isroel* lost one, *Misrachi* won an additional seat, while the others kept one each. In the fourth parliament, *Zeire Zion* and the *Bund* were no longer represented. *Agudas Isroel* had two and *Misrachi* one representative.

In Estonia, the Germans had three and the Russians one member in the Constituent Assembly. In the first parliament (1920) the Germans won four seats and the Russians one. In the second, the German number dropped to three and the Russian increased to four. In the third, the Germans again dropped to two and the Russians to three. In the fourth and last democratic parliament (1929–1932) the Germans and the Russians had two seats each. In addition, the Swedes won one seat. See Ewald Ammende, ed., *Die Nationalitäten in den Staaten Europas. Sammlung von Lageberichten* (Vienna-Leipzig, 1931), 14–19, 30–33; *Die Nationalitäten in den Staaten Europas Ergänzungen* (Vienna-Leipzig, 1932), 4–7; Michail Kurchinskii, "Russen und Ukrainer," *Süddeutsche Monatshefte* (1928/29):717–18; Albert Salts, *Die politischen Parteien Lettlands*, Lettland-Bücherei, 7 (Riga, 1926):42–47.

3. *Rigasche Rundschau*, 3 June 1931.

4. Wolfgang Wachtsmuth, *Von deutscher Arbeit in Lettland*, Vol. 3: *Das politische Gesicht der deutschen Volksgruppe in Lettland in der parlamentarischen Periode 1918–1934* (Cologne, 1953), 351–52. For minority activities in the parliaments see ibid., 374–424.

5. Georg von Rauch, "Schweden und Russen in Estland," *Baltische Monatshefte* 5 (1936):216.

6. Wachtsmuth, 349; Ammende (1931), 32–33.

7. Baron Wilhelm von Fircks, "Volkstum und Bodenständigkeit," *Baltische Monatsschrift* 58 (1927): 35–43.

8. Letter from Lothar Schoeler, 7 June 1921; Friedrich W. Just [Wolfgang Wachtsmuth], *Von deutscher Arbeit in Lettland*, unpublished manuscript, 2 (Riga, 1939), 39; Protocol of the Baltic German Democratic Party, 10 January 1924, in Just, 2:65.

9. Protocol of the Committee of the Baltic German Parties, 20 and 26 November 1925, in Just, 2:93–95.

10. Protocol of the People's Party, 20 March 1930, in Just, 2: 101.

11. Protocol of the Baltic German Democratic Party, 20 August 1919, in Just, 1:216; Wachtsmuth, 134.

12. Complete text is given in Just, 1:220–21.

13. Wachtsmuth, 129–30; Hans von Rimscha, "Paul Schiemann als Minderheitenpolitiker," *Vierteljahrshefte für Zeitgeschichte* 4 (1956):51.

14. *Revaler Bote*, 15 June 1923.

15. *Revaler Bote*, 22 March 1923.

16. For preparations for elections, demands, and committee assignments see Wachtsmuth, 356–60; Just, 1:589.

17. As it did later on in the Committee, the Baltic German Progressive party preferred a presidency that would change hands every month, while Schiemann, Baron Fircks, and the Jews pleaded for a permanent one (Just, 1:364–65). The Progressive party had first objected to the forming of the minority bloc as "an activity tending towards the government" (Protocol of the Reform Party, 6 May 1920, in Wachtsmuth, 358). This opposition was quite different from that of the Conservatives.

18. Protocol of the Reform Party, 20 May 1920, in Wachtsmuth, 361.

19. Circular issued at its founding, Protocol of the Minority Committee, 13 May 1920; Protocol of the Reform Party, 15 April and 6 August 1920; in Just, 1:368–69. *Rigasche Rundschau*, 18 June 1920.

20. Paul Schiemann, in *Jahrbuch des baltischen Deutschtums* (1923), 33; Wachtsmuth, 361–62; in September 1920 a delegation consisting of Edwin Magnus, Moritz Mintz, and A. Bochagov appeared before the minister of education, Juris Plahkis, and protested against the government's intention of reviewing the school system of the minorities (Protocol of the Reform Party, 24 September 1920, in Just, 2:261).

21. Riots occurred on June 1 and 2; a call for boycotting the "Hebrews" appeared in *Latvijas Kareivis*, 10 June 1920 (Just, 1:378–79).

22. Protocol of the Minority Committee, 23 and 24 July 1920, in Just, 1:380–81.

23. The government had the right only to certify or not to certify the changes proposed by the minorities (Protocol of the Committee of Baltic German Parties, 6 December 1920; Protocol of the Minority Committee, 8 December 1920, in Just, 1:386).

24. Protocol of the Minority Committee, 26 May 1920, in Just, 1:387.

25. Protocol of the Minority Committee, 7 November 1921. Hellmann made his attacks against the Germans in a speech on 25 December 1920 (ibid.). See the press controversy between Schiemann, Hellmann, and a second Jewish delegate in *Rigasche Rundschau*, 5, 8, and 10 January 1921. Protocol of the Reform Party, 14 January 1921, in Just, 1:388.

26. *Rigasche Rundschau*, 1 and 2 October 1921. Protocol of the Minority Committee, 3 October 1921, in Just, 1:393.

27. Schiemann, in *Jahrbuch des baltischen Deutschtums* (1928):30; Fritz Wertheimer, *Von deutschen Parteien und Parteiführern im Ausland* (Berlin, 1930), 54–55.

28. See Wertheimer, 41; Oswald Hartge, in *Jahrbuch des baltischen Deutschtums* (1930): 71–72.

29. *Rigasche Rundschau*, 22 April 1931.

30. Arthur Mägi, *Das Staatsleben Estlands während seiner Selbständigkeit* (Stockholm, 1967), 321.

31. Wertheimer, 41.

32. *Rigasche Rundschau*, 11 May 1921.

33. Ibid., 14 November 1931; they were the Russians Jānis Pommers, Kornilev, and Leontin Shpolianskii.

34. *Revaler Bote*, 6 and 13 December 1921; 7, 9, and 10 March 1923; 30 August 1923.

35. Protocol of the Minority Committee, 26 May 1921; 12 and 20 December 1921; 3 April 1922; in Just, 2:38.

36. Schiemann, *Jahrbuch des baltischen Deutschtums* (1928), 30; Wachtsmuth, 370.

37. Protocol of the Minority Committee, 15 November 1923; 7 and 21 December 1923; 7, 22, and 23 January 1924; in Just, 2:328–30.

38. Protocol of the Democratic Party, 14 February 1924; Stavenhagen report of 8 February 1924; in Just, 2:330–31.

39. Schiemann, in *Königsberger Hartungsche Zeitung*, 13 January 1927; *Jahrbuch des baltischen Deutschtums* (1928):31; Wertheimer, 57–60.

40. *Revaler Bote*, 2 June 1921; Wachtsmuth, 186.

41. *Neue Zeit*, 2 February 1935.

42. Text of proceedings discussed in Wachtsmuth, 187–88.

43. Protocol of the Minority Committee, 18 October 1927, in Just, 1:401.

44. For detailed literature about the *coups d'état* and the development of new constitutional conditions see Michael Garleff, *Deutschbaltische Politik zwischen den Weltkriegen* (Bonn, 1976).

The Baltic States between Nazi Germany and Soviet Russia

1. For a summary of the foreign relations of the Baltic States see Leonas Sabaliūnas, *Lithuania in Crisis* (Bloomington, Indiana, 1972), ch. 2. On the Baltic Entente see, e.g., Louis Tissot, *La Baltique* (Paris, 1940), 91–131; Edgar Anderson, "Toward the Baltic Union," *Lituanus* 12:2 and 13:1 (1966–1967); William F. Reddaway, *Problems of the Baltic* (London, 1940), 34ff; Benjamin Akzin, "Choices Before the Baltic States," *Foreign Affairs*, April 1937, 495–508. On the Vilnius problem see Alfred E. Senn, *The Great Powers, Lithuania and the Vilna Question* (Leyden, 1966); also Josef Korbel, *Poland Between East and West* (Princeton, 1963), ch. 10. For background see also Hugh Rodgers, *Search for Security . . . 1920–1934* (Hamden, Conn., 1975), and Piotr Łossowski, *Kraje bałtyckie na drodze od demokracji do dyktatury* (Warsaw, 1972).

2. On Soviet-Baltic relations see Albert Tarulis, *Soviet Policy Toward the Baltic States . . . 1918–1940* (South Bend, Indiana, 1959); Stuart Schram, "L'Union Sovietique et les Etats Baltes," in Jean-Baptiste Duroselle, ed., *Les frontieres europeennes de l'URSS 1917–1941* (Paris, 1957), 25–166; Boris Meissner, *Die Sowjetunion, die baltischen Staaten und das Völkerrecht* (Cologne, 1956), ch. 1; Gregory Rutenberg, "The Baltic States and the Soviet Union," *American Journal of International Law* 29 (October 1935):598–615.

3. USSR, Ministerstvo inostrannykh del, *Dokumenty vneshnei politiki SSSR*, XVII (Moscow, 1971): 214–17, 260–61, 787; V. Sīpols, "Bor'ba SSSR za mir v Pribaltike v 1933–40 gg.," *Kommunist Sovetskoi Latvii*, no. 9 (1959):25–32; Bohdan Budurowycz, *Polish-Soviet Relations, 1932–1939* (New York, 1963), ch. 2.

4. Georg von Rauch, *Geschichte der Baltischen Staaten* (Stuttgart, 1970), 161–62, 211; Schram, 113–14; Tarulis, 92; Max Beloff, *The Foreign Policy of Soviet Russia* (New York, 1949), 2:78–79.

5. Hitler order, in Jodl notes, IMT Document 1781-PS; also cited in Hans Roos [Hans-Otto Meissner], *Polen und Europa* (Tübingen, 1957).

6. The Lithuanian envoy was told that Moscow had no grounds to object to the normalization of relations (Roos, 315). See also Budurowycz, 110–12. But according to Davies, Litvinov told him "that his government was concerned lest still more serious

demands should be made by Poland if Lithuania should accede to the present demand, under some similar 'innocuous dress' which would in effect destroy Lithuanian independence." Davies to Hull, March 26, 1939, in Joseph E. Davies, *Mission to Moscow* (New York, 1941), 294–95.

7. Davies, 289, 193–94.

8. *DBFP*, 3rd ser., III, 640; also in Tarulis, 98.

9. Rauch, 167–69; Tarulis, 115.

10. *Pravda*, 21 June 1938, cited in Tarulis, 98.

11. Alfred Bilmanis, comp., *Latvian-Russian Relations: Documents* (Washington, 1944), 193. See also Hans von Rimscha, "Die Baltikumpolitik der Grossmächte," *Historische Zeitschrift*, 177, no. 2 (April 1954): 281ff. The Lithuanian Premier later quoted Molotov as telling him in June 1940: "You must take a good look and understand that in the future small nations will have to disappear" (Tarulis, 212).

12. Some skepticism is in order with regard to the various Polish memoirs asserting that in 1938–1939 Litvinov asked Warsaw for a free hand in the Baltic or proposed to divide the Baltic States with Poland. See Budurowycz, 145; Józef Beck, *Dernier Rapport* (Neuchâtel, 1951), 157.

13. *DBFP*, 3rd ser., 36–37.

14. U.S. Department of State, *Nazi-Soviet Relations* (Washington, 1948), 34–35.

15. Rauch, 172; Rimscha, 287.

16. See Tõnu Parming, "Reinterpreting Aspects of Estonia's Incorporation into the Soviet Union" (paper, Conference on the Baltic Area in World War II, San Jose, Calif., 1973); Schram, 67, 106, 141; Rauch, 169–70. British consul Gallienne reported from Tallinn in July 1939 that the Estonian foreign minister Kaarel Selter found Soviet Russia showing aggressive tendencies whereas Germany was not. Gallienne countered that by its behavior Estonia was "doing much to justify a Soviet contention that the Baltic States could not be trusted to ask for help before it was too late. Prominent Estonian statesmen had told me at various times that they would accept German help to repel any Soviet aggression, but would refuse Soviet help to repel German aggression." Gallienne pointed to business circles, propertied classes, and army officers as particularly pro-German. (*DBFP*, 3rd ser., VI, 325–27.)

17. Ibid., VI, 40.

18. On the Baltic States in the 1939 negotiations see, e.g., E. Čeginskas, *Die Baltische Frage in den Grossmächteverhandlungen 1939. Commentationes Balticae*, XII/XIII, 1967; Schram, 131–51; Tarulis, ch. 5; Rimscha, 298ff; B. Meissner, 45–46; Hans Rothfels, "Das Baltikum als Problem internationaler Politik," in *Zur Geschichte und Problematik der Demokratie: Festgabe für Hans Herzfeld* (Berlin, 1958), 608–10; *DBFP*, 3rd ser., V–VI; Boris Ponomarev et al., eds., *History of Soviet Foreign Policy* (Moscow, 1969), 1:360–77.

19. Ponomarev, 368.

20. *DBFP*, 3rd ser., VI, 423.

21. *Nazi-Soviet Relations*, 34.

22. Ibid., 36–43, 52, 57, 58, 63.

23. Ibid., 71, 78.

24. Ibid., 103–4, 107.

25. Ibid., 112–17.

26. Munters quotes Stalin as telling him: "As far as Germany is concerned, we could occupy you" (Bilmanis, 193).

27. See, e.g., Thomas Remeikis, "The Impact of Internal Politics on Response Capabilities of the Lithuanian Regime, 1938–1940" (paper presented at the Conference of Baltic Studies at the Hoover Institution, Stanford, Calif., 1973).

28. Rimscha, 305.

29. Bilmanis, 193.

30. Statement of Krėvė-Mickevičius (1950), reprinted in U.S. Congress, House of Representatives, 83d Cong., 2d sess., Select Committee on Communist Aggression, *Third Interim Report* (Washington, 1954), 450–63; Tarulis, 212–15, 270; Rauch, 188. Even if it may be an overstatement to assert (Tarulis, 215) that "the truthfulness of Krėvė's statement is beyond a doubt," there is no reason to question these particular recollections.

Great Britain and the Baltic States, 1938–1939

1. Arnold J. Toynbee, *Survey of International Affairs, 1920–1933* (London, 1925), 245.

2. *The Foreign Office List and Diplomatic and Consular Year Book, 1920–1940* (London, 1920–1940), 38–582 *passim*.

3. Ibid., 38–582 *passim*.

4. Royal Institute of International Affairs, *The Baltic States* (London, 1938), 164–65.

5. Ernst-Albrecht Plieg, *Das Memelland, 1920–1939* (Würzburg, 1962), 3–24 *passim*; Royal Institute, *Baltic States*, 94–101 *passim*; Henry de Chambon, *La Lithuanie pendant la Conférence de la Paix, 1919* (Paris, 1931), 59–60; H.W.V. Temperley, ed., *A History of the Peace Conference of Paris*, vol. 2: *The Settlement with Germany* (London, 1920), 383, and vol. 3: *Chronology, Notes, and Documents* (London, 1920), 168; Alfred Erich Senn, *The Emergence of Modern Lithuania* (New York, 1959), 121; Toynbee, 258–59; Great Britain, Foreign Office, *British and Foreign State Papers, 1924* (London, 1927), CXIX, 502–15.

6. R. G. D. Laffan et al., *Survey of International Affairs, 1938* (London, 1953), 3:357–390 *passim*.

7. *DBFP*, 3rd ser., I, 108: Henderson to Halifax, 1 April 1938, and I, 625: Henderson to Halifax, 13 April 1939; PRO, FO, 371/23599, 16: Preston to Halifax, 16 January 1939.

8. *DBFP*, 3rd ser., V, 638: Collier to Halifax, 7 December 1938; V, 640: Preston to Halifax, 7 December 1938; 639n: Collier Minute; IV, 639: Phipps to Halifax, 7 December 1938; 640: Phipps to Halifax, 8 December 1938; PRO, FO, 371/23607, 21: Preston to Halifax, 16 January 1939.

9. *DBFP*, 3rd ser., IV, 642: Halifax to Ogilvie-Forbes, 10 December 1938.

10. PRO, FO, 371/23600, 65n: Campbell to Halifax, 22 March 1939.

11. Ibid., 66: Preston to Halifax, 29 December 1938.

12. PRO, FO, 371/23599, 22: Collier to Preston, 20 January 1939; 19: Preston to Collier, 21 December 1938.

13. Ibid., 234–35: Collier Minute, 4 January 1939.

14. Great Britain, *Parliamentary Debates, Commons*, 5th ser., CCCXLIII, 180–81.

15. PRO, FO, 371/23599, 297: Seeds to Halifax, 30 January 1939; 34: Orde to Halifax, 21 February 1939; *DBFP*, 3rd ser., IV, 121: Henderson to Halifax, 18 February 1939.

16. Martin Gilbert and Richard Gott, *The Appeasers* (Boston, 1963), 192–93; PRO, FO, 371/23653, 15–16: Collier Minute, 7 January 1939.

17. PRO, FO 371/23600, 80: Collier Minute, 17 March 1939; 145–46: Henderson to

Halifax, 27 March 1939; 36: Halifax to Phipps, 18 March 1939.

18. Ibid., 80–81: Collier Minute, 17 March 1939.

19. Ibid., 43n: Ogilvie-Forbes to Halifax, 20 March 1939.

20. Ibid.

21. PRO, FO, 371/23086, 123–24: Speaight to Halifax, 26 April 1939; 117: Halifax to Phipps/Kennard, 10 May 1939; 130: Halifax to Henderson, 13 May 1939.

22. Arnold J. Toynbee, ed., *Documents on International Affairs, 1939–1946*, Vol. 1: *March-September, 1939* (London, 1951), 113–14; *DBFP*, 3rd ser., IV, 453: Kennard to Halifax, 22 March 1939.

23. *DBFP*, 3rd ser., V, 228–29: Seeds to Halifax, 18 April 1939.

24. PRO, FO, 371/23064, 150: Collier to Halifax, 26 April 1939.

25. PRO, FO, 371/23655, 167–68: Gallienne to Halifax, 16 May 1939; 86: Gallienne to Halifax, 15 May 1939.

26. Ibid., 84n and 87: Gallienne to Halifax, 19 May 1939.

27. Ibid., 87: Halifax to Gallienne, 18 May 1939.

28. *DBFP*, 3rd ser., V, 669: Halifax to Orde, 24 May 1939; PRO C 7727/3356/18, 235, 246: Cabinet Conclusions: 24 May 1939.

29. PRO, FO, 371/23067, 5: Foreign Policy Committee Meetings, 5 June 1939.

30. *DBFP*, 3rd ser., V, 737: Phipps to Halifax, 1 June 1939.

31. Ibid., 350: Orde to Halifax, 27 April 1939; PRO, FO, 371/23068, 207–8: Collier to Halifax, 16 June 1939; NA, 760P. 62/56, 1–2: Packer to Hull, 20 April 1939.

32. PRO, FO, 371/23069, 324–25: Clive to Halifax, 23 June 1939.

33. Ibid., 67–69: Orde to Halifax, 29 June 1939.

34. Ibid., 249–51: Seeds to Halifax, 4 July 1939.

35. Arnold J. Toynbee, *Survey of International Affairs: The Eve of War* (London, 1951), 473.

General Hans von Seeckt and the Baltic Question

1. Hans von Seeckt, *Aus seinem Leben*, Friedrich von Rabenau, ed. (Leipzig, 1940), 130–31.

2. Hajo Holborn, "Diplomats and Diplomacy in the Early Weimar Republic," in Gordon Craig and Felix Gilbert, eds., *The Diplomats: 1919–1939* (New York, 1967), 1:123–71.

3. Seeckt, 252.

4. Otto Becker, *Bismarcks Ringen um Deutschlands Gestaltung* (Heidelberg, 1958).

5. Hajo Holborn, *A History of Modern Germany, 1840–1945* (New York, 1969), 234.

6. Otto Fürst von Bismarck, *Gedanken und Erinnerungen* (Stuttgart, 1922), 2:299–301.

7. Josef Korbel, *Poland Between East and West* (Princeton, 1959), 118.

8. Harold J. Gordon, *The Reichswehr and the German Republic 1919–1926* (Princeton, 1957), 226–27.

9. Hans von Seeckt, "Antwort auf ein Promemoria des Grafen Brockdorff-Rantzau und den Reichskanzler," in Harry Pross, ed., *Die Zerstörung der deutschen Politik* (Frankfurt a.M., 1960), 298.

10. Rudolfas Valsenokas, *Klaipėdos problema* (Klaipėda, 1932), 84. Also R. Žiugžda,

"Klaipėdos kraštas lietuvių tautos žemė," in A. Petraitis, ed., *Klaipėda* (Vilnius, 1965), 38.

11. An article by Galvanauskas on Klaipėda as reprinted from *Draugas*, in Petras Mačiulis, *Trys ultimatumai* (Brooklyn, N.Y., 1962), 63–64.

12. Aleksandras Merkelis, *Antanas Smetona* (New York, 1964), 281.

13. Note printed in June Degras, ed., *Soviet Documents of Foreign Policy* (London, 1951), 1:358–59.

14. See excerpts of Krėvė's memoirs as published by Aleksandras Marcinkevičius, in Petras Petrušaitis, ed., *Nepriklausomai Lietuvai* (Chicago, 1965), 345–46.

15. Ibid.

16. Ibid.

17. Romuald J. Misiunas, "Versailles and Memel," *Lituanus*, 14, no. 1 (Spring 1968):90.

18. Francis L. Carsten, *Reichswehr und Politik 1919–1933* (Cologne, 1964), 155.

19. Hans von Seeckt, "Wege deutscher Aussenpolitik," *Schriftenreihe der Weltwirtschaftlichen Gesellschaft zu Münster* 26 (1931):11–15.

20. On the friction between the two personalities see H. R. Berndorff, *General zwischen Ost und West* (Hamburg, 1951), 141.

21. Seeckt, "Wege deutscher Aussenpolitik," 33.

The Baltic Entente: Phantom or Reality?

1. *DBFP*, 2d ser., E. L. Woodward and Rohan Butler, eds., 7 (London, 1946–1958): 736, 738 (Sir Hugh Montgomery Knatchbull-Hugessen).

2. PRO, FO, 371 (Northern Europe), 9273, 3 November 1923; 9252-N8875/39/59, 12 November 1923 (Gregory); HA, LSS, box 3, no. 2498/sl. (G. V. Bisenieks, 12 November 1923); British Documents, ser. Ia, I, 846, 865–67 (Gregory).

3. *FRUS, Russia, 1918* (Washington, 1931–1932), III, 841–42; Edgar Anderson, "Die Baltische Frage und die Internationale Politik der Alliierten und Assoziierten Mächte bis zum November 1918," in Jürgen von Hehn, Hans von Rimscha, and Hellmuth Weiss, eds., *Von den baltischen Provinzen zu den Baltischen Staaten* (Marburg/Lahn, 1971), 271.

4. Léon Noël, *L'Agression allemande contre la Pologne. Une Ambassade à Varsovie 1935–1939* (Paris, 1946), 98–100—the Polish-French military alliance was signed on February 19, 1921; Vilnis Sīpols, *Slepenā diplomātija* (Riga, 1965), 90–91.

5. Frank P. Chambers, *This Age of Conflict* (New York, 1962), 155; Alfred Erich Senn, *The Emergence of Modern Lithuania* (New York, 1959), 224–25; Edgar Anderson, *Latvijas vēsture 1914–1920* (Stockholm, 1967), 609–14; Sīpols, *Slepenā diplomātija*, 132–45.

6. AA, Microcopy T-120, ser. K243, R. 3875, K071356, K071341; ser. 3015, R. 1466, D596051; "Foreign Policy of the USSR," *European Economic and Political Survey*, 1, no. 7 (1 December 1925): 10; Jane Degras, ed., *Soviet Documents on Foreign Policy*, 2 (London, 1951–1953):104, 112–13; HA, LSS, box 12, no. 0/8sl. p. 205/ 1134, no. 3.

7. Germany, Aussenministerium, *DGFP*, ser. C, II, 421, no. 219—the treaty was signed on 26 January 1934; LSS, box 11, no. 5452 (13 February 1934); box 6, no. 197/21/sl. (30, January 1934); Vilnis Sīpols, *Dzimtenes nodevība* (Riga, 1963), 165—the Baltic States tried to find a way out in a complete neutrality.

8. Edgar Anderson, "Toward the Baltic Entente—the Initial Phase," in Jüri G. Poska, ed., *Pro Baltica, Mélanges dédiés à Kaarel R. Pusta* (Stockholm, 1965), 42–54.

9. Ibid., 52; Edgar Anderson, "Toward the Baltic Union, 1920–1927," *Lituanus* 12, no. 2 (Summer 1966):31, 33.

10. Anderson, "Baltic Union, 1920–1927," 36–37, 42–45; Edgar Anderson, "Toward the Baltic Union, 1927–1934," *Lithuanus* 13, no. 1 (Spring 1967):21–22.

11. Anderson, "Baltic Union, 1927–1934," 6–7, 17, 22–24.

12. NA, Record Group 84, 860n.01/23 (Young); Arthur Brown Ruhl, *New Masters of the Baltic* (New York, 1921), 151ff; M. Peltier, "Campagne en Mer Baltique. Souvenirs," *La Revue maritime*, no. 225 (October 1965):1126; Sir Hugh Montgomery Knatchbull-Hugessen, *Diplomat in Peace and War* (London, 1949), 62–63; HA, LSS, box 14, no. 197/621 (K. Freimanis, 30 March 1933), PRO, FO, 371-17185, N3076/N2667/59 (8 April 1933).

13. HA, LSS, box 12, no. 1656/sl. (Bilmanis, 9 June 1934); Sīpols, *Dzimtenes nodevība*, 85–86; AA, T-120, ser. 6611, R. 3073, E498135 (Martius); PRO, FO, 371-18231, N3658/13/59; NA, Record Group 84, 760i.00/34.

14. NA, Record Group 59, 860i.01/57.

15. Sīpols, *Dzimtenes nodevība*, 84.

16. Anderson, "Baltic Union, 1927–1934," 25–28.

17. Edgar Anderson, *Die militärische Situation der baltischen Staaten* (Königstein im Taunus, 1968), 130–35, 137–42, 145–47, 151; reprinted in *Acta Baltica* 8 (1968); Jürg Meister, "Was kostet die Freiheit?" *Allgemeine Schweizerische Militärzeitschrift* 137, no. 12 (December 1971):865–76.

18. Anderson, *Die militärische Situation*, 135, 137, 142–43, 146, 148.

19. Anderson, "Baltic Entente," 48.

20. Anderson, "Baltic Union, 1927–1934," 15.

21. Anderson, *Die militärische Situation*, 149–55.

22. NA, Record Group, Mil. Int. Div., 2584—3/2, 44/10, 67/2; 2587—52/6; 2621—41/1, 74/1; 10641—242/3, 355/5; PRO, FO 371-17181, N658/527/59; 19401, N2742/2742/59; 21060, N1188/792/59; 22229, N445/445/59; 22226, N5272/154/59; 23607, N976/59.

23. Anderson, *Die militärische Situation*, 131, 138, 145, 147.

24. PRO, FO, 371-18231, N7122/131/59 (19 December 1934).

25. Stasys Lozoraitis, letter, 5 January 1959; NA, Record Group 59, 760i.60m/15 (14 December 1934).

26. NA, Record Group 165, Mil. Int. Div., 2584-67/1 (8 March 1935).

27. AA, T-120, ser. 1751, R. 1027, 403837-49; NA, Record Group 84, 860i.00/386.

28. Royal Institute of International Affairs, *The Baltic States* (London, 1938), 85.

29. NA, Record Group 165, 20 November 1937; PRO, FO, 371-21059, N3993/346/59.

30. PRO, FO, 371-21060, N1188/792/59—11 February 1937.

31. HA, LSS, box 6, 197/207/sl.—11 April 1935.

32. NA, Record Group 165, 2584/67/1, 2—15 April 1935.

33. Stasys Lozoraitis, personal letter, 5 January 1959.

34. NA, Record Group 165, 2621-74/1; 2584-67/2; 2587-52/6, 53/7; 10641-342/2.

35. Stasys Lozoraitis, personal letter, 5 January 1959; Anderson, *Die militärische Situation*, 149–51.

36. NA, Record Group 84, 760n.00/136 (Carlson).

37. Ibid., Record Group 165, 20 November 1937.

38. AA, T-120, ser. 1751, R. 1027. 403837-49.

39. PRO, FO, 371-21062, N6436/4257/59.

40. Thomas Russel Ybarra, "The Self-Extermination of Self-Determination," *New York Times Book Review and Magazine* (23 October 1921), 7.

41. PRO, FO, 371-2229, N558/349/59; 2226, N155/155/59.

42. NA, Record Group 165, 20 November 1937: AA, T-120, ser. 1807, R. 1037, 411555-58; PRO, FO, 371-21059, N3993/346/59.

43. Anderson, *Die militärische Situation*, 131ff.

44. Ibid., 142–45.

45. Ibid., 148–49.

46. Tõnu Parming, "Reinterpreting Aspects of Estonia's Incorporation into the Soviet Union," unpublished manuscript, 2:9–10, 16–18, 20–21, 25–31, 43, 46—Estonian military leaders at that time were under strong German influence and simultaneously controlled the Estonian foreign policy.

47. *FRUS, The Soviet Union 1933–1939*, 954–55.

48. Anderson, *Die militärische Situation*, 155.

49. Parming, 49–50.

50. The Estonian and Latvian chiefs of staff met on November 18–23, 1939, from November 29 to December 1, 1939, and on December 16, 1939. On January 24, 1940, the Estonian chief of staff visited Riga, and the Latvian and Lithuanian military leaders visited Tallinn in February 1940, followed by another meeting in Riga on March 14–16.

51. Tarulis, 186, 191–92.

The Baltic Question in World Politics

1. Cf. Stanley W. Page, *The Formation of the Baltic States* (Cambridge, Mass., 1959); J. Hehn, H. Rimscha, H. Weiss, eds., *Von den baltischen Provinzen zu den baltischen Staaten* (Marburg/Lahn, 1971); G. von Rauch, *Geschichte der baltischen Staaten* (Stuttgart, 1970).

2. Cf. H. Rodgers, *Search of Security: A Study in Baltic Diplomacy 1920–1934* (Hamden, Conn., 1975); H. Wehberg, "Das Problem der internationalen Organisation in der Entwicklung der Ostsee-Maechte," *Friedenswarte* 40 (1940): 13ff. See also the chapter by Edgar Anderson in J. G. Poska, ed., *Pro Baltica: Melanges dediés à Kaarel R. Pusta* (Stockholm, 1965), 41ff.

3. Cf. W. W. Hartlieb, *Das politische Vertragssystem der Sowjetunion 1920–1935* (Leipzig, 1936); A. N. Tarulis, *Soviet Policy toward the Baltic States* (Notre Dame, Indiana, 1959), 62ff.

4. *Osteuropa* 12 (1936/37):264; Tarulis, 22ff.

5. Cf. G. Rhode, *Kleine Geschichte Polens* (Darmstadt, 1965), 496ff.; H. Laeuen, *Polnisches Zwischenspiel* (Berlin, 1940), 164ff.; R. Breyer, *Das Deutsche Reich und Polen 1932–1937* (Würzburg, 1955).

6. Hans J. Morgenthau has discussed the difficulty of correctly appraising national power in his book *Macht und Frieden* (Gütersloh, 1963).

7. M. Freund, ed., *Geschichte des Zweiten Weltkrieges in Dokumenten*, 2d ed. (Freiburg im Breisgau, 1954), 1:394.

8. Cf. *FRUS, 1939*, I, 195ff.; also E. Raczynski, *The British-Polish Alliance* (London, 1948), 14ff.

9. Cf. A. J. Taylor, *Die Ursprünge des Zweiten Weltkrieges*, 2d ed. (Gütersloh, 1962).

10. On the question of negotiations see B. Meissner, *Die Sowjetunion, die baltischen Staaten und das Voelkerrecht* (Cologne, 1956), 26ff.; Tarulis, 101ff.; Rauch, 168ff. From the Soviet point of view see M. Pankrashova and V. Sīpols, *Pochemu ne udalos' predotvratit' voinu. Moskovskie peregovory SSSR, Anglii i Frantsii 1939 goda* (Moscow, 1970).

11. G. Bonnet, *Vor der Katastrophe. Erinnerungen des französischen Aussenministers 1938–1939* (Cologne, 1951), 179.

12. Cf. Meissner, 45ff.

13. Ibid., 57ff.; E. Anderson, "The Pacts of Mutual Assistance between the USSR and the Baltic States," in A. Ziedonis, Jr., W. L. Winter, and M. Valgemae, eds., *Baltic History* (Columbus, Ohio, 1974), 239ff.

14. Cf. B. J. Kaslas, "The Lithuanian Strip in Soviet-German Secret Diplomacy, 1939–1941," *Journal of Baltic Studies* 4, no. 3 (Fall 1973): 211ff.

15. Cf. Meissner, 78ff.; Tarulis, 200ff.; U.S. Congress, House of Representatives, 80th Cong., 1st sess., *Baltic States Investigation. Hearings,* Part 1 (Washington, 1954).

16. Sh. P. Sanakoev and B. J. Tsybulevsky, eds., *Tegeran-Yalta-Potsdam,* 3rd ed. (Moscow, 1971), 96.

17. Cf. Meissner, 112ff.

18. Cf. H. Paechter, *Weltmacht Russland. Aussenpolitische Strategie in drei Jahrhunderten* (Oldenburg-Hamburg, 1968).

19. Meissner, 82.

20. Ibid., 62; K. Selter, "Die Sowjetpolitik und das Baltikum," *Monatshefte für Auswärtige Politik* 18 (1944): 201ff.

21. For a detailed documentation of the illegal character of Soviet intervention and the following annexation of the Baltic States see Meissner, 194ff., and the literature listed there; H. J. Uibopuu, *Die völkerrechtliche Stellung der baltischen Staaten* (Stockholm, 1965).

22. Meissner, 291ff.; L. Juda, "United States' Nonrecognition of the Soviet Union's Annexation of the Baltic States: Politics and Law," *Journal of Baltic Studies* 6, no. 4 (Winter 1975): 272ff.

23. Letter of Dean Rusk to Johannes Kaiv, Acting Consul General of Estonia at New York City in Charge of Legation, 15 February 1963.

24. Cf. Meissner, 304ff.; B. Meissner, "Die Bundesrepublik Deutschland und die baltische Frage," *Jahrbuch des baltischen Deutschtums* 24 (1976).

25. Text in B. Meissner, *Moskau-Bonn, Die Beziehungen zwischen der Sowjetunion und der Bundesrepublik Deutschland 1955–1973* (Cologne, 1955), 1:124.

26. *Baltische Briefe* (September 1970), 1.

27. Cf. B. Meissner, "Die Prinzipienerklärung der KSZE und ihre völkerrechtliche Bedeutung," *Politik und Kultur* 4 (1975): 60ff.

28. H. Rothfels, *Reich, Staat und Nation in deutsch-baltischen Denken* (Halle, 1930), 119[1].

The Catholic Church and the Soviet Government in the Baltic States, 1940–1941

1. A reference to a reputed 1935 statement by Stalin denigrating the Pope's "lack of power." When asked by Pierre Laval to make some concessions to the Catholic Church,

Stalin is reported to have replied: "How many divisions does the Pope have?"

2. Albert Galter, *The Red Book of the Persecuted Church* (Westminster, Md., 1957), 64; Vittorio Vignieri, "Soviet Policy Toward Religion in Lithuania: The Case of Roman Catholicism," in V. Stanley Vardys, ed., *Lithuania Under the Soviets* (New York, 1965), 215–16. The figures take into account the incorporation of Vilnius with its many Polish Catholics and the loss of Klaipėda with its many German Lutherans. For a good picture of general politics and history in Lithuania on the eve of the war see V. Stanley Vardys, "Independent Lithuania: A Profile," *Lithuania Under the Soviets*, 21–46; see also Henry de Chambon, *La Lithuanie moderne* (Paris, 1933); Owen J. C. Norem, *Timeless Lithuania* (Chicago, 1943); Alfred E. Senn, *The Emergence of Modern Lithuania* (New York, 1959); Romuald J. Misiunas, "Fascist Tendencies in Lithuania," *Slavic and East European Review*, 48, no. 110 (January 1970): 88–109.

3. Galter, 56–57, 64; Walter Kolarz, *Religion in the Soviet Union* (New York, 1962), 206; Paul Mailleux, S.J., "Catholics in the Soviet Union," in Richard H. Marshall, ed., *Aspects of Religion in the Soviet Union 1917–1967* (Chicago, 1971), 365.

4. Galter, 53.

5. Pierre Blet et al., eds., *Actes et documents du Saint Siège relatifs à la seconde guerre mondiale* (Vatican City, 1967–1973), 7 vols. to date.

6. Ibid., III, part 1: *Le Saint Siège et la situation religieuse en Pologne et dans les Pays Baltes (1939–1945)*, nos. 153, 160, 165, 166 and note 1, p. 257.

7. Radio Moscow, *Daily Digest of Foreign Broadcasts*, BBC, Part I, 1 July 1940, 4B, iii–iv.

8. Blet et al., III, part 1, nos. 167, 170, 179.

9. Ibid., no. 174.

10. There were demonstrations against the Soviet incorporation of Lithuania. See Blet et al., III, part 1, no. 187.

11. Radio Vatican, BBC, 29 July 1940, 3C, i.

12. Blet et al., III, part 1, no. 187.

13. Radio Vatican, BBC, 13 August 1940, 3C, ii.

14. Blet et al., III, part 1, no. 191.

15. Ibid., IV: *Le Saint Siège et la guerre en Europe (juin 1940–juin 1941)* (Vatican City, 1967), nos. 43, 44.

16. Ibid., nos. 46, 47.

17. Galter, 57. Monsignor Centoz went directly to Rome where he was placed in charge of a newly founded commission for combating Communism. See *New York Times*, 3 October 1940.

18. Blet et al., III, part 1, no. 199.

19. Radio Vatican, BBC, 17 September 1940, 3C, ii.

20. Blet et al., III, part 1, nos. 208, 214.

21. Ibid., nos. 217, 219, 226.

22. Radio Vatican, BBC, 12 December 1940, 3C, i.

23. Such reproaches were so common in the Papal media that only representative examples are listed here: Radio Vatican, BBC, 31 January, 3C, i; 27 February, 3C, iii; 28 February, 3C, i; 27 March, 3C, i; 9 July, 3C, i; 29 July, 3C, i; 16 September, 3C, i–ii; 11 November, 3C, i; 18 December, 3C, i–ii (1940).

24. Cardinal Maglione to Myron Taylor, 26 April 1940, PSF 43, FDR Library; Cordell Hull to Commission for Polish Relief, Inc., 18 June 1940, PSF 43, FDR Library; Blet

et al., I: *Le Saint Siège et la guerre en Europe* (*mars 1939–juin 1940*) (Vatican City, 1967), nos. 286, 292, 317, 324, 329; *FRUS*, 1940, II, 686–93, 705–6.

25. Radio Vatican, BBC, 9 January, 2C, i; 17 January, 2C, ii (1940).

26. Ibid., 17 January 1940, 2C, ii.

27. Ibid., 12 July, 3C, i; 29 July, 3C, i (1940).

28. Blet et al., I, no. 360.

29. Ibid., no. 365.

30. Ibid., IV, nos. 116, 117, 216.

31. Through most of 1940, Stalin, as in 1939, seemed oblivious to the Vatican's anti-Soviet efforts. Communist news media continued to portray the Catholic Church as an anachronistic lackey of the capitalists or, as *Izvestiia* phrased it on 23 January, "a living corpse." For some examples of the anti-Catholic propaganda, see Radio Moscow, BBC, 15 February, 4A, ii; 17 March, 4A, ii; 28 April, 4A, i (1940); *Izvestiia*, 24 February 1940; *Pravda*, 13 January, 20 March, 9 May, 1940; *Bezbozhnik*, 28 July, 11 August, 1940.

32. Ulam, 305.

33. It is generally assumed that Stalin was caught off guard by the Nazi invasion. That charge, however, must be modified in the light of two facts. First, his expropriation of housing from the Catholic Church in Eastern Europe very likely was in response to a need for more quarters to house the additional troops that had been moved into the area. Moreover, he did strengthen his border defenses by building antitank and other fortifications and, in a negative sense, by removing *en masse* the people that he considered untrustworthy. Obviously, he could not dramatically improve his military posture in the west, in a positive way, by deploying large numbers of troops, for that in itself could have irritated the Germans and stimulated an immediate Nazi attack.

34. Blet et al., IV, no. 257; also p. 378, note 1.

35. Ibid., no. 227.

36. Ibid., III, part 1, nos. 265, 270.

37. Ibid., no. 307.

38. Ibid., nos. 310, 316, 400, 425; part 2, no. 355.

39. Ibid., IV, no. 309.

40. Volodymyr Kubijovyč, *Ukraine: A Concise Encyclopedia* (Toronto, 1971), 174.

41. For some good studies on the details of the first Soviet occupation and the deportations in Eastern Europe see Irina Saburova, "The Soviet Occupation of the Baltic States," *Russian Review* 14, no. 1 (January 1955): 36–49; V. Stanley Vardys, "Aggression, Soviet Style, 1939–1940," *Lithuania Under the Soviets*, 47–60; V. Stanley Vardys, "The Partisan Movement in Postwar Lithuania," *Lithuania Under the Soviets*, 87–91; Zenonas Ivinskis, "Lithuania During the War: Resistance Against the Soviet and Nazi Occupants," *Lithuania Under the Soviets*, 61–84; Eugen Glowinskyi, "The Western Ukrainians," 149–51; Simon Kabysh, "The Belorussians," in *Genocide in the USSR* (New York, 1958), 84–86.

42. Blet et al., III, part 1, no. 191, note 3.

43. The memoirs of Leopold Braun (unpublished ms., 1961, located in the Assumptionist Archives, Assumptionist Provincial House, New York), 371–81.

44. Ibid., 10–12. For representative examples in 1941 see Radio Vatican, BBC, 10 January, 3C, i; 5 February, 3C, i; 2 April, 3C, ii; 21 June, 3C, i (1941).

45. Blet et al., IV, no. 258.

46. Ibid., nos. 331, 403, 411.

Morality or Expediency? The Baltic Question in British-Soviet Relations, 1941–1942

1. For a good example of the difference of opinion see PRO, FO, Group 371, General Correspondence, N 411/3/38, Foreign Office, Cripps Correspondence; D. Dilks, ed., *The Diaries of Sir Alexander Cadogan 1938–1945* (London, 1971), 321. For further details of the Baltic question in British-Soviet relations, 1940–1941, see David Kirby, "Sir Stafford Cripps and the Baltic question 1940–1942," a paper presented at the Second Baltic Conference in Stockholm, June 1975.

2. PRO, FO, N3607/3/38: Churchill to Eden, 9 July 1941. Churchill's statement to the House is in *Parliamentary Debates, Fifth Series, Volume 365. House of Commons Official Report* (London, 1940), 39.

3. PRO, CP, WM 67 (41), CAB 65/19; Sir Llewellyn Woodward, *British Foreign Policy in the Second World War* (London, 1971), 2:12–13.

4. Woodward, 2:220. For a Soviet view of British-Russian relations between July and November 1941 see V. Trukhanovsky, *British Foreign Policy during World War II* (Moscow, 1970), 213–19.

5. *FRUS*, 1941, I, 194: Hull to Winant, 5 December 1941; Sir John Wheeler-Bennett and A. Nicholls, *The Semblance of Peace: The Political Settlement after the Second World War* (London, 1972), 45.

6. Woodward, 2:205.

7. PRO, FO, N563/5/38: Eden's memorandum, 28 January 1942.

8. The Rt. Hon. Earl of Avon, *The Eden Memoirs: The Reckoning* (London, 1965), 284, 289.

9. I. Maisky, *Memoirs of a Soviet Ambassador: The War 1939–43*, (London, 1967), 230–32.

10. See Woodward, 2:226–33, for the text of the December 17 discussions. The Foreign Office attitude toward the question of *de facto* sovereignty is discussed in Kirby, "Sir Stafford Cripps."

11. Woodward, 2:233–35. PRO, FO, N109/5/38 contains Eden's record of the Moscow talks.

12. PRO, CP, WM 131 (41), CAB 65/21.

13. W. Churchill, *The Second World War* (London, 1950), 3:559.

14. PRO, FO, N106/86/38: Eden to Churchill: 5 January 1942.

15. Churchill, 3:615–16. PRO, FO, N109/86/38, gives a slightly fuller version of Churchill's reply than the former prime minister himself chose to publish.

16. See Cadogan, 437, diary entry for 24 February 1942; Eden, 317.

17. PRO, FO, N563/5/38: Eden's memorandum of 28 January 1942; Eden, 318–20.

18. PRO, CP, WM, 17 (42), CAB 65/29. Eden does, however, speak of some hesitance among his cabinet colleagues (p. 320).

19. *FRUS*, 1942, III, 510–12: Hull to Roosevelt, 4 February 1942; Cordell Hull, *The Memoirs of Cordell Hull* (London, 1948), 2:1167–70.

20. *FRUS*, 1942, III, 513–20: memorandum of a conversation between Welles and Halifax, 18 February 1942. PRO, FO, N1024/5/38: Halifax to Foreign Office, 20 February 1942.

21. *FRUS*, 1942, III, 521–24: memorandum of a conversation between Welles and Halifax, 20 February 1942; PRO, FO, N1025/5/38: Halifax to Foreign Office, 21 Feb-

ruary 1942. Maisky recalls that Roosevelt was hinting at a meeting à deux with Stalin at this time (p. 262).

22. PRO, CP, WM 24 (42), CAB 65/29.

23. PRO, FO, N1115/5/38: Eden to Halifax, 26 February 1942. For the aide-mémoire of February 25 see FRUS, 1942, III, 524–26; Eden, 323.

24. Churchill, 4:293.

25. PRO, FO, N1279/5/38: Halifax to Foreign Office, 9 March 1942.

26. Ibid., 1331/5/38: Halifax to Foreign Office, 12 March 1942; Wheeler-Bennett, 48–49.

27. PRO, FO, N1364/5/38: Halifax to Foreign Office, 14 March 1942. This telegram was heavily marked by Foreign Office clerks. The use of the phrase "legitimate security" was taken as a bad sign.

28. Ibid., N1526/5/38: Eden to Halifax, 23 March 1942.

29. Cadogan, 442–43.

30. PRO, FO, N1653/5/38, contains the draft dispatch; PRO, CP, WM 37 (42), CAB 65/29; Cadogan's comment was "I expect they'll [i.e., the cabinet] get an outsize raspberry from Roosevelt" (p. 444).

31. PRO, FO, N1653/5/38: Eden to Halifax, 27 March 1942.

32. Ibid., N1737/5/38: Halifax to Foreign Office, 2 April 1942; FRUS, 1942, III, 536–38: Welles' memoranda of conversations with Halifax, 30 March and 1 April 1942.

33. Ibid., 1942, III, 539–42: Berle-Welles correspondence, 3–4 April 1942.

34. PRO, FO, N1921/5/38: Halifax to Foreign Office, 12 April 1942. See also ibid., N1832/5/38: letter from Edw. Montgomery of the News Chronicle; N1835/5/38, in which Nevile Butler of the North American department laid down possible lines of defense of British policy. He urged that the Charter and the July elections in the Baltic States be played down and the modest and limited nature of Soviet demands stressed; it was also in the interests of the United Nations that the Soviet Union emerge as the major Baltic power after the war.

35. Ibid., N2426/5/38: Machtig (Dominions Office) to Cadogan, 6 May 1942.

36. Cadogan, 446, 449.

37. Ibid., 437.

38. PRO, FO, N6756/174/59: Dew's comment on Kaarel Pusta's note on Estonian independence, 1 December 1941. See also ibid., N4784/44/59: Eden's comment on a note presented to the Foreign Office by the Estonian minister A. Torma in August 1941, seeking confirmation that Article 2 of the Atlantic Charter would apply to the Baltic States. Eden disliked notes of this nature from men "who represent nothing but themselves," and feared trouble if Washington was encouraging the Baltic legations in the United States to believe that the Allies were "necessarily pledged to restore their independence."

39. Ibid., N1881/5/38: draft treaties annexed to Eden's memorandum of 10 April 1942; ibid., N2963/5/38: Foreign Office memorandum, 6 May 1942; Woodward, 2: 245–46.

40. PRO, FO, N1993/5/38: Eden to Clark Kerr, 16 April 1942. See also ibid., N1939/5/38: Smuts to Eden, 10 April 1942, for the original suggestion for guarantees of local autonomy for the Baltic States.

41. Ibid., N2336/5/38: Eden to Clark Kerr, 1 May 1942; PRO, CP, WM 56 (42), CAB 65/30; Maisky was also pesseimistic about the chances of agreement over the drafts (p. 263).

42. Cadogan, 449–50; Woodward, 2: 247–48; PRO, FO, N2497/5/38: Eden's memorandum to the War Cabinet, 6 May 1942; Eden, 326–27.

43. PRO, FO, N2500/5/38: Eden's memorandum to the War Cabinet, 12 May 1942; ibid., N2646/5/38: Eden's memorandum to the War Cabinet, 18 May 1942.

44. Maisky, 266–67; PRO, FO, N2901–04/5/38, contains the protocols of the meetings, 21–23 May 1942.

45. Cadogan, 455; Hull, 2:1173; FRUS, 1942, III, 559–64: Winant to Hull, 24 and 25 May 1942. PRO, CP, WM 66, 67 (42), CAB 65/30.

46. Wheeler-Bennett, 50.

47. FRUS, 1942, III, 613: Standley to Hull, 22 July 1942; Eden, 330; Trukhanovksy, 252.

48. J. Gaddis, The United States and the Origins of the Cold War 1941–1947 (New York, 1972), 113; Eden, 373.

49. Gaddis, 138–39; Wheeler-Bennett, 148, 162–63.

50. PRO, FO, N665/506/59: Churchill's personal minute to Eden, 16 January 1944.

51. Churchill, 5:252.

52. PRO, FO, N665/506/59: Warner's draft reply to Churchill, January 1944.

Soviet Historiography on World War II and the Baltic States

1. M. P. Gallagher, The Soviet History of World War II (New York, 1963).

2. Joseph Stalin, The Great Patriotic War of the Soviet Union (English ed., New York, 1945).

3. "Velikaia otechestvennaia voina Sovetskogo Soiuza," in S. I. Vanilov, ed., Bol'shaia sovetskaia entsiklopediia (Moscow, 1951), 7:157–208.

4. Gallagher, 81.

5. Dokumenty i materialy kanuna Vtoroi Mirovoi Voiny (Moscow, 1948), 2 vols.

6. Of particular interest in this connection is the collection of short stories by Vasilii Grossman, Gody voiny (Moscow, 1946), 148, 155, which refers to disloyalty and German collaborators among the populace; also Konstantin Simonov, Dni i nochi (Moscow, 1944), 42, which portrays the ineptitude of the Red Army during the initial stage of the war.

7. Gallagher, 58–59.

8. A. V. Karasev, "Kratkii obzor literatury po istorii Velikoi Otechestvennoi Voiny," Voprosy istorii, no. 6 (1961):116–19.

9. Lietuvos TSR istorijos bibliografija, 1940–1965 (Vilnius, 1969).

10. The figures for each year are: 1946 (6), 1947 (1), 1948 (4), 1949 (1), 1950 (0), 1951 (2), 1952 (2), 1953 (2), 1954 (4), and 1955 (7).

11. V. I. Savchenko, "Ob izuchenii istorii Latviiskoi SSR perioda Velikoi Otechestvennoi Voiny," in A. A. Drizul [Drīzulis], ed., V dni voiny, 1941–1945 gg. (Riga, 1964), 5–26.

12. E. A. Zhagar [Žagars], "Nekotorye voprosy klassovoi borby v Latviiskoi SSR nakanune Velikoi Otechestvennoi Voiny," in Drizul, V dni voiny, 1941–1945 gg., 27–28.

13. A. K. Biron and V. V. Doroshenko, Sovetskaia istoriografiia Latvii (Riga, 1970).

14. Juozas Žiugžda, *Tarybų Sąjungos pagalba lietuvių tautai apginant savo laisvę ir nepriklausomybę 1939 ir 1940 metais* (Vilnius, 1949). It is tempting to assume that a corresponding Latvian work is that by A. Drīzulis, *Cīņa par fašistiskās diktatūras gāšanu un Padomju Latvijas nodibināšanu 1940 gadā* (Riga, 1951). Neither work is readily available in any major reference library in the United States. The copy of Žiugžda used in this study is part of a private English collection.

15. *Falsificators of History* (Washington, D.C.: Information Bulletin of the Embassy of the Union of Soviet Socialist Republics, February 1948); also published as *Falsifiers of History*, with an introduction by Frederick L. Schuman, by the Committee for the Promotion of Peace (New York, [1948]).

16. Ibid., 49–51.

17. Žiugžda, 5, 54, 55 (citation).

18. Vladimir Dedijer, *The Battle Stalin Lost* (New York, 1971), 113ff.

19. M. Požarskas, *Tarybų valdžios atkūrimas Lietuvoje, 1940–1941 metais* (Vilnius, 1955), 4.

20. Cited in L. Tillett, *The Great Friendship* (Chapel Hill, N.C., 1969), 199.

21. N. Heer, *Politics and History in the Soviet Union* (Cambridge, Mass., 1971), 76.

22. Gallagher, 178.

23. D. I. Kovalevskii, *Velikaia otechestvennaia voina Sovetskogo Soiuza, 1941–1945. Posobie dlia uchitelia* (Moscow, 1959). A team of distinguished diplomatic historians did virtually the same research in 1967: V. L. Israelian and L. N. Kutakov, *Diplomatiia agressorov* (Moscow, 1967), 7; English ed.: V. Issraeljan and L. Kutakov, *Diplomacy of Aggression* (Moscow, 1970).

24. G. A. Deborin, *Vtoraia mirovaia voina, voenno-politicheskii ocherk* (Moscow, 1958), 31, 51, 77–78. Deborin reiterates his claim that the mutual-aid pacts prevented the seizure of the Baltic States by the Germans, who were "already poised to overrun them," in his recent English edition: G. Deborin, *Secrets of the Second World War* (Moscow, 1971), 44. Aleksandr Moisevich Nekrich is the author of *1941–22 iunia* (Moscow, 1965), in which he castigated Stalin for lack of war-preparedness. The book was criticized among official military historians and was withdrawn. Nekrich was subsequently expelled from the Communist Party and emigrated to the United States.

25. Institut Marksizma-Leninizma pri TsK KPSS. Otdel Istorii Velikoi Otechestvennoi Voiny, *Istoriia velikoi otechestvennoi voiny Sovetskogo Soiuza, 1941–1945 gg.*, 1:171ff.

26. Ibid., 4:337.

27. Heer, 248.

28. V. Petrov, *"June 22, 1941"*: *Soviet Historians and the German Invasion* (Columbia, S. C., 1968), 12.

29. P. G. Grigorenko, *Sokrytie istoricheskoi pravdy—prestuplenie pered narodom! Pis'mo v redaktsiiu zhurnala "Voprosy istorii KPSS"* (London, Canada, 1970).

30. L. Pern, *V Vikh're voennykh let* (Tallinn, 1969); V. Karvialis [Karvelis], "Osvobozhdenie sovetskoi Litvy," in *Gitlerovskaia okkupatsiia v Litve, sbornik statei* (Vilnius, 1966), 281–359; V. Vitkauskas, "Paskutinieji buržuazijos valdymo metai Lietuvoje. Iš mano atsiminimų," *Švyturys* (1958), no. 1:11–12; no. 6:16–17. E. Dirvelė et al., *Kovų keliais, lietuviškoji divizija didžiajame tėvynes kare, Tarybų Lietuvos išvadavimas* (Vilnius, 1965).

31. The story of E. V. Nikonov, the heroic sailor defender of Tallinn in N. G. Nemirov et al., *Vo slavu rodiny (1941–1945)*, Sbornik dokumentalnykh materialov voennykh muzeev (Moscow, 1961), 29–32; *Tallinn v ogne*, Sbornik statei veteranov voiny i vospo-

minaniia uchastnikov geroicheskoi oborony Tallina i Moonzundskogo Arkhipelaga 7 Iulia–2 Dekabria 1941 goda (Tallinn, 1971, 2d ed.); *Na pravyi boi, na smertnyi boi, Sbornik vospominanii i dokumentov o vooruzhennoi bor'be fashistskikh zakhvatchikov* (Riga, 1968). The latter relates a curious incident, which could be connected to the contemporary campaign for "Soviet" patriotism. Fedor Soprunov of the 227th Regiment of the 183rd Rifle Division of the Latvian Territorial Corps remembers a student's query to a politruk why Riga was not being defended. The latter answered that the German attack was too strong, but that Moscow would not be given up. "But my home is in Riga not Moscow," replied the student. The politruk answered, "I say Moscow not because I happen to be Russian but because I am a Communist." The war was an ideological one against fascism, and the capital of Communism happened to coincide with the capital of Russia and the Soviet Union.

32. A. A. Kursonov and E. S. Lagutin, "K voprosu ob effektivnosti partizanskogo dvizheniia na territorii Sovetskogo Soiuza," in A. M. Nekrich et al., eds., *Protiv falsifikatsii istorii vtoroi mirovoi voiny* (Moscow, 1964), 269.

33. I. Kasnickis and V. Meščeriakovas, *Kovos puslapiai* (Vilnius, 1961); E. Martinson, *Poka dyshat' ia umeiu* (Tallinn, 1968); A. Rashkevits [Raškevics], *Zapiski partizana* (Riga, 1963); A. P. Semonov, *Neustrashimye* (Riga, 1963); P. Staras, *Partizaninis judėjimas Lietuvoje didžiojo tėvynės karo metu* (Vilnius, 1966).

34. *Ognennye gody, Dokumenty i materialy ob uchasty komsomola v velikoi otechestvennoi voine* (Moscow, 1971), 426–28.

35. Institut Marksizma-Leninizma, 1:176; A. A. Drizul [Drīzulis] et al., eds., *Borba latyshskogo naroda v gody velikoi otechestvennoi voiny, 1941–1945* (Riga, 1970), 13.

36. V. Sīpols, *Tainaia diplomatiia—Burzhuaznaia Latviia v antisovetskikh planakh imperialisticheskikh derzhav, 1919–1940 gg.* (Riga, 1968), 314.

37. A. A. Drizul [Drizulis], *Latviia pod igom fashizma, 1934–1940 gg.* (Riga, 1960).

38. R. Medvedev, *Let History Judge* (New York, 1971), 442.

39. Grigorenko, 85.

40. G. N. Reutov, *Pravda i vymysel o vtoroi mirovoi voine* (Moscow, 1967), 76–77; 2d ed., 1970, 132–33.

41. *Ocherki istorii velikoi otechestvennoi voiny, 1941–1945* (Moscow, 1955), 34.

42. B. S. Telbukhovskii, *Velikaia otechestvennaia voina Sovetskogo Soiuza, 1941–1945* (Kratkii ocherk) (Moscow, 1959), 15.

43. V. Maamiagi [Maamägi], "Protiv falsifikatsii istorii Estonii burzhuaznonatsionalisticheskimi emigrantskimi istorikami," *Sovetskaia Pribaltika v bratskoi seme narodov SSSR* (Riga, 1960), 4:50.

44. S. Atamukas, *Kompartiia Litvy v borbe za sovetskuiu vlast'* (Moscow, 1961), 223.

45. V. V. Gushchin, "Borba rabochego klassa Litvy protiv antinarodnoi vneshnei politiki burzhuaznogo pravitelstva (1939–1940 gg.)," in V. T. Fomin et al., eds., *Voprosy sovremennogo kommunisticheskogo i rabochego dvizheniia* (Moscow, 1961), 213.

46. Sīpols, 321.

47. L. N. Ivanov, *Ocherki mezhdunarodnykh otnoshenii v period vtoroi mirovoi voiny (1939–1945 gg.)* (Moscow, 1958), 29. He does not seem to be very good at geography, and has the Hitlerites occupying, in September 1939, the northern Polish communication centers Grodno and Kaunas (p. 48); Sīpols, 299; Iu. V. Borisov, *Sovetsko-frantsuzkie otnosheniia i bezopasnost' Evropy* (Moscow, 1960), 91.

48. A. M. Nekrich, *Politika angliiskogo imperializma v Evrope (Oktiabr', 1938–Sentiabr', 1939)* (Moscow, 1955).

49. A. M. Nekrich, "Politika angliiskogo pravitel'stva na severo-zapade Evropy (Sentiabr', 1939–Ianvar', 1940)," *Novaia i noveishaia istoriia*, no. 5 (1962):24–25; 29.

50. Deborin, 78.

51. V. A. Sekistov, *Bolshaia lozh' o voine: kritika noveishei burzhuaznoi istoriografii Vtoroi Mirovoi Voiny* (Moscow, 1971), 149.

52. Nekrich, *Politika*, 344.

53. J. Bulavas, *Vokiškųjų fašistų okupacinis Lietuvos valdymas (1941–1944 m.)* (Vilnius, 1969), 33.

54. Sīpols, 338.

55. *Lietuvos TSR Aukščiausiosios Tarybos III-ji Sesija, 1944 m. rupjūčio men. 29–30 d. stenografinė apyskaita* (Vilnius, 1947).

56. Gushchin, 213; A. Bulota, *Nuo balto žirgo iki svastikos* (Vilnius, 1962), 154.

57. R. Zhiugzhda [Žiugžda], "Ruka pomoshchi v groznyi chas," *Kommunist* [Litvy], no. 10 (1972):15–23.

58. Bulota, 159.

59. K. Tiškevičius, "Fašistinės santvarkos krizė Lietuvoje tarybų valdžios atkūrimo išvakarėse (1938–1940 m.)," in J. Žiugžda et al., eds., *Už socialistinę Lietuvą* (Vilnius, 1960), 289.

60. *Istoriia Latviiskoi SSR, sokrashennyi kurs* (Riga, 1971, 2d ed.), 554ff.; Sīpols, 323–36; Petrov, 145–46; Bulota, 161; Petrov, 77.

61. Gushchin, 213.

62. P. A. Larin, *Estonskii narod v velikoi otechestvennoi voine, 1941–1945 gg.* (Tallinn, 1964).

63. Gushchin, 183.

64. *Ocherki Istorii Velikoi Otechestvennoi Voiny*, 37.

65. V. A. Maamiagi [Maamägi], "O nekotorykh osobennostiakh perekhoda pribaltiiskikh sovetskikh respublik k stroitelstvu sotsializma (1940–1941 gg.)," *Istoriia SSSR*, no. 6 (1962):27–43; *Istoriia Latviiskoi*, 590–91, 583–84; Biron, 390.

66. V. Kancevičius, "Revoliucinės situacijos peraugimas į socialistinę revoliuciją Lietuvoje 1940 metais," *Spalio revoliucija ir visuomeniniai mokslai* (Vilnius, 1967), 110–11. Elsewhere the same author has also made an attempt to classify Lithuanian social groups in 1940 as "top" and "bottom" categories in the events of 1940. V. Kancevičius, " 'Viršūnės' ir 'apačios' 1940 m. socialistinės revoliucijos Lietuvoje išvakarėse," *Už socializmo sukūrimą Lietuvoje* (Vilnius, 1969), 199–207.

67. V. Kancevičius, *1940 metų birželis Lietuvoje* (Vilnius, 1973). The same year also saw the publication of two military accounts of the war years by Lithuanians: [Gen.] V. Karvelis, *Lietuvos TSR išvadavimas iš hitlerinės okupacijos, 1944–45* (Vilnius, 1973) and J. Arvasevičius, *1418 dienų mūšiuose* (Vilnius, 1973). G. Abramavičius, *Nuo Kauno iki Vilniaus 1502 dienos* (Vilnius, 1974) is a similar memoir-type military account by a former political officer.

68. Kancevičius, *1940 metu*, 54.

69. H. Šadžius, "Buržuazinės istorijografijos koncepcijų kritika 1940 metų socialistinės revoliucijos Lietuvoje klausimu," *Ideologinė kova ir jaunimas* (Vilnius, 1972), 60–61.

70. Ivan Maisky, *Memoirs of a Soviet Ambassador: The War, 1939–1943*, trans. A. Rothstein (New York, 1967), 139–40.

71. K. Navickas, *Leninės nacionalinės politikos istorinė reikšmė lietuvių tautai* (Vilnius, 1960), 71. The justice of the Soviet demands on the Baltic governments in June 1940 is

also educed from the mutual-aid pacts by J. Žiugžda," Buržuazinės santvarkos Lietuvoje krizė ir fašistinės diktatūros nuvėrtimas (1939–1941 metai)," *Mokslas tarybų Lietuvoje* (Vilnius, 1961), 5–29.

72. K. Navickas, *TSRS vaidmuo ginant Lietuvą nuo imperialistinės agresijos, 1920–1940 metais* (Vilnius, 1966), 322–23.

73. Zhagar, 27–28;30–34.

74. Ibid., 34–35:40–41; *Istoriia Latviiskoi*, 614, mentions the distrust on the part of the Northwest Military Command of the units of the former Latvian army and their demobilization upon rumors of large-scale defections in the Lithuanian Territorial Corps.

75. Zhagar, 46–48 (citation); election figures:37, 54–55.

76. Cited by A. Werth, *Russia at War, 1941–1945* (New York, 1964), 125.

77. Ibid., 55; Maamägi, "O nekotorykh," 32.

78. *Borba za sovetskuiu Pribaltiku v velikoi otechestvennoi voine, 1941–1945* (Riga, 1966), 1:24.

79. Zhagar, 55.

80. See E. Martinson, *Slugi svastika* (Tallinn, 1962), K. Lemmik and E. Martinson, *12,000* (Tallinn, 1962), for the cases of Linnas and Viiks. Some of this literature was intended for foreign consumption, such as [Anon.], *Do You Know This Man?* (Vilnius, 1963), in the case of A. Impulevičius of Philadelphia. The Latvian effort, J. Silabriedis and B. Arklans, *Political Refugees Unmasked* (Riga, 1965), stresses the interconnection between atrocities and the wartime collaboration of various bourgeois nationalists. Among the Russian document collections of this nature note E. A. Bolton et al., eds., *Prestupnye tseli—prestupnye sredstva, Dokumenty ob okkupatsionnoi politike fashistskoi Germanii na territorii SSSR (1941–1944 gg.)* (Moscow, 1968), which is more scholarly and contains numerous Baltic documents.

81. Also of note is the two-volume collection G. Ersvilaitė et al., eds., *Masines žudynės Lietuvoje*, 2 vols. (Vilnius, 1965, 1973).

82. A. Gaigalaitė, "Buržuaziniai nacionalistai hitlerinės Vokietijos tarnyboje, 1939–1941 m.," *LTSR Mokslų Akademijos darbai*, Serija A 2 (9), 1960, 145–46.

83. J. Dobrovolskas, "Lietuviškųjų buržuazinių nacionalistų antiliaudinis veikimas okupaciniame hitlerininkų valdžios aparate, 1941–1944 m.," *LTSR Mokslų Akademijos darbai*, Serija A 2 (13), 1962.

84. B. Baranauskas et al., eds., *Documents Accuse* (Vilnius, 1970), 93–101; 55.

85. Iu. Butėnas, "Burzhuaznye natsionalisty—posobniki gitlerovskikh okkupantov," in *Gitlerovskaia okkupatsiia v Litve, sbornik statei* (Vilnius, 1966), 37, 43–44.

86. J. Aničas, Katalikiškasis klerikalizmas Lietuvoje 1940–1944 metais (Vilnius, 1972); J. Aničas, "Pasauliečių klerikalų reakcinė veikla Lietuvoje hitlerinės okupacijos metais (1941–1944)," *LTSR Mokslų Akademijos darbai*, Serija A 4 (41), 1972, 71–81. Among the sources cited by Aničas, the following were unavailable for consideration in this study: P. Bagackas, "Lietuvos reakcinė katalikų dvasininkija hitlerinių okupantų tarnyboje," *LKP istorijos klausimai*, 5 (5), 1966; A. Bulota, "Katalikų bažnyčia hitlerinės okupacijos metais Lietuvoje," *Religija, ateizmas, dabartis*, 5 (1966).

87. Bulavas, 33, 47, 271.

88. A. A. Drizul [Drīzulis] et al., eds., *Borba latyshskogo naroda v gody velikoi otechestvennoi voiny 1941–1945 gg.* (Riga, 1970), 96–99;900–901.

89. *Bor'ba za sovetskuiu Pribaltiku*, 1:24, 18; 3:206, 208, 211, 218. Mention of bourgeois Estonian insurrectionists occasionally occurs in other contexts. The verdict of one of

the show trials, that of Jüriste et al., mentions armed diversionary bands during the early part of the war formed by reactionary members of the officer corps of the former bourgeois army and the military-nationalistic organization Kaitseliit—Lemmik and Martinson, 161. The 1st Latvian Workers' Regiment fought bands of bourgeois Estonian nationalists in the vicinity of Piltsama during the summer of 1941—*Istoriia latviiskoi*, 614.

90. *Bor'ba za sovetskuiu Pribaltiku*, 3:227–29;244–47.

91. *Eesti riik ja rahvas teises maailmasöjas* (Stockholm, 1954–62), vols. 1–10. The series was continued in the same format, though not on the same quality paper, in Soviet Estonia so as to present the Soviet side; *Eesti riik ja rahvas teises maailmasöjas* (Tallinn, 1964–1972), vols. 11–15.

92. *Bor'ba za sovetskuiu Pribaltiku*, 3: 250.

93. *Bor'ba za sovetskuiu Pribaltiku*, 3:250.

94. Ibid., 3:252; Maamiagi, "Protiv," 52.

95. The book by P. Larin, a combined work in Russian of two earlier Estonian works, is quite brief on the events of 1939–1940 (first 37 pages out of 352). Most of the work is a paean to Soviet Estonian military heroism. And there is little detraction from that lofty theme by any discussion of disloyal elements. Series B of the Works of the Tallinn Polytechnical Institute for 1960 contains two rather esoteric articles of the war on the preparation of Soviet teachers in Estonia in 1940–1941 and on the role of the Baltic fleet in the defense of Estonia.

Frequently Used Baltic Geographical Names

Before 1917 most places in Estonia, Livonia, and Courland—the three provinces that were merged into the independent states of Estonia and Latvia—were officially known by their German names. The Russian varieties were generally transcriptions into Cyrillic from the German. In Lithuania, the officially used names were Russian. Generally, these constituted derivations of Polish rather than Lithuanian names. The Soviets officially use indigenous names transcribed into Cyrillic.

Indigenous	German	Russian	Polish
Cēsis	Wenden		
Kurzeme*	Kurland	Kurliandiia	
Daugava	Düna	Dvina	
Daugavpils	Dünaburg	Dvinsk	
Hiiuma	Dagö		
Jelgava	Mitau	Mitava	
Kaunas	Kowno(Kauen)	Kovno	Kowno
Klaipėda	Memel		
Latgale*	Lettgallen	Latgaliia	
Liepāja	Libau	Libava	
Nemunas	Memel	Nemen	Niemen
Peipsi	Peipus	Chudskoe ozero	
Pärnu	Pernau	Pernov	
Panevėžys	Ponewesch	Ponevezh	
Šiauliai	Schaulen	Shavli	
Tallinn	Reval	Revel	
Tartu	Dorpat	Iurev	
Ukmergė	Wilkomir	Vilkomir	Wilkomierz
Valga/Valka	Walk	Valk	
Ventspils	Windau	Vindava	
Vilnius	Wilna	Vilno	Wilno
Žemaitija*	Schemaiten	Zhmud'	Żmudź

*The majority of historians writing in English use the historical Latinized forms of these names, Courland, Latgalia, and Samogitia, respectively. These Latinized names, furthermore, signify not merely geographic provinces but also certain historical entities.

Notes on Contributors

Edgar Anderson is Professor of History at San Jose State University (California). He is the author of twelve books and scores of articles in books and journals on Baltic and West Indian topics. His numerous professional activities include past service as President of the Association for the Advancement of Baltic Studies.

Olavi Arens is Assistant Professor of History at Armstrong State College (Savannah, Georgia). He is an Associate Editor of the *Journal of Baltic Studies* and writes on Baltic affairs.

David M. Crowe, Jr., formerly associated with the National Archives, now teaches at Elon College. He has written a series of articles, reviews, and abstracts on Baltic history in the *Journal of Baltic Studies* and elsewhere.

Alexander Dallin is Professor of History and Political Science at Stanford University and Senior Research Fellow at the Hoover Institution. He was Director of the Russian Institute and Adlai E. Stevenson Professor of International Relations at Columbia University. His nine books include *German Rule in Russia, 1941–1945* (1957), *The Soviet Union at the United Nations* (1962), *Political Terror in Communist Systems* (1970), and other studies.

Dennis J. Dunn is Associate Professor of History at Southwest Texas State University. He is the author of *The Catholic Church and the Soviet Government, 1939–1949* (1977) as well as of articles on church-state relations in European Communist states.

Michael Garleff is Lecturer in the Department of History at the University of Kiel (Germany). He is the author of *Deutschbaltische Politik zwischen den Weltkriegen* (1976) and of articles on minority politics in the Baltic States.

David Kirby is Lecturer in Baltic History at the School of Slavonic Studies of the University of London (England). He edited a collection of documents, *Finland and Russia 1808–1920*, and is the author of numerous articles on Finnish socialism.

Boris Meissner is Professor at the University of Cologne (Germany) and Director of the University's Institute for Eastern Law. He has served as counsellor at the West German Embassy in Moscow and continues serving as a member of several West German research and publishing institutions. His numerous books include *Russland, die Westmächte und Deutschland* (1953), *Die Sowjetunion, die baltischen Staaten und das Völkerrecht* (1956), and *Sowjetgesellschaft im Wandel* (1966).

Romuald J. Misiunas is Assistant Professor of History at Williams College. He is a past Vice-President of the Association for the Advancement of Baltic Studies and has written several articles and reviews on Baltic and Russian history.

Julius P. Slavenas is Associate Professor of History at the State University of New York at Buffalo. He has published numerous articles and reviews on Baltic history.

Aba Strazhas is Professor of History at Haifa University (Israel). Between 1947 and 1973 he occupied various positions in Soviet educational institutions, including that of Dean of the Faculty of History at Vilnius Pedagogical Institute. He has written numerous articles on modern German and Lithuanian history that were published, among others, in Moscow's *Voprosy istorii*.

Charles L. Sullivan is Chairman of the Social Studies Department at Leland High School (San Jose, California) and is the author of several articles on Baltic history.

V. Stanley Vardys is Professor of Political Science at the University of Oklahoma and former director of its center for Russian area studies in Munich. An author of numerous articles mainly on Soviet nationality questions, he co-wrote and edited *Lithuania under the Soviets* (1965) and *Karl Marx: Scientist? Revolutionary? Humanist?* (1971), and wrote *The Catholic Church, Dissent and Nationality in Soviet Lithuania* (1978). He is past President of the Association for the Advancement of Baltic Studies.

Index